AF594921

What is Gilbert & George?

HENI

For more pictures and information go to:

www.gilbertandgeorge.co.uk

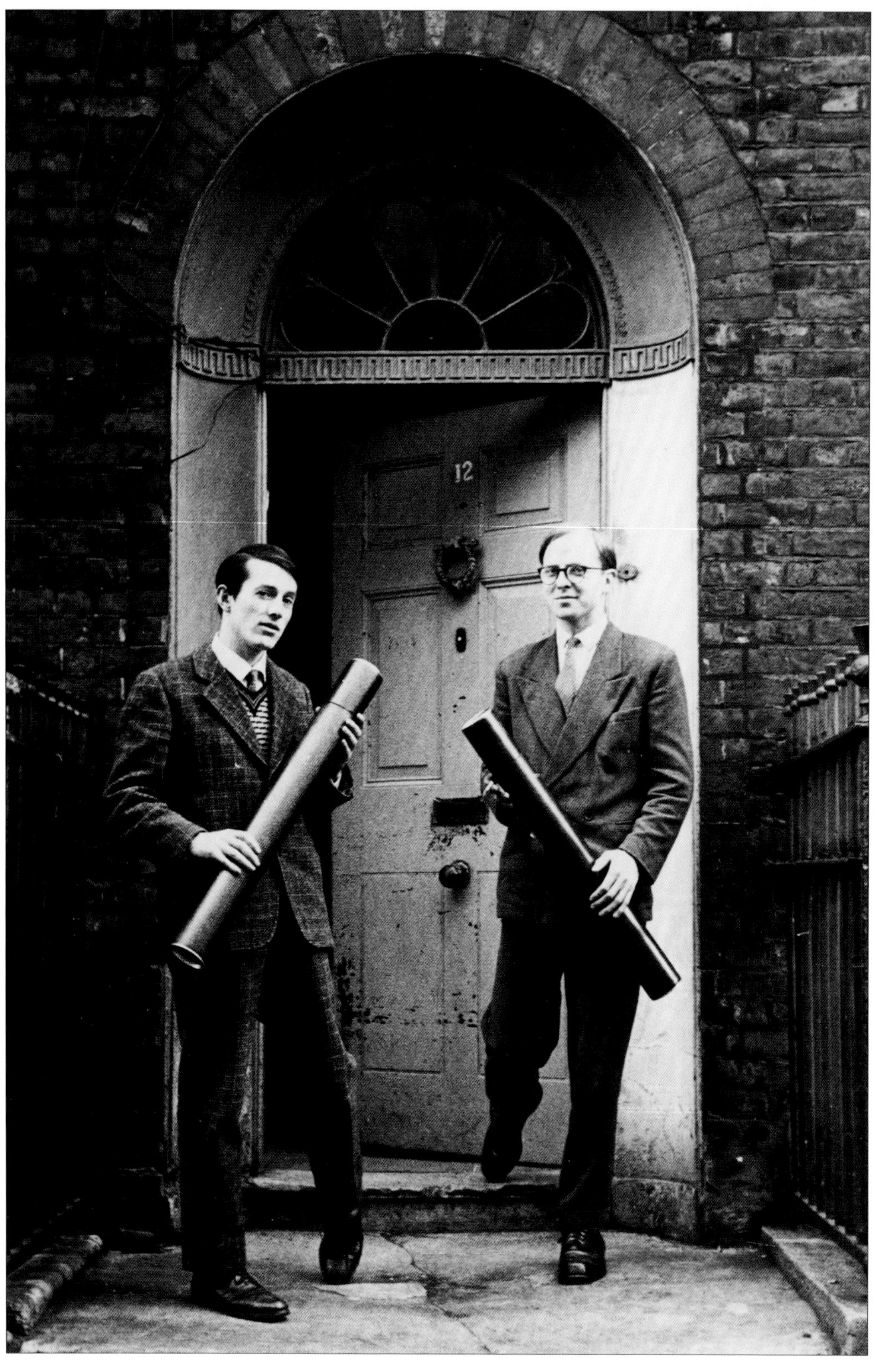

1969. Off to post CHARCOAL ON PAPER SCULPTURE for the Paris 14 Group Exhibition.

What is Gilbert & George?

Michael Bracewell

HENI

We just want this clear simple vision of ourselves. We don't have to meet all those philosophers in France to understand what we're doing.

Gilbert & George, 1995

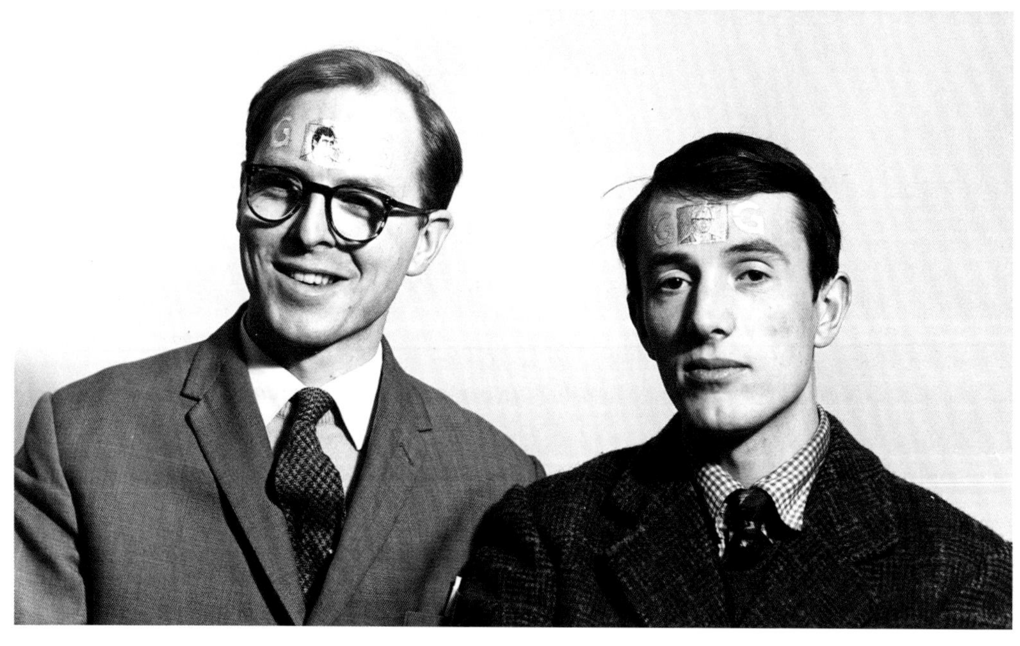

1969. DESIGNS FOR FOREHEADS.

Contents

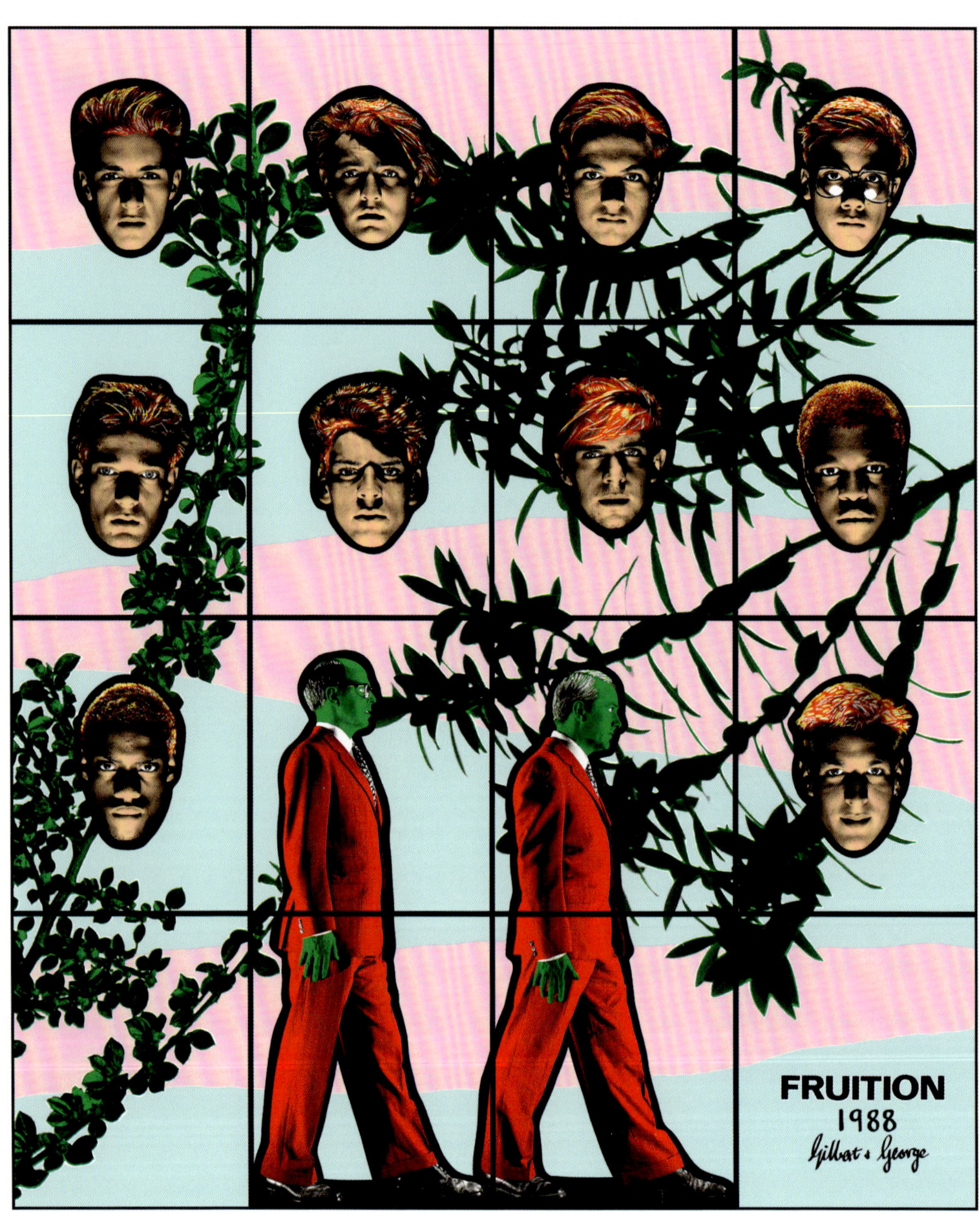

FRUITION. 1988. 302 x 254 cm

One
What is Gilbert & George?

Gilbert and George are two men who together are one artist: Gilbert & George.

The vision of Gilbert & George is their art, of which they are the embodiment. Therefore Gilbert & George are the art of Gilbert & George. The art of Gilbert & George is based upon feelings rather than intellect.

Gilbert & George are a total modern independent visionary artist, alone.

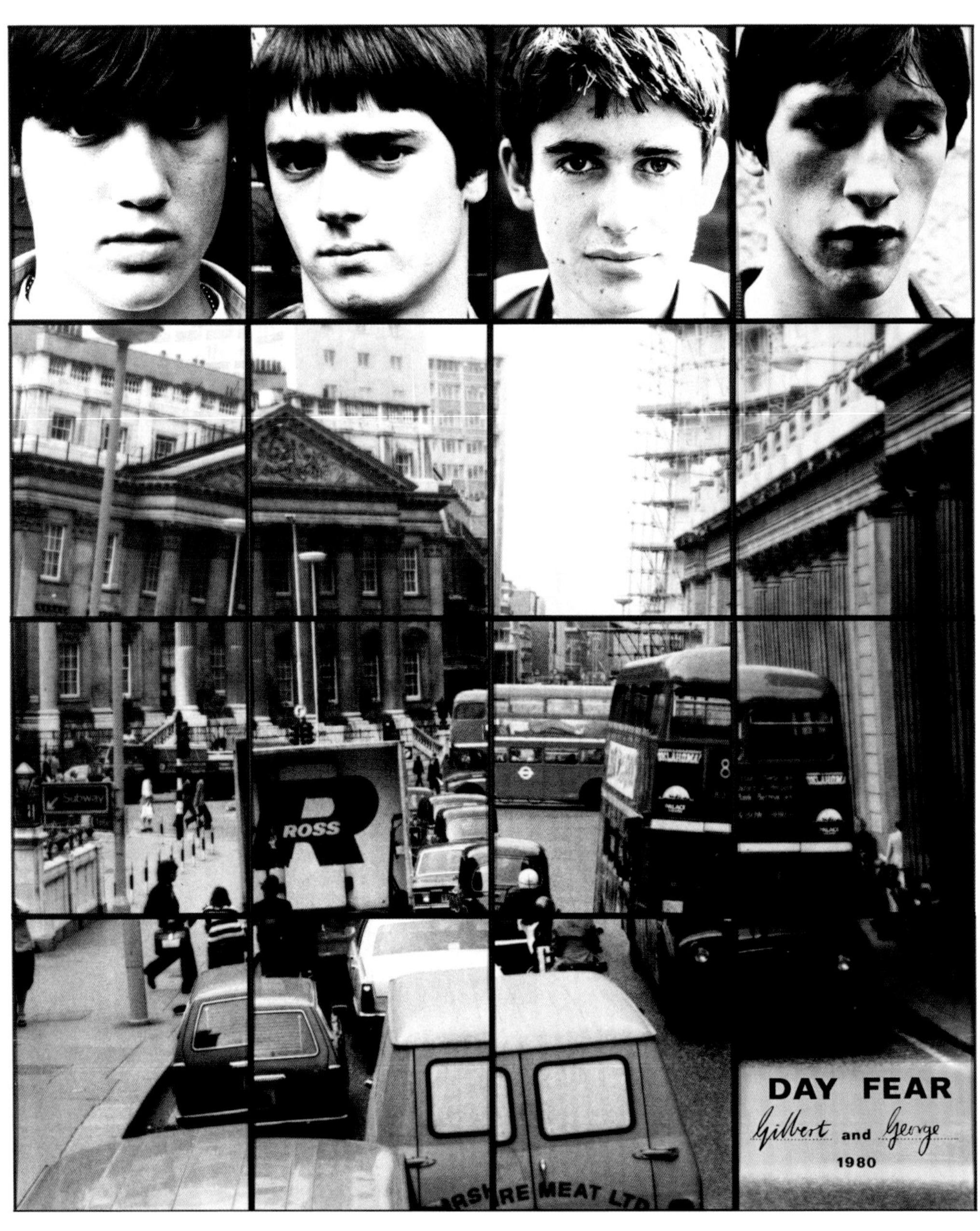

DAY FEAR. 1980. 241 x 201 cm

Two
What is the Vision of Gilbert & George?

The vision of Gilbert & George is firstly their singular and particular way of seeing, experiencing and celebrating life.

The vision of Gilbert & George is also and simultaneously their way of seeing and making art.

The inspiration and subject of the art of Gilbert & George is modern life.

The life of Gilbert & George is art.

Gilbert & George, with the viewer, explore and test their feelings in their art.

On walks around their home in the East End of London, Gilbert & George see the modern human condition. Acceleration, religion, politics, business, dullness, leisure, celebration, violence, money, history, poverty, age, sex, work, hope, newness, sickness, desire, intoxication, beauty, dereliction, love, despair, the radicalised world, the virtual world. They see the daily routines and feelings of their fellow citizens, from all backgrounds: the fast, modern, multi-cultural and multi-technological world. Office workers and junkies. They see the spectrum of human behaviour.

Gilbert & George observe the constantly changing life of the city the way one might observe the weather, or study the ceaseless current of a vast river.

The vision of Gilbert & George is committed to raw realism, but is also deeply romantic: finding heightened or disturbed emotion in ordinary things, in a way that renders the subjects of their art extraordinary and richly atmospheric; individual, yet connected by common feelings.

The vision of Gilbert & George derives from the union of lucidity and heightened feeling; their art from the balance of control and loss of control.

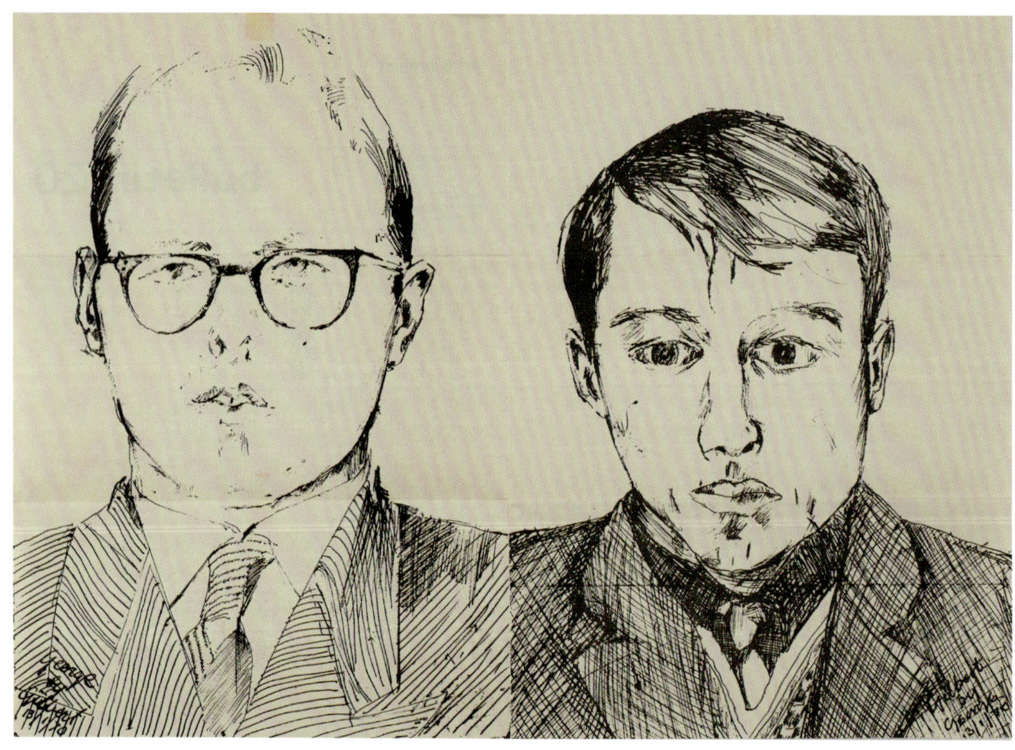

1970. GEORGE BY GILBERT AND GILBERT BY GEORGE.
Ball pen drawing made for *Art and Project Bulletin* N° 20, Amsterdam.

Three
To the Power of Two

Early photos of Gilbert & George show two very glamorous young men: calm, cheerful, resolute. The bond between them looks profound and absolute.

Their duality infers the idea of two men brought together by fate, as outsiders, as seekers-of-truth, as outcasts, as companion-lover-fellow travellers, as witnesses of life, together in their vulnerability and the climate of their feelings. Dualism structures the vision and art of Gilbert & George: two men, one artist; control and loss of control; reactionary and radical; traditional and ultra-modern.

The singularity of Gilbert & George, therefore, derives from their duality.

There is a magical quality to the union of Gilbert & George, as communicated by their art.

The notion of two tramps, always on the outside, with only each other, journeying through life. At times they seem to be stooges of fate, at others, cosmic travellers, or old fashioned song-and-dance men: mystical, vulnerable, desiring, supernatural, suffering, ritualistic, universal in their contradictions as much as their constancy. These roles and qualities comprise a powerful modern archetype: part seer, part common man, part poet, part rebel-disrupter of complacencies. More fancifully: melancholy ghost and mischievous poltergeist.

The duality of Gilbert & George enables and articulates reflection, opposites, unity, solidarity, disturbance, love, comedy and myth.

The art of Gilbert & George is the epic story of two seekers-of-truth and all that they encounter, all that occurs to them, always alone, always together.

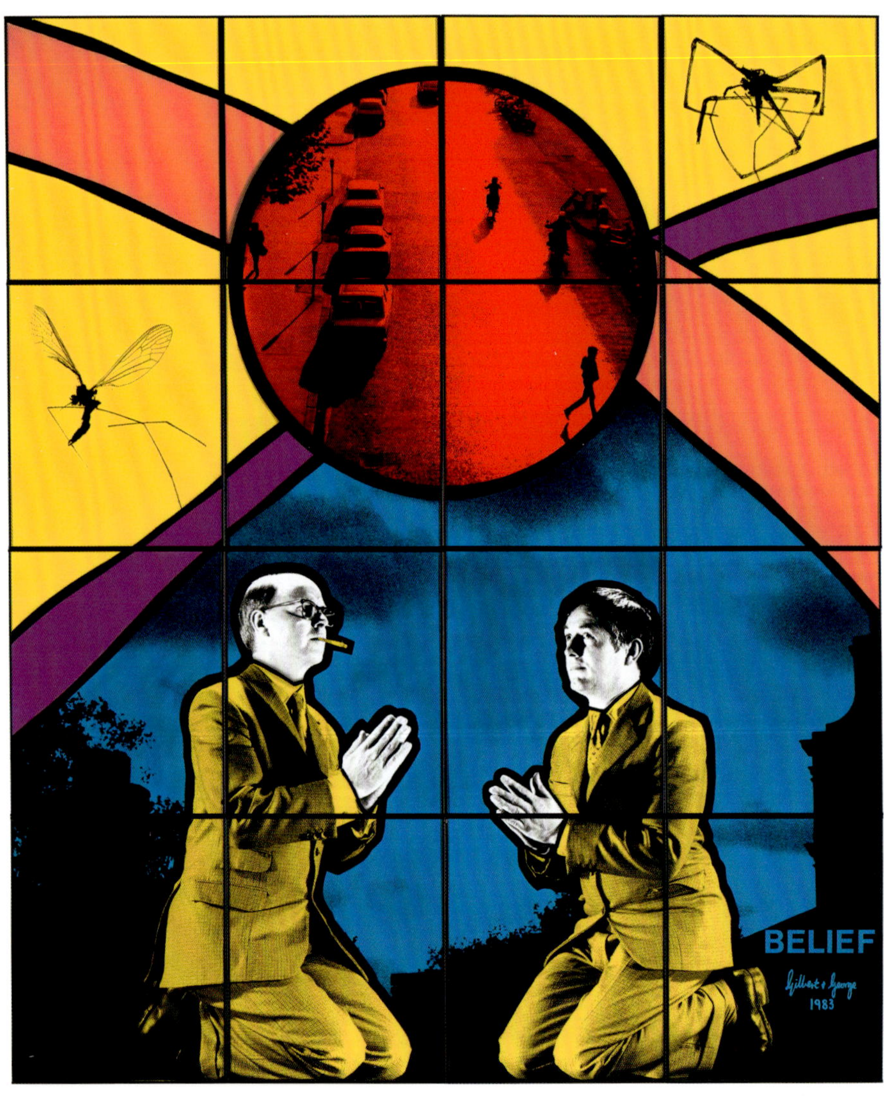

Four
Gilbert & George are Anti-Theoretical

Gilbert & George repudiate the reach and influence of art theory as a means of conceiving, creating, solving or explaining a work of art.

Gilbert & George maintain an ideological opposition to art theory and the reference of art to the history or theory of art.

Their art asserts instead the powers of emotion and actuality, and the confluence of these living forces. It does this in ways that are variously and in combination violent, mysterious, comical, poetic, brutal, absurd, sexual, ugly, mystical, monstrous, loving, visionary, prurient, shocking and rich with ceremonial and symbolic meaning.

Gilbert & George want their art to be a living art, which suggests feelings to each viewer, and poses questions that may or may not be answerable, but are personal, piercing and vital as questions. Their art addresses particularly subjects that are culturally occluded or disowned. Their art questions social taboos and morality. The vision and art of Gilbert & George is relentless and uncompromising.

By looking at difficult subjects in a humanistic way, the art and vision of Gilbert & George, however extreme, is intended to 'de-

← BELIEF. 1983. 241 x 201 cm

shock' rather than seeking to shock. The aim of Gilbert & George is not the simple task of 'shocking' a viewer, but the difficult task of interrogating a subject and themselves.

Crucially, the art of Gilbert & George, however poetic or spectacular an individual picture or sculpture may be, is not intended to be an aesthetic, formalist or conceptual statement of any kind, or to be admired for qualities such as colour, composition or artistic reference.

The art of Gilbert & George is intended to confront, entrance, interrogate, inspire, disrupt certainties, create difficulties, amuse, mystify, amaze, shock, move, confound and above all prompt the viewer to question life and art within themselves and their own experience.

Often dogmatic, combative, crude, crazed, grotesque, unfathomable, blasphemous, theatrical and troubling; often joyous, inspiring, generous, funny, beautiful and strange, the art of Gilbert & George has always invited the viewer, intimately and forcefully, to search for and question their own truth, and find their own answers.

If you believe in God, or not; if you cannot comprehend the current of events that seems to be sweeping you away; if you are the whole of boredom; if you think you're cool; if you feel secure in your authority; if you find yourself ridiculous; if you are in or out of love; rich or poor – the art of Gilbert & George addresses you directly, as an equal within a democracy of modern equals, each a vessel of amazing potential, and doesn't pay heed to your cynicism or pride, because the river runs on.

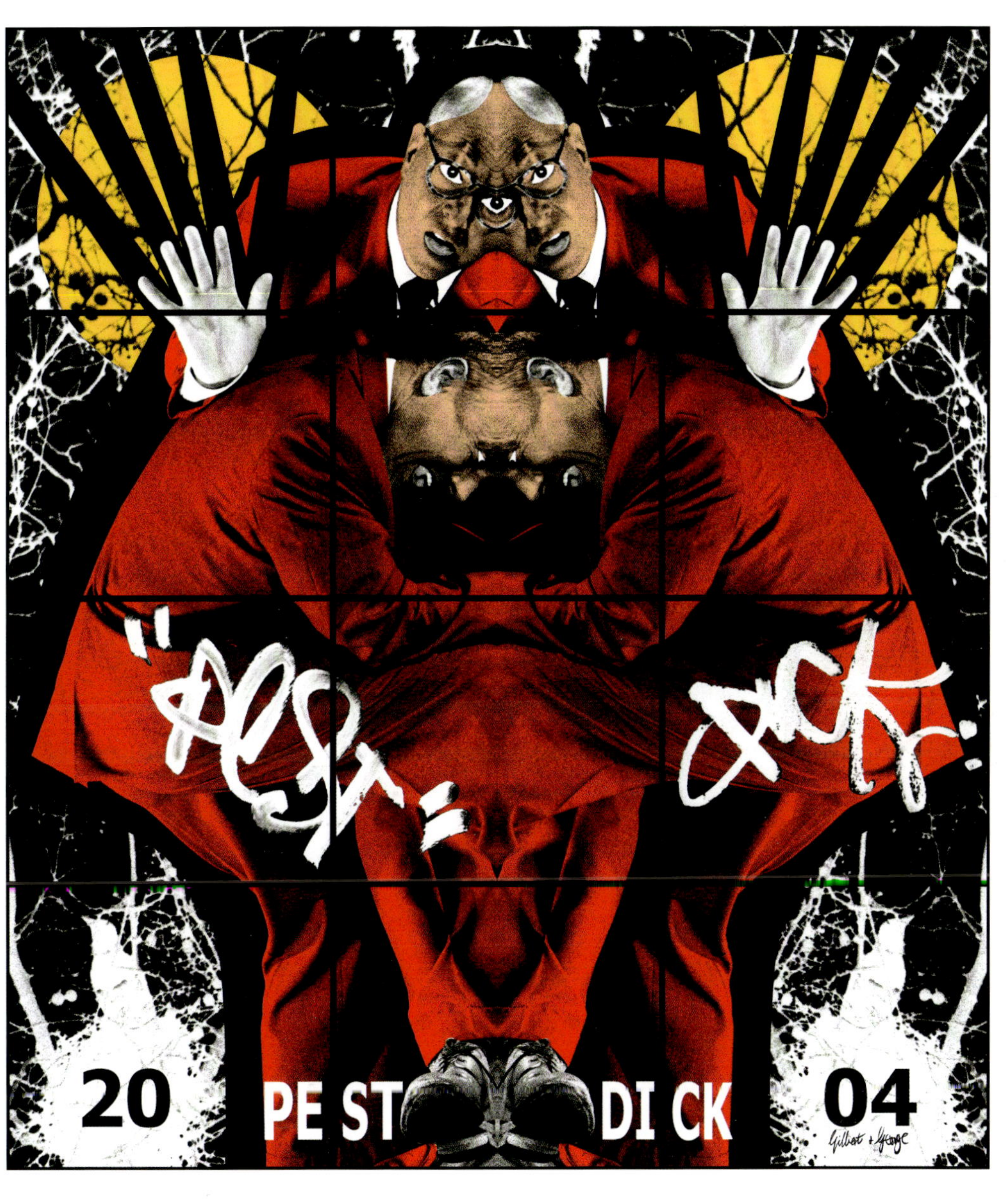

PEST DICK. 2004. 252 x 225 cm
One of THE PERVERSIVE PICTURES.

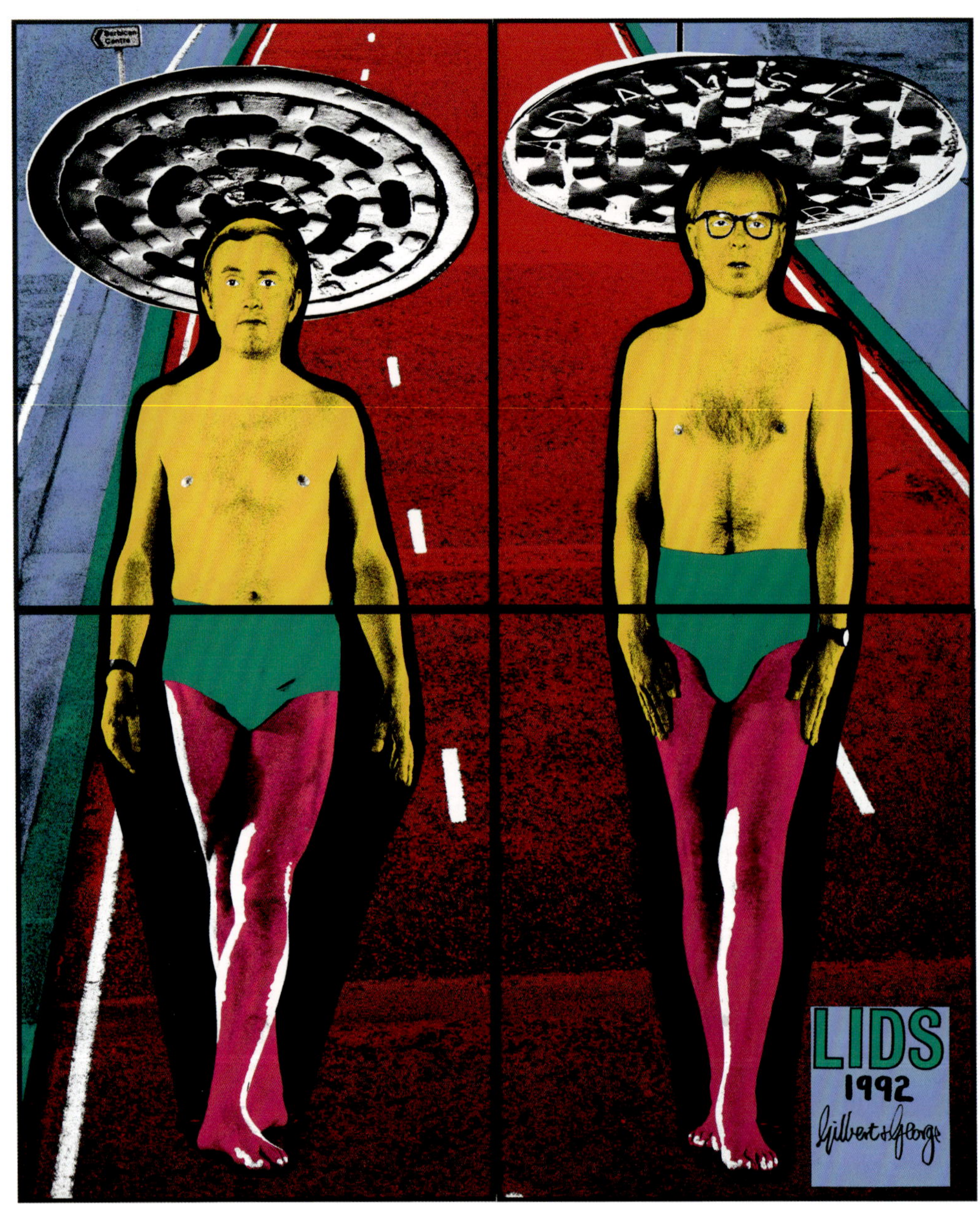

LIDS.   1992.   169 x 142 cm

Five
Always Begin with a Joke

From their earliest days, Gilbert & George have advanced and empowered their art with the assistance of both overt and ambiguous humour and paradox.

The modern archetype of the same-sex double act relates to the modern archetype of the prankster, comedian and stooge of fate. The lives of the same-sex double acts – from Bouvard *et* Pécuchet to Laurel and Hardy – become parables of meaning. Tricks, jokes, poses, pastiche and slapstick-melancholy-absurdist-comedy dramas can become agents of opposition, manifestos and declarations of independence. In Britain, comedy is the nearest thing we have to a national avant-garde.

Humour, like glamour, spectacle and shock, communicates directly and alluringly, its charm drawing the viewer into the deeper and more serious world of a vision, statement or argument.

The art and vision of Gilbert & George is not ironic but is drawn from a concept of irony: contrast, reversal, paradox, multi-faceted and layered. In their art, the funny can be sad; the absurd can be serious; the stark and lonely can be beautiful; the uproarious and hilarious can be threatening and fearful.

In communicating their feelings and beliefs, Gilbert & George can be funny in conjunction with being violent, melancholy, disturbing, disturbed, glamorous, dead-pan, ghostly, prurient. Humour is an intense shade on the palette of emotions from which the art of Gilbert & George is created.

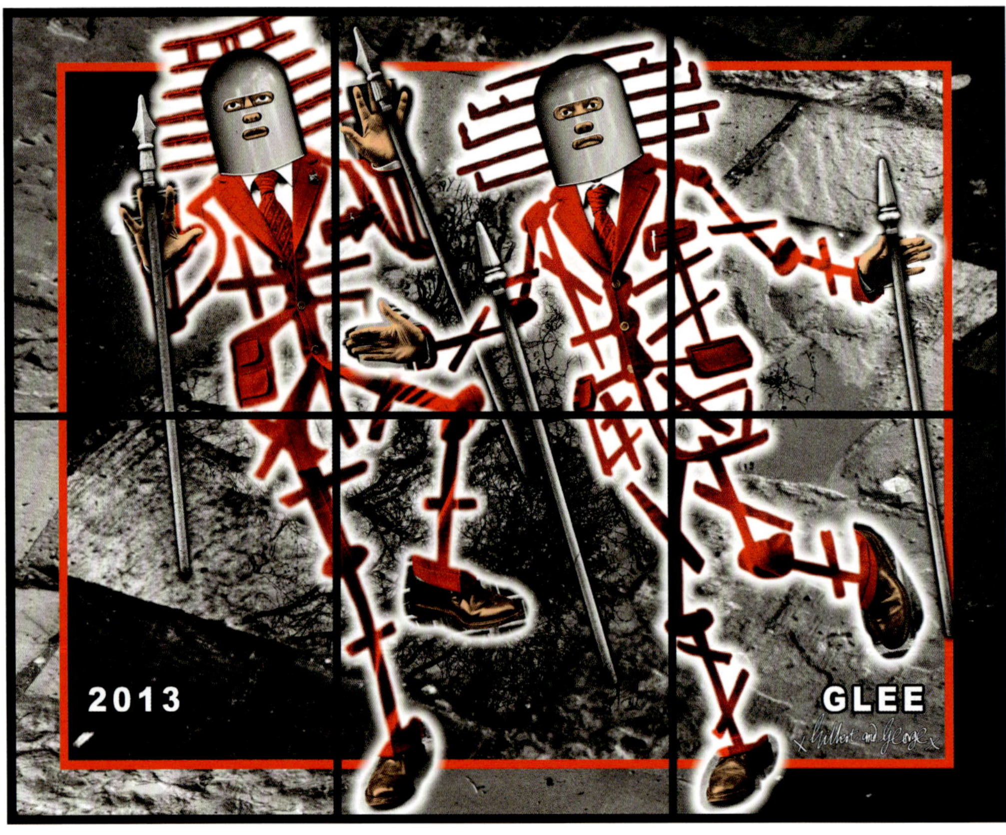

GLEE. 2013. 151 x 191 cm
One of THE SCAPEGOATING PICTURES.

Six
The 'Moral Dimension' of the Art of Gilbert & George

The art of Gilbert & George is the moral and emotional expression of their vision.

For Gilbert & George, the 'moral dimension' in their art conveys the imprint of time and human activity on all things. It is fundamental to the vision of Gilbert & George to experience and transcribe in their art the strange, alluring eloquence of this imprint – its truth.

The 'moral dimension' in the art of Gilbert & George is therefore powerfully empathetic, as though all phenomena were sentient: the sadness of the old wall, the desire of the leaves, the personalities of street names, the temper of graffiti, the loneliness of broken glass.

Further examples in the art of Gilbert & George might be the image of a wet and empty street, the postmark on an old letter, or a padlocked steel door. Each image brings its own world, of which it is eloquent when un-muted by our openness to its call.

We think of all the life that has taken place along the street, the activity and event, drama and nothingness, that have soaked like rain into the asphalt and the buildings and the pavements and the trees. We think of place absorbing time, of time ventriloquising place, and vice versa. The overlapping commentaries of memory and mood, the chasm of the past from which we are constantly emerging. The 'moral dimension' in the vision and art of Gilbert & George is to acknowledge the continuum of mortality: all those people, all those lives, where are they now?

The vision of Gilbert & George is therefore the first principle by which their art is inspired and created. The moral vision of Gilbert & George is the beating heart of their art's truth.

The art of Gilbert & George conveys the symbolic power of its subjects as a crucial aspect or its psychological and emotional impact. For example, the ruin in one of their pictures (the broken concrete and rusted steel cables in a demolished building) is the ruin inside all of us. The street in East London with its cyclists and street signs and litter and scratched stickers on lamp posts, is the universal street. The stranger stands for the mystery and anonymity of all strangers. The leafless branch leads the viewer's thoughts to sadness or hope, loneliness, the nature of faith or love, the passing of the seasons, the speed and colour of days. The desire to do nothing but look at the sky.

Shit, tears, traffic, drunkenness, clowning or clouds, anonymous youths, luxuriant blossoms, snow, classified advertisements, old statues, newspaper headlines. All of the image-subjects in the art of Gilbert & George are configured to create pictures that resemble fantastical tableaux: declamatory, elegiac, crazy lucid-dreaming scenes of modern life.

The viewer experiences the drama, temper or strangeness of the art of Gilbert & George as a glimpse of some mad-mystical-visionary commentary upon the mood of the modern world – as though looking through a portal into a wonderland or a parallel dimension within our common reality. A place where archetypes and symbols create their own strange pageantry. Here's where the story ends: the rain, the street, the psychic force-field of a million strangers, the collapse of meaning into primal forces.

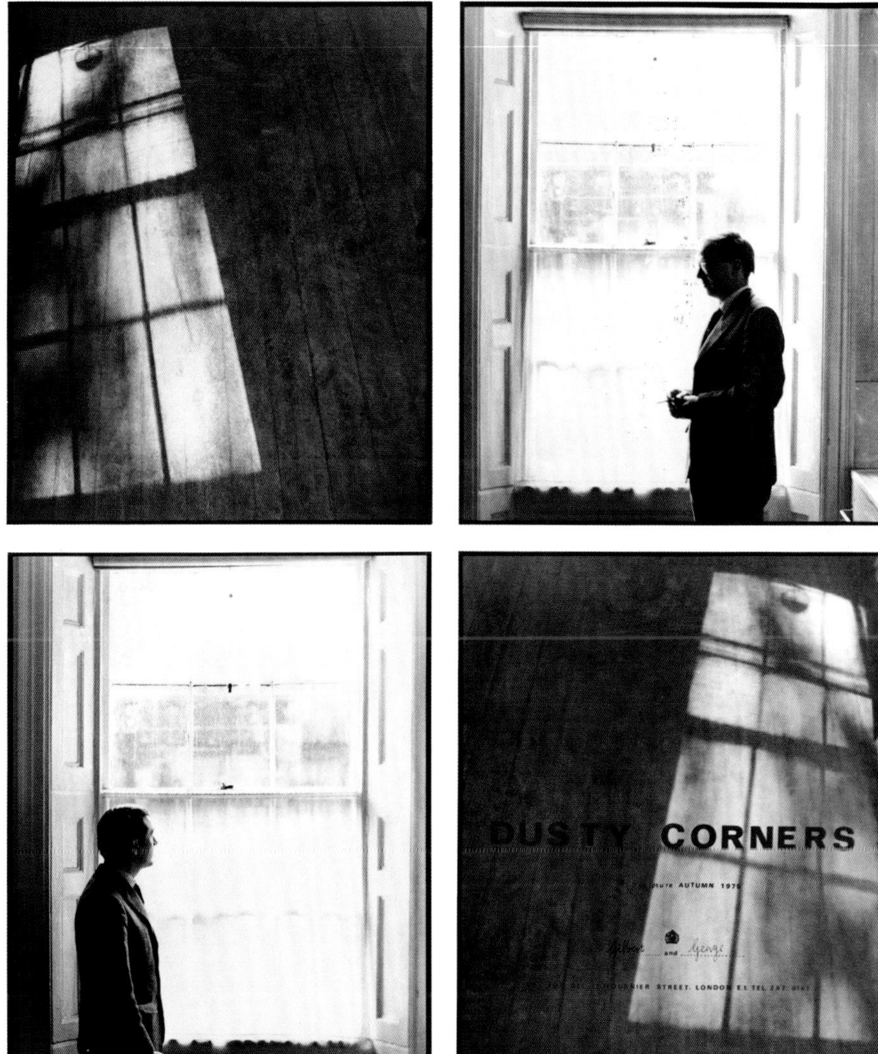

DUSTY CORNERS Nº 10. 1975. 124 x 104 cm

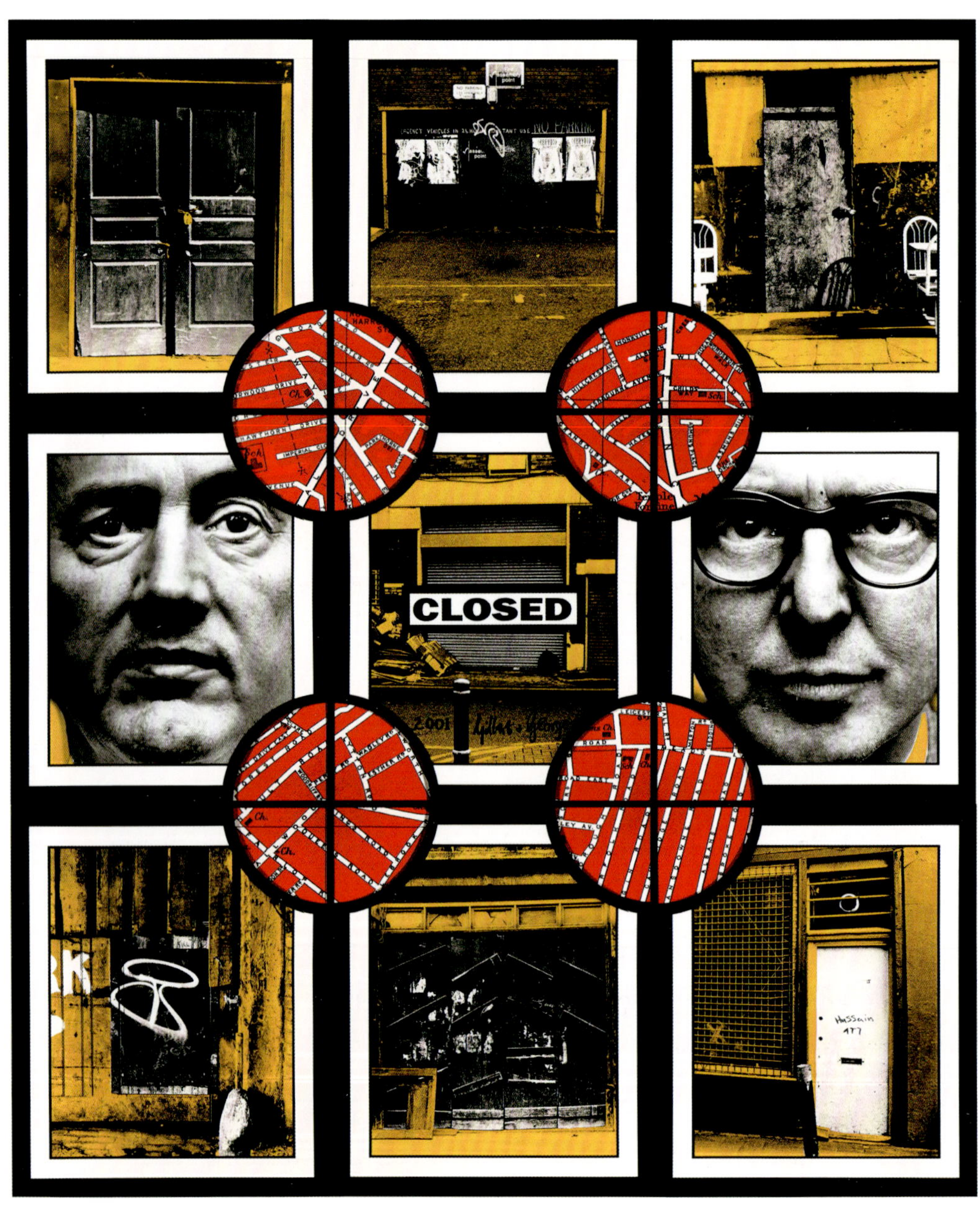

CLOSED. 2001. 226 x 190 cm
One of THE NINE DARK PICTURES.

Seven

Qualitative Judgements Don't Apply

The art of Gilbert & George – absurdist, eerie, sexy, moody, insolent, angry, mad and inscrutable – has never been created by the artists to be 'good' or 'bad' as art, in artistic terms.

If a classically modern and modernist view of art can be summarised as the translation, through art, of individual experience into universal truth, then the art of Gilbert & George could be said to exclude and deny that act of artistic translation, seeking rather to report or 'channel' their feelings, which are their vision, directly.

The art of Gilbert & George therefore seeks and selects forms, elements and visual language solely on the basis of their immediacy, accuracy and efficiency as communicators of feeling and belief.

In this, Gilbert & George resemble more spirit mediums or a psychic media, reporting on life. They are communicators of states and moods that can be likened to music or the weather: sometimes melodious and harmonic, at others atonal and discordant; calm and mild, then humid and stormy.

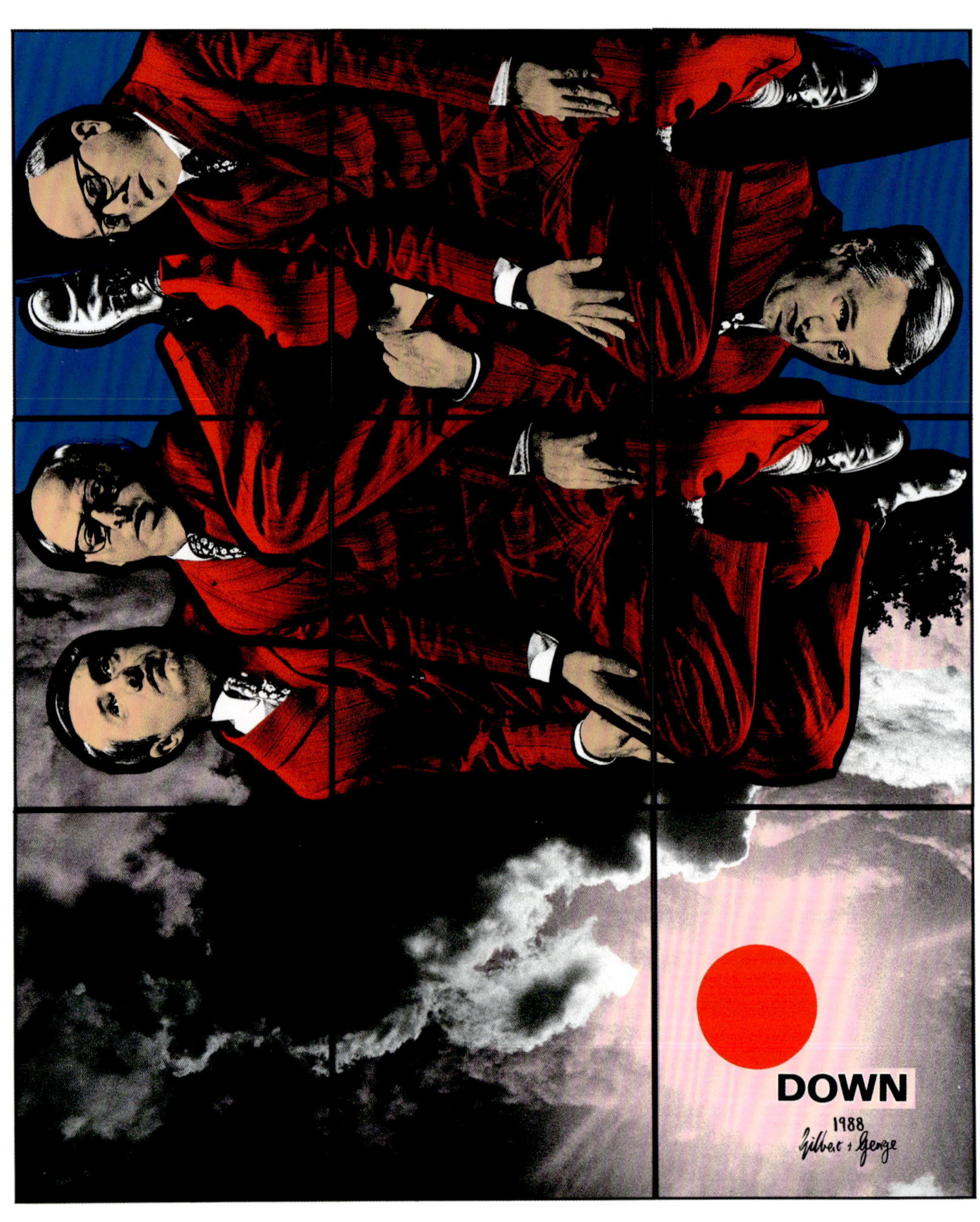

DOWN. 1988. 253 x 213 cm

Eight
Gilbert & George is Paradox and Phantasmagorical Realism

Gilbert & George want their art to communicate their experience of witness as directly as possible.

Pictorially, this communication appears as visionary, symbolic and archetypical tableaux: absurd, monstrous, crazy, dream-like, corporeal, hallucinogenic, portentous – at times inferring stories, encounters or adventures. Time, place, activity and incident combine and mutate into strange new alloys of feeling and experience.

The art of Gilbert & George makes use of this hybridisation, contrast, paradox and confluence to articulate drama, mystery, urgency, stillness, tragedy, hysteria – heightened emotion, the moods of life.

The balance of 'madness' and 'normality' empowers their art. In the art of Gilbert & George, visionary spectacle occurs within landscapes of modern urban realism. The conservative dress and demeanour of Gilbert & George, as they take their places in their art, is in sharp contrast to the extreme states they witness, attend, embody, depict. The art of Gilbert & George reveals the turbulence of thought, prejudice and feeling concealed within rational human behaviour.

These contrasts, confluences, contradictions and conflations of time, place and image create the formidable paradox of 'phantasmagorical realism' ('phantasmagorical', adjective: 1. Having a fantastic or deceptive appearance, as something in a dream or created by the imagination. 2. Having the appearance of an optical illusion, especially one produced by a magic lantern. 3. Changing or shifting, as a scene made up of many elements).

The art of Gilbert & George is not concerned with formalist artistic problems but ethical provocation, experiential sensation and empathy. How does their art make the viewer feel? Jubilant or angry, confused or entranced? And how does their response speak to their sense of themselves? How is the viewer changed by their experience of looking at the art?

For Gilbert & George, such self-questioning and questioning of art is the function of art and also their statement on the role of art. All of their art is and always has been therefore a 'manifesto' (noun: 'a public declaration of policy and aims') as well as an account of their emotional experience of the modern world.

As such, the art of Gilbert & George is also avant-garde in the original meaning of that term: 'an agent of reform'.

The vision of Gilbert & George is therefore a moral and emotional experience of the modern world, communicated in a form that combines the visionary with the paradoxical, and as an artistic principle. These forms and functions are interlinked and interdependent, and have been expressed in the art of Gilbert & George, over the years, in many different but unified media: posing, drawing, inviting, drinking, painting, dancing, writing, filming and the creation of thousands of pictures.

The vision of Gilbert & George, which is also the art of Gilbert & George, is a visionary, avant-garde, anti-art manifesto.

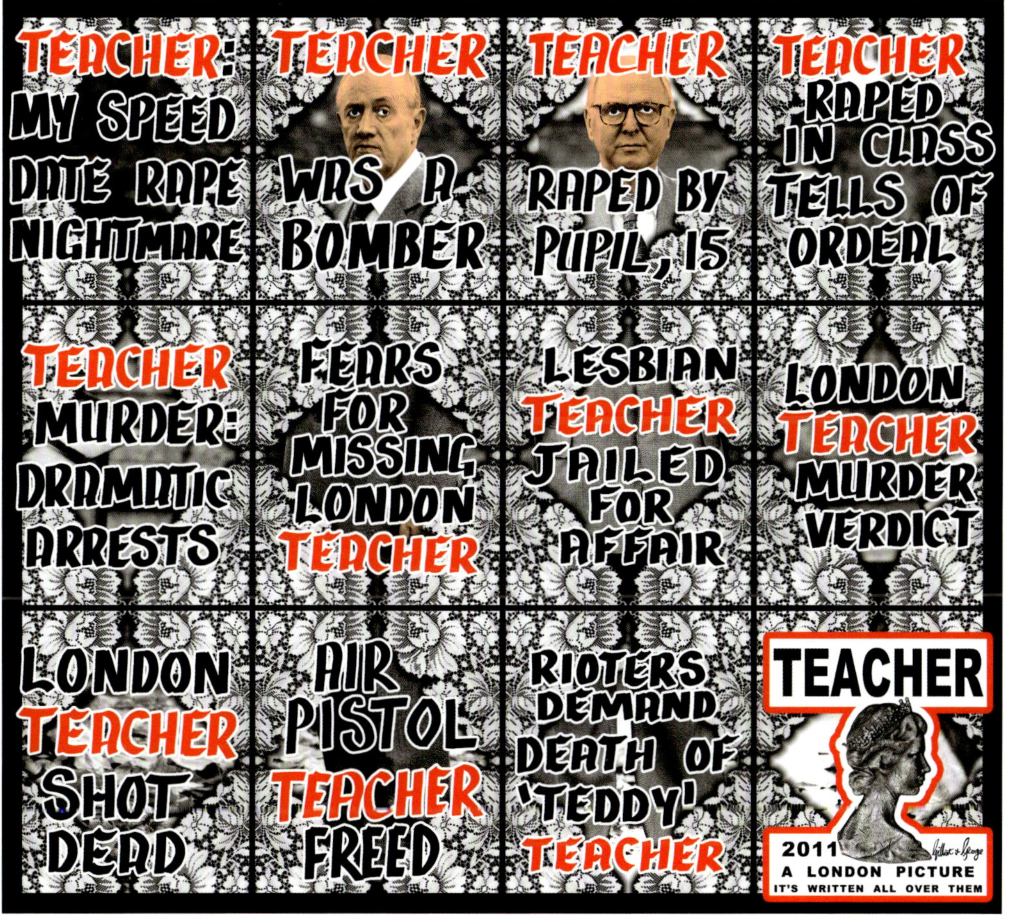

TEACHER. 2011. 226 x 254 cm
One of THE LONDON PICTURES.

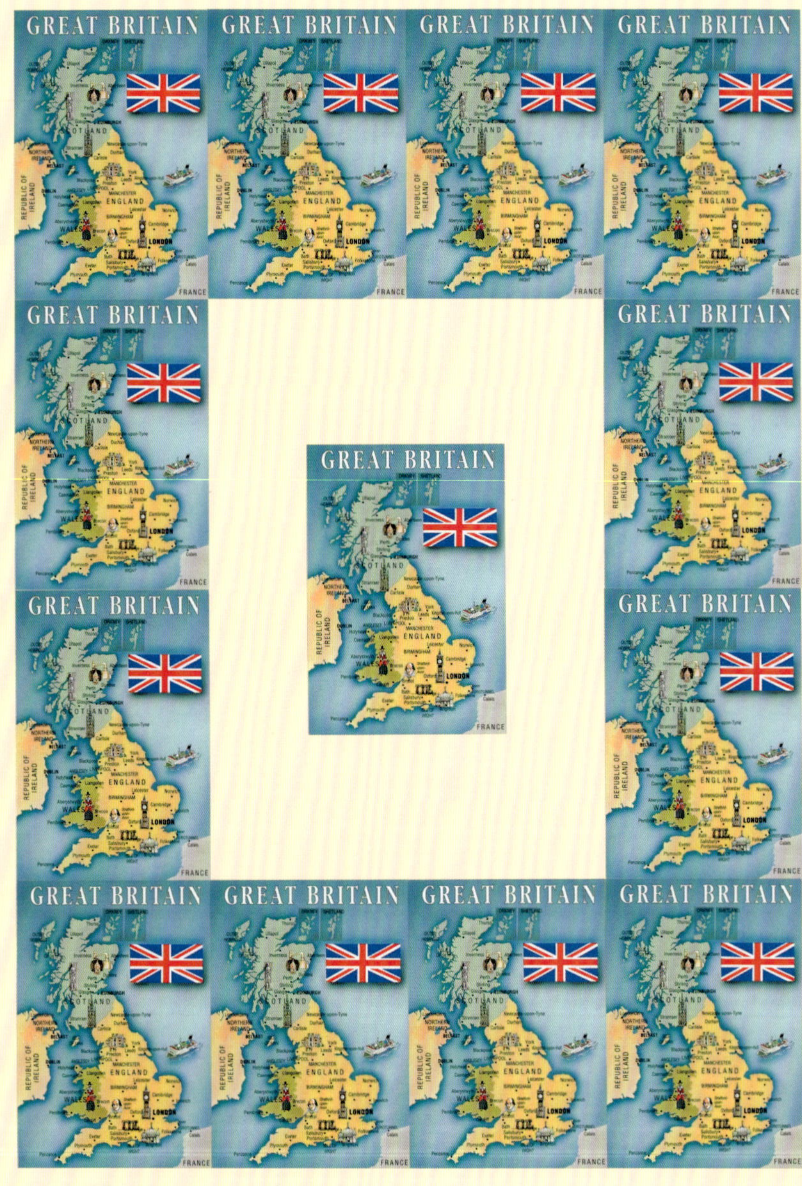

GB

A UNION FLAG PICTURE POSTCARD PICTURE

13 IDENTICAL CARDS ARRANGED TO FORM AN ANGULATED VERSION ⊡ OF THE SIGN OF THE URETHRA ⊙

Gilbert 2009 and George

TRAD VER CONT

Nine
Modern Efficiency

Gilbert & George have always wanted to use the most efficient and up-to-date means of making their art.

The appearance of their art, in terms of medium and design, is dictated by the criteria of clarity, impact and modernity.

When Gilbert & George began to make their art, having nothing – no tools, no studio, no money, no support – they realised that they were their own medium and found ways to communicate their vision in the most direct and emphatic manner: as LIVING SCULPTURES, by means of POSTCARD SCULPTURES and courteous formal invitations.

They made their DRAWING SCULPTURES by working very fast on large sheets of paper that could be assembled to create a dramatic and atmospheric enfolding and immersive experience for the viewer. Like standing in a clearing in the forest. The drawings were not made to be 'good' as drawings, but to communicate feelings and thoughts as powerfully and directly as possible.

← GB. 2009. 123 x 88 cm A URETHRA POSTCARD PICTURE.
Gilbert & George began creating POSTCARD SCULPTURES in 1972.

When viewers began to admire these drawings as drawings, aesthetically, Gilbert & George ceased to make them.

Other efficient media for communicating their vision of life and art included making books, and making pictures in the medium of composite photographic panels, that could be adaptable in size, easily assembled and stored for transport. This design system, which Gilbert & George developed as early as 1971 and had perfected as their iconic 'grid' form by 1974, communicates their vision in a form that is monumental, timelessly modern and emotionally emphatic.

Since 2000, Gilbert & George have used computers to replicate the image-making process they had used to create their earlier pictures. And in updating the technology of their process, Gilbert & George continue to imbue their art with the 'mood' and spirit of that technology. Also, computers reduce even further the chance of 'artistic process' coming between the vision of Gilbert & George and the communication of that vision as art.

Gilbert & George create their art automatically, as a classification system that is shaped in turn by the cataloguing of data: alphabetically by subject, by cross-reference, by type, by frequency. Thus, the explosion of feeling is triggered. This is seen overtly in many groups of pictures, including the TWENTY LONDON EAST ONE PICTURES (2003), the POSTCARD (and related) PICTURES of 2009, and THE LONDON PICTURES of 2010 – all of which are created or 'ordered' by classification, cataloguing, index or directory. These processes of ordering data also have the effect of inferring the vastness, the infinity, of lives, activities and identities.

The means by which Gilbert & George create their art always

informs and deepens the spirit, mood, imagistic and emotional reach of their subject matter. The art of Gilbert & George has always been created in accordance with the most up-to-date and efficient technology available, by the conflation of a rigidly systematic process and volatile, moral, visionary subject matter and by the collision of cold objectivity and deep subjectivity.

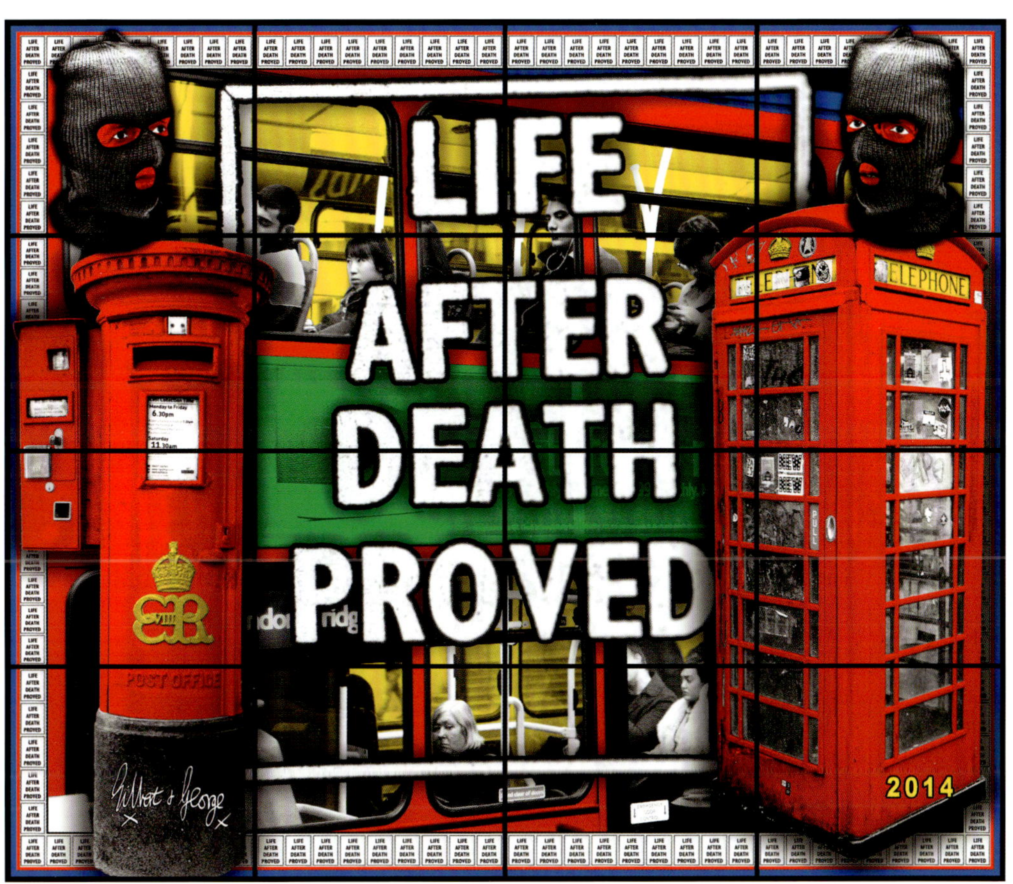

LIFE AFTER DEATH PROVED. 2014. 254 x 302 cm
One of THE UTOPIAN PICTURES.

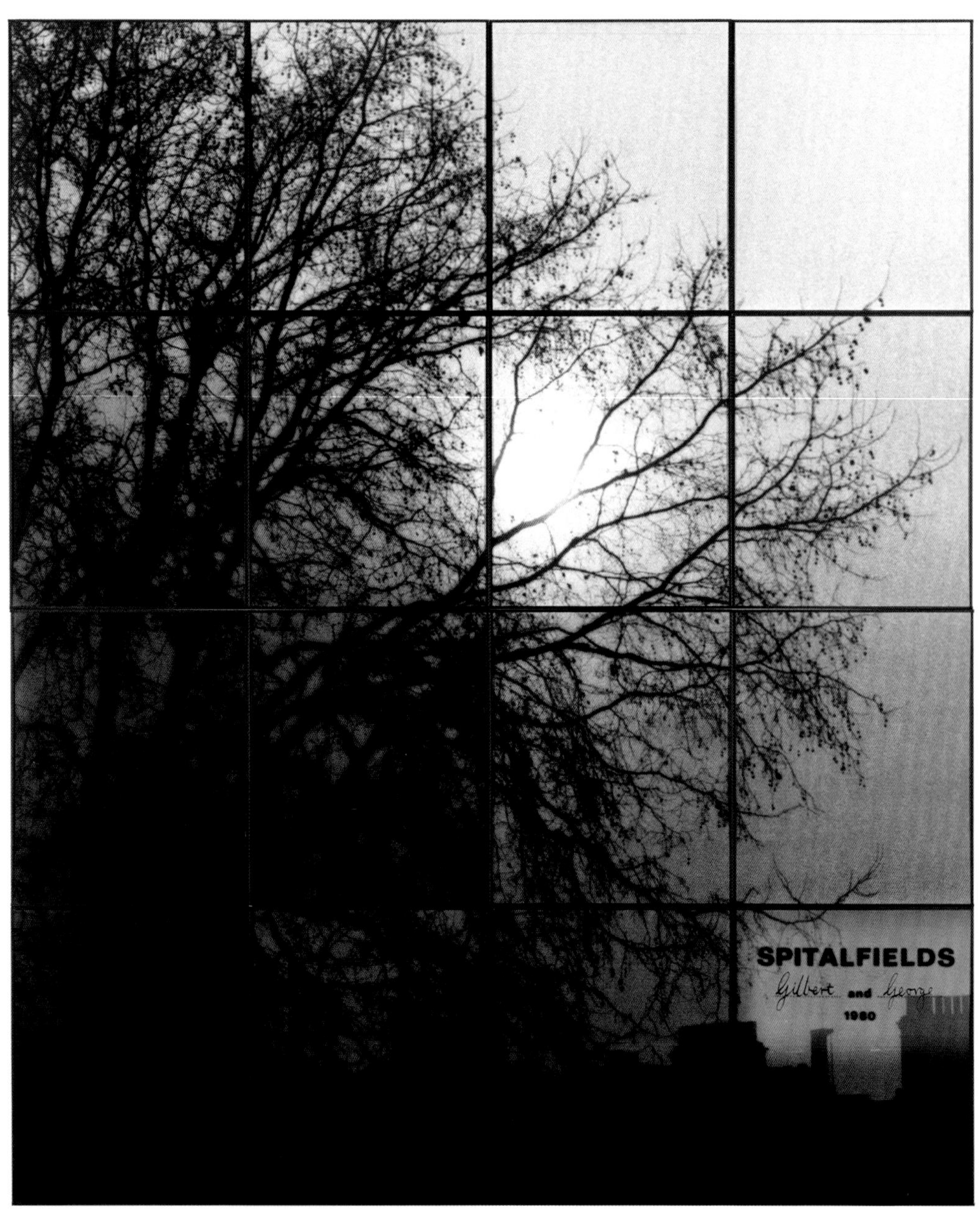

SPITALFIELDS. 1980. 241 x 201 cm

Ten
Looking at the Art of Gilbert & George: 'How is my nature modified by its presence?'

The art of Gilbert & George invites the viewer to look and examine the experience of looking. The quotation below, from the writings of the Victorian critic Walter Pater, offers an astute account of this process:

'To see the object as in itself it really is,' has been justly said to be the aim of all true criticism whatever, and in aesthetic criticism the first step towards seeing one's object as it really is, is to know one's own impression as it really is, to discriminate it, to realise it distinctly. The objects with which aesthetic criticism deals – music, poetry, artistic and accomplished forms of human life – are indeed receptacles of so many powers or forces: they possess, like the products of nature, so many virtues or qualities. What is this song or picture, this engaging personality presented in life or in a book, to me? What effect does it really produce on me? Does it give me pleasure? And if so, what sort or degree of pleasure? How is my nature modified by its presence, and under its influence? The answers to these questions are the

original facts with which the aesthetic critic has to do; and, as in the study of light, of morals, of number, one must realise such primary data for one's self, or not at all.

Walter Pater, *The Renaissance: Studies in Art and Poetry* (1873)

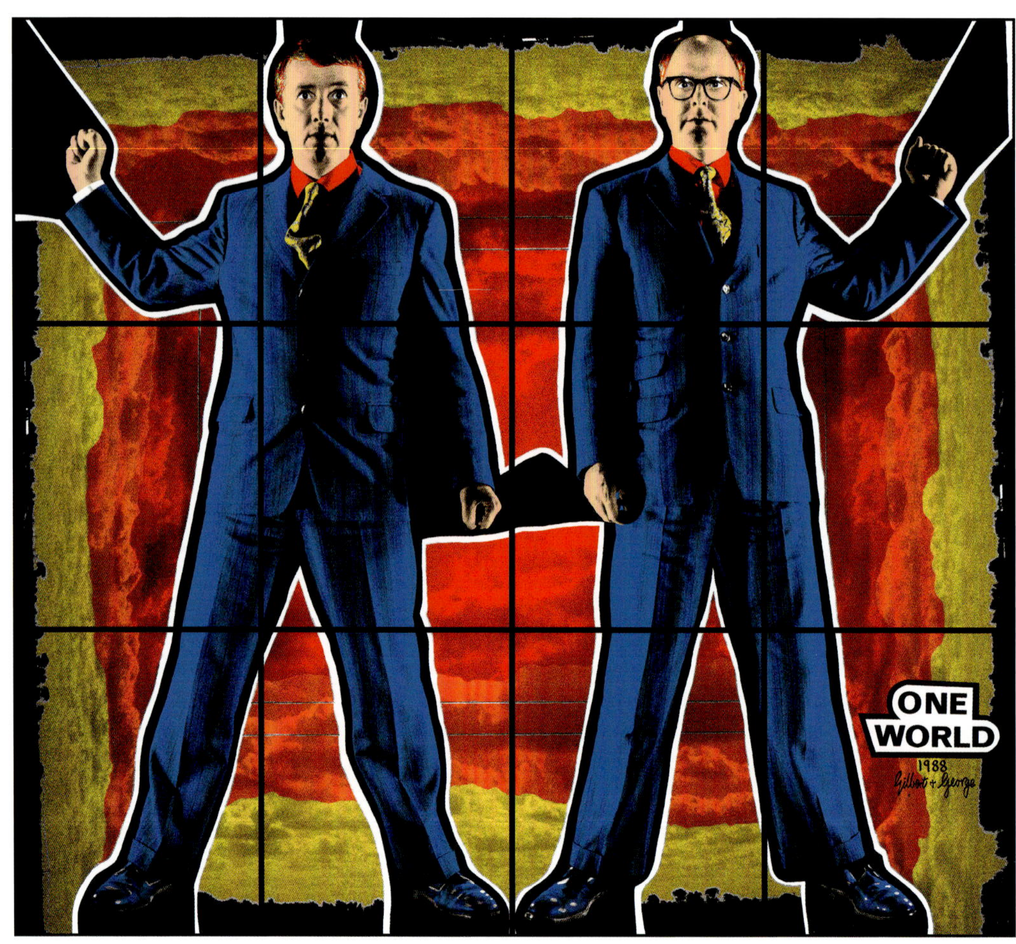

ONE WORLD. 1988. 226 x 254 cm

Eleven
Gilbert & George Contra Mundum

Soon after meeting at St Martin's School of Art, London, in 1967, Gilbert & George knew that they had an opposing view of art to that held by most of their teachers and even their fellow students.

In particular, Gilbert & George rejected the history of modern art as a formalist and aesthetic lineage, rooted in the European Old Masters of the Renaissance, descending down the centuries – with scant regard (as taught at that time) for the history of British art – to Impressionism, Post-Impressionism, Abstraction, Pop art, Minimalism and Conceptualism.

This history and these terms, these schools of art, seemed not only meaningless to Gilbert & George, but decadent, irrelevant and elitist. To Gilbert & George this was a history and ideology of art that addressed only other artists and those educated in the history and theory of art.

Gilbert & George opposed and confronted the academic vision of art that their generation had inherited. They did not believe, for example, that an abstract steel sculpture, however minutely or cleverly discussed, had any relevance whatsoever to the lives of the 'majority' of people sitting on a bus in the street below the art school studio windows.

Nor did Gilbert & George believe in the anarchic, reforming zeal of Conceptual art in Britain in the late 1960s and early 1970s. They considered its mission to be obscure, incomprehensible to those outside the village of the art world, and solely concerned with, and of relevance to, art and other artists, to the discourse of contemporary art.

The earliest art of Gilbert & George, therefore, opposed the conceptualism of their contemporaries by subverting or confounding its strategies while diverting its processes, subjects and ideologies to the exact reverse of their intended aims and asserted values. Thus Gilbert & George would embroil the elevated discourse of contemporary art in traditionalism, common actuality, populism, conservatism, gin and days out in the country – in all the things that contemporary art was unable or unprepared to process – and they achieved this with extraordinary poetry and transcendent outsider pathos.

Thus, the art and vision of Gilbert & George, so gentle and well-mannered, took shape as a form of class war.

Gilbert & George wanted an independent art of their own, that addressed modern life – chaotic, messy, mysterious, dull, impassioned, vulnerable, busy, contradictory, vulgar, driven and challenged – as it existed on any city street; an art that in addition, as a consequence of this vision, had neither dependency upon, nor affiliation to, any other school or history of art. The art of Gilbert & George would be modern, literal and visionary, simultaneously.

To realise this art, and as a vital aspect of this realisation, they chose isolation, independence and solitariness: Gilbert & George *contra mundum*.

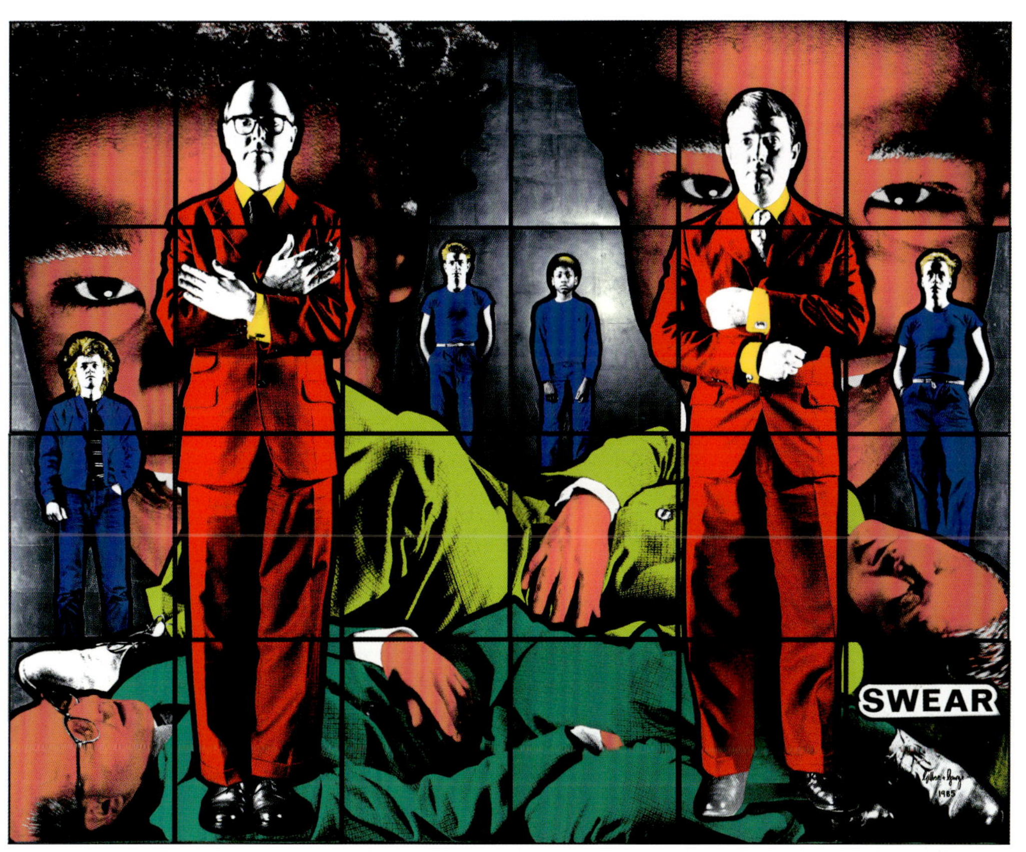

SWEAR. 1985. 251 x 301 cm

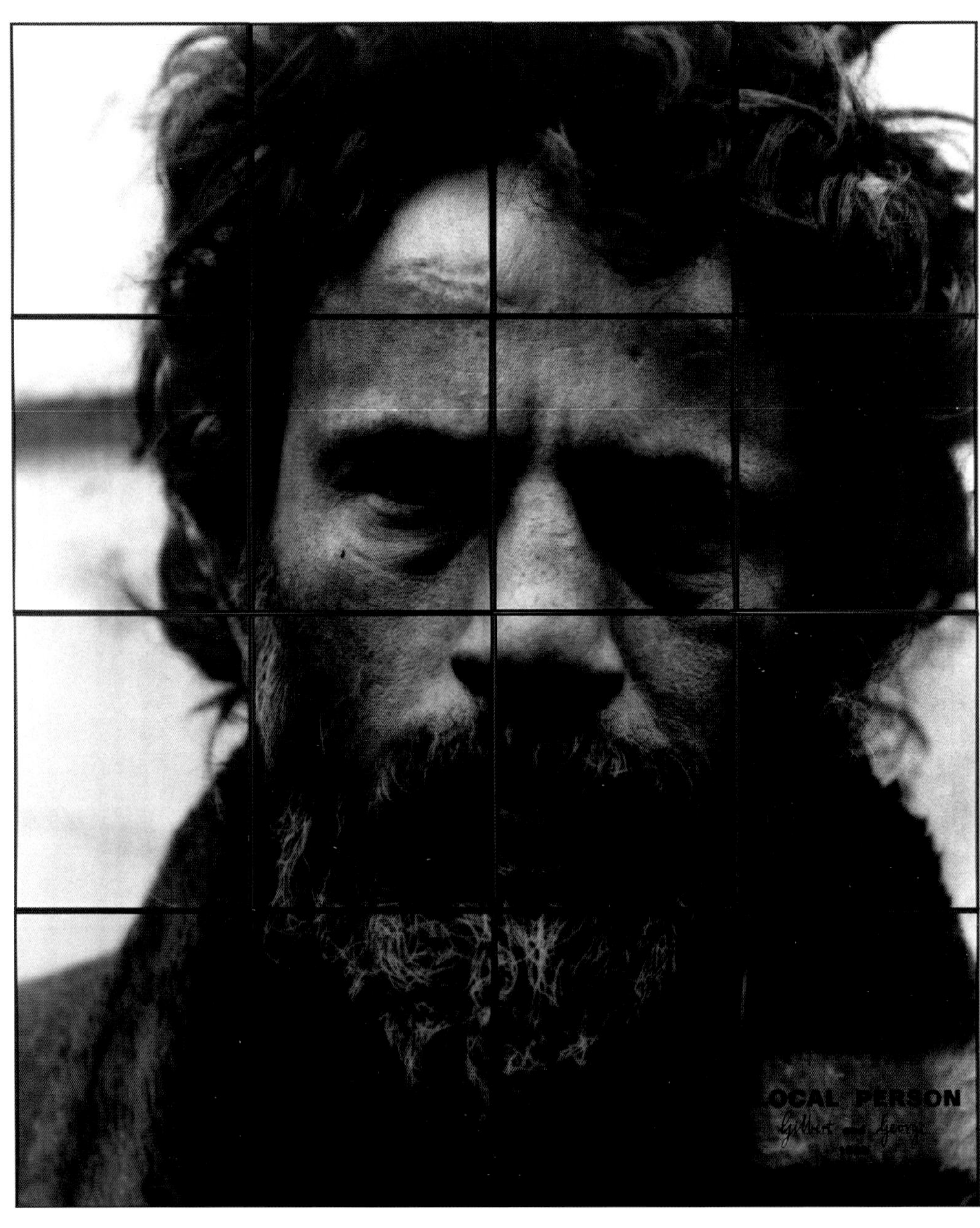

LOCAL PERSON. 1980. 241 x 201 cm

Twelve
Gilbert & George: Avant-Garde Traditionalist Revolutionaries

And so, Gilbert & George set themselves apart from all other artists, young or old. As students, even, they set themselves apart geographically, sartorially, emotionally, socially, artistically and, above all, ideologically.

Gilbert & George did not and do not want to be distracted from their calling and creed as artists by any other artists or artistic institutions or discussion of art.

They moved to what were then the slums and desolation of East London. Here was their subject. Their subject was life, not art.

Having nothing but each other and the streets they walked, Gilbert & George realised – had the life-changing revelation – that 'they' were their art. They named themselves LIVING SCULPTURES and dedicated their lives to the ceaseless, arduous, all-consuming task of being Gilbert & George. They were their own medium, unique. They needed nobody and nothing and still don't. Their beliefs and activities as artists, appropriating forms of conservatism and traditionalism (then regarded as artistically heretical) to their own radical ends, were increasingly opposed to those of most, if not all, of their tutors and contemporaries. In the vision and art of Gilbert & George, as embodied by Gilbert & George, the reactionary became radicalised.

The art of Gilbert & George was thus the reverse of 'contemporary art'. And in this reversal, it was avant-garde.

As reversal is said to be a mainstay of practical magic, so this reversal of contemporary artistic vision, ideals and values conjured into being the single and singular artist, Gilbert & George. From the moment of this realisation, Gilbert & George knew their transformation into the single artist Gilbert & George was absolute and complete.

Gilbert & George were born of opposition and reversal as avant-garde traditionalist revolutionaries.

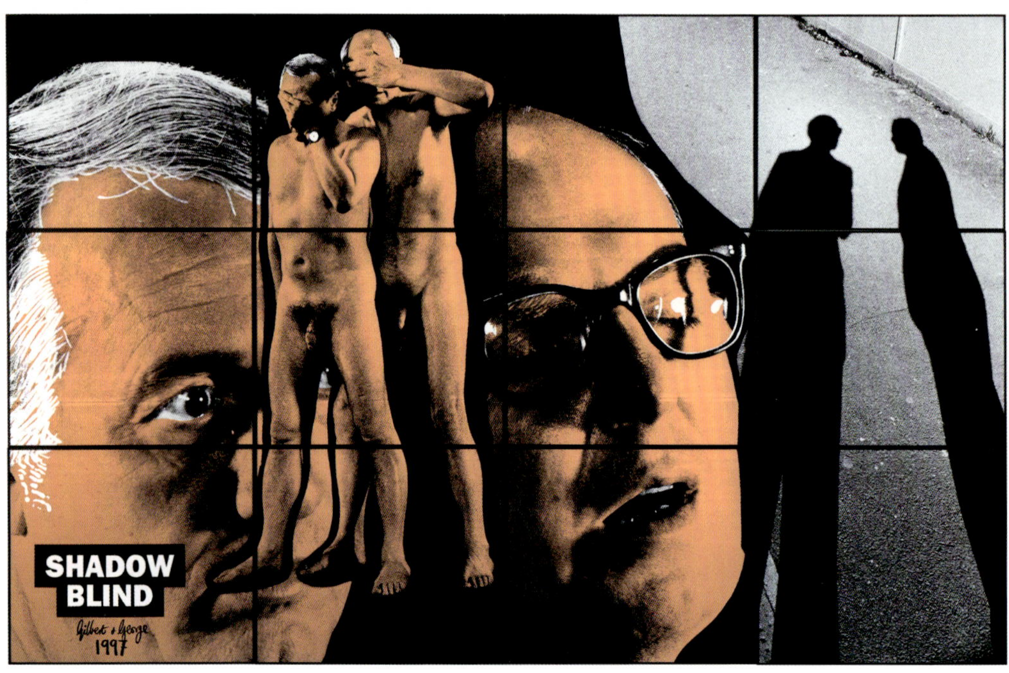

SHADOW BLIND. 1997. 190 x 302 cm

Thirteen
Countering the Counterculture and Radicalising the Reactionary

Countercultural and artistic activities and attitudes – that doubled as ideals and dogma – fashionable in London during the late 1960s, included: unbounded or intuitive creative experimentalism, protest politics, improvisation, 'free' love, motifs of psychedelic introspection, sexual politics, informality, communal living, psychological exploration, dense systemics, Eastern mysticism, Marxist-Leninist-Trotskyite studies, hallucinogenic drugs, a widening use of heroin, iconoclasm, heavy rock, art theory and the espousal of Euro-Maoist revolutionary directives.

All of the above dedicated primarily, in deed or spirit, to the indiscriminate dismantling, and/or reform, of existing authority of all kinds and its iconography.

As counterculture historically asserts and administrates an opposition and alternative to what are perceived to be the established cultural mores of a society at a given period, so the art and vision of Gilbert & George offered a further, equally oppositional and alternative view to the countercultural and artistic beliefs, values, theories and practices of their contemporaries. In confounding the counterculture, Gilbert & George reinforced the creation of their own independent avant-garde and honed the concision of their visual language.

Gilbert and George were becoming Gilbert & George in 1968. This was the year when The Rolling Stones recorded 'Street Fighting Man' and international student anger towards the war in Vietnam was at its height.

Within this broader context, the art of Gilbert & George commenced its mission to disrupt and rearrange the ethical space between authority and dissent. Meaning: that the art of Gilbert & George seeks to depose the policing of personal choice and artistic freedoms by ideologies, be they political, religious or cultural.

The art of Gilbert & George reflects the schisms, passions, questions, convictions, frailties, compromise, fears, contradictions, delusions, anger, irrationalities, beliefs and flux that comprise the relationship between attitude and identity, and between a person and 'the people'.

When The Rolling Stones played their free concert in Hyde Park in the summer of 1969, Gilbert & George walked through the crowd as LIVING SCULPTURES. They looked extreme, possessed and provocative. Were they challenging the counterculture or the most intense expression of it?

Such is the power of paradox that their hybridisation of ultra-conservatism and de-personalised other-worldliness made their 'aura' as much as their appearance mesmeric, alluring and alarming. When Gilbert & George 'performed' their SINGING SCULPTURE in

Australia in 1973, the organiser noted: 'It is very interesting to watch the spectators, too. They seem scared to go near Gilbert & George.'

Having become LIVING SCULPTURES, Gilbert & George seemed supernatural, alien, seer-like. People asked them questions about life and meaning. The more they looked like Young Conservatives gone mad, the more Gilbert & George created a vision and art that was extreme, singular, weird, modern, individualist, open, visionary and Libertarian.

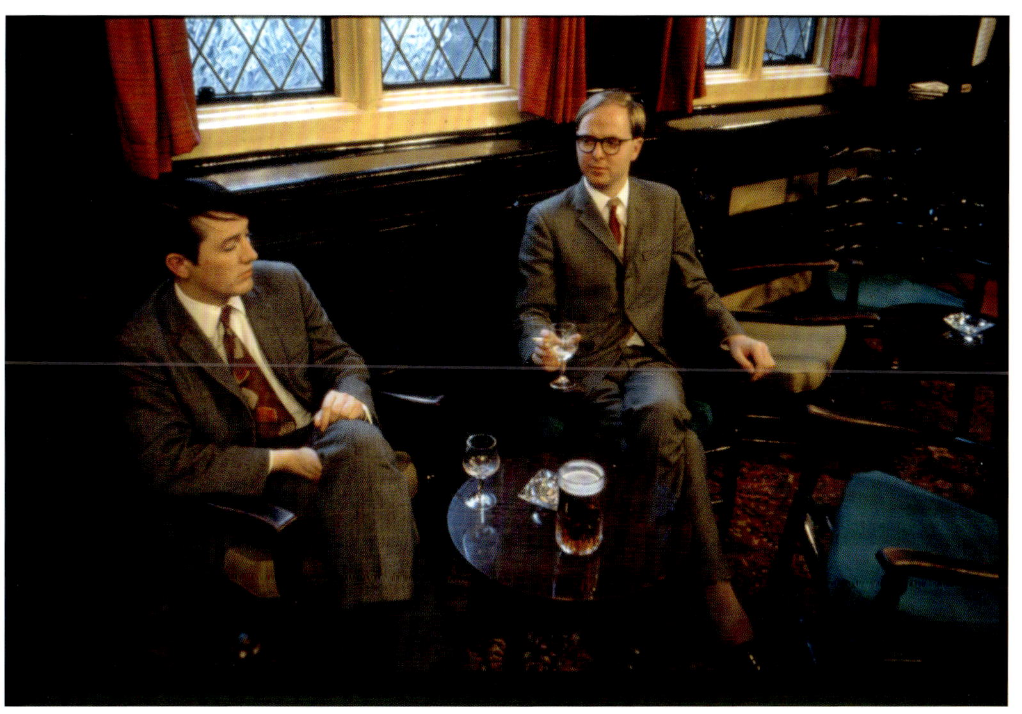

A drink at The Abercorn Bar, London, 1972.

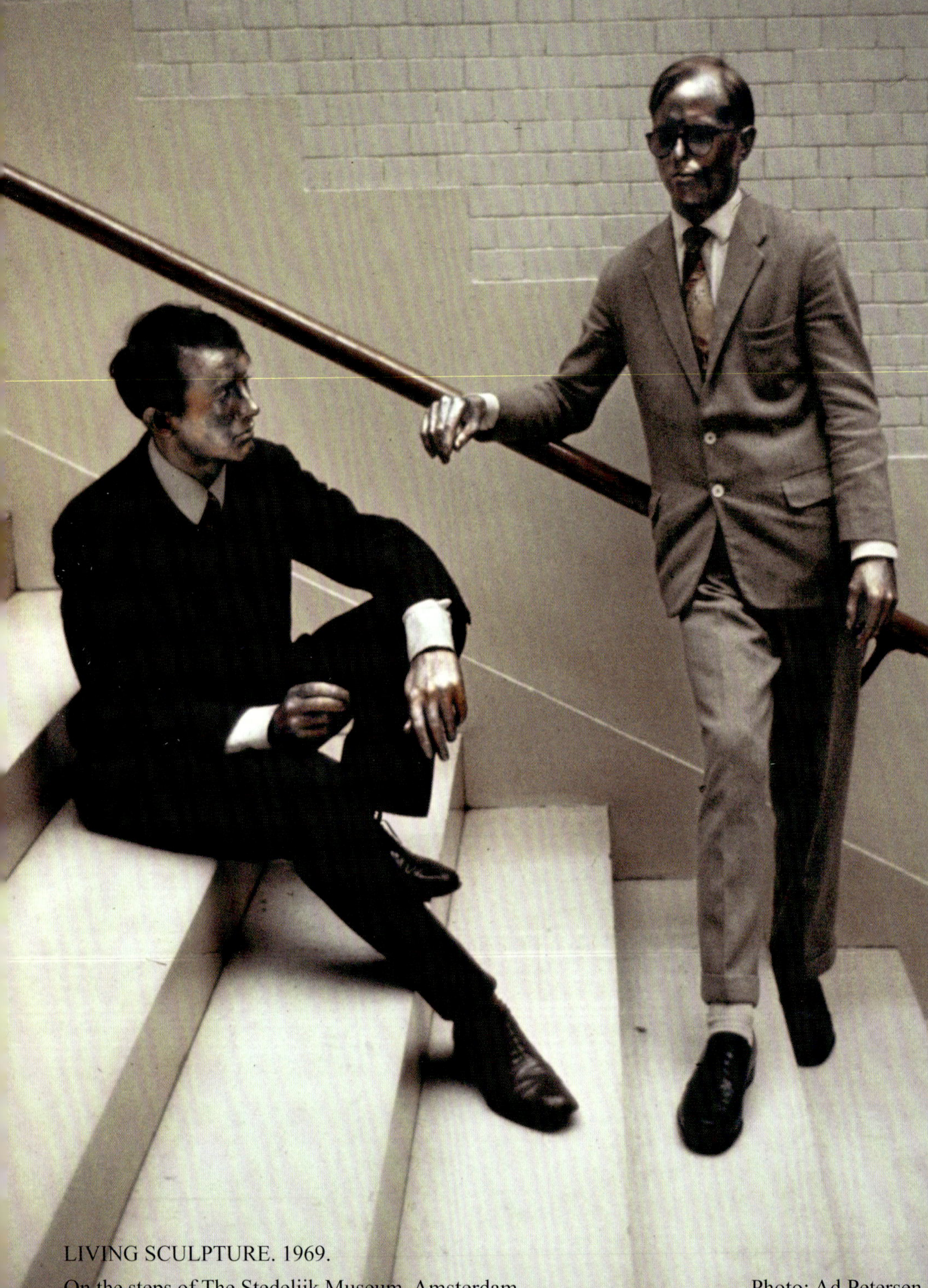

LIVING SCULPTURE. 1969.
On the steps of The Stedelijk Museum, Amsterdam. Photo: Ad Petersen

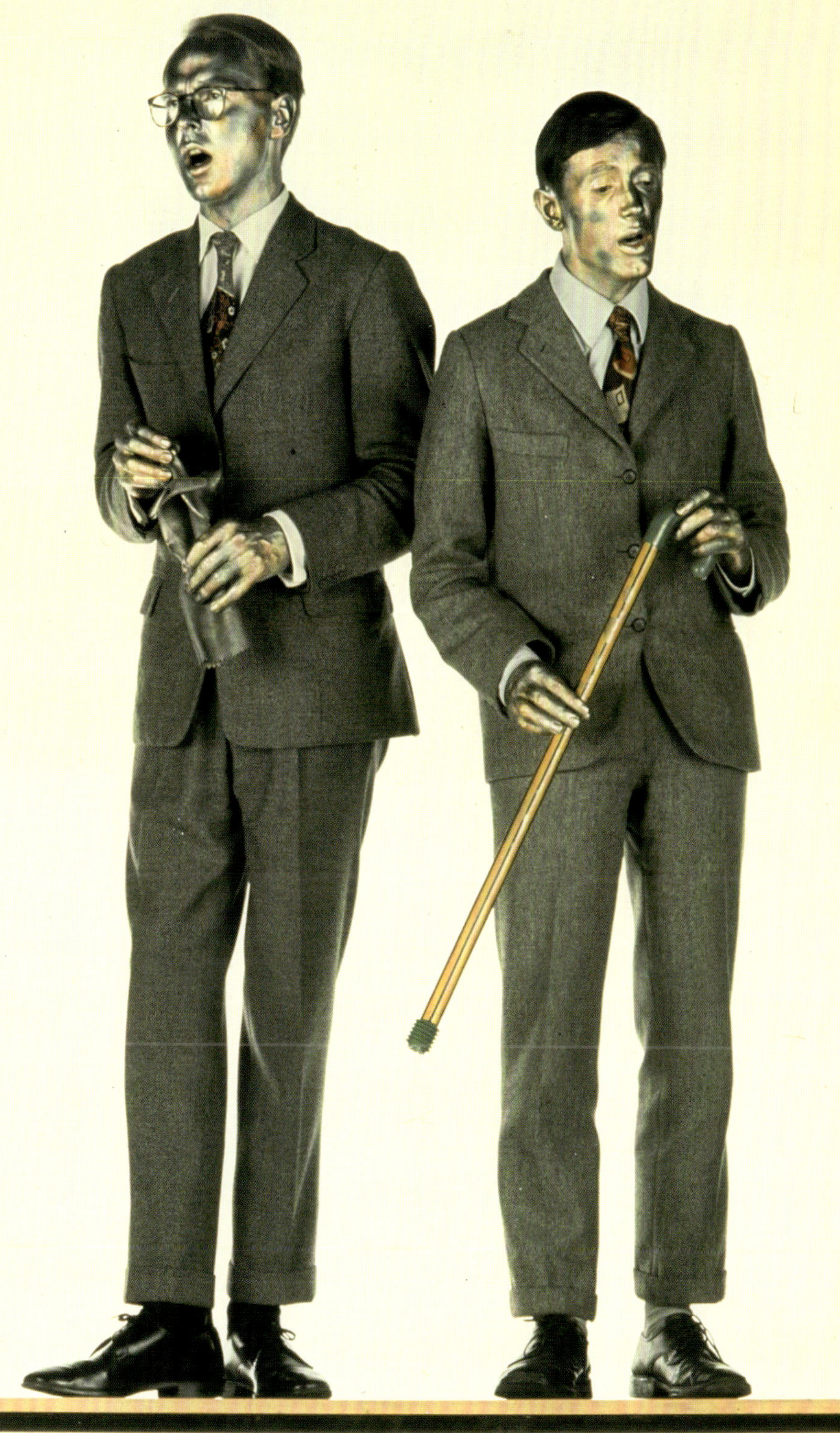

SINGING SCULPTURE. 1970. London. Photo: Snowdon

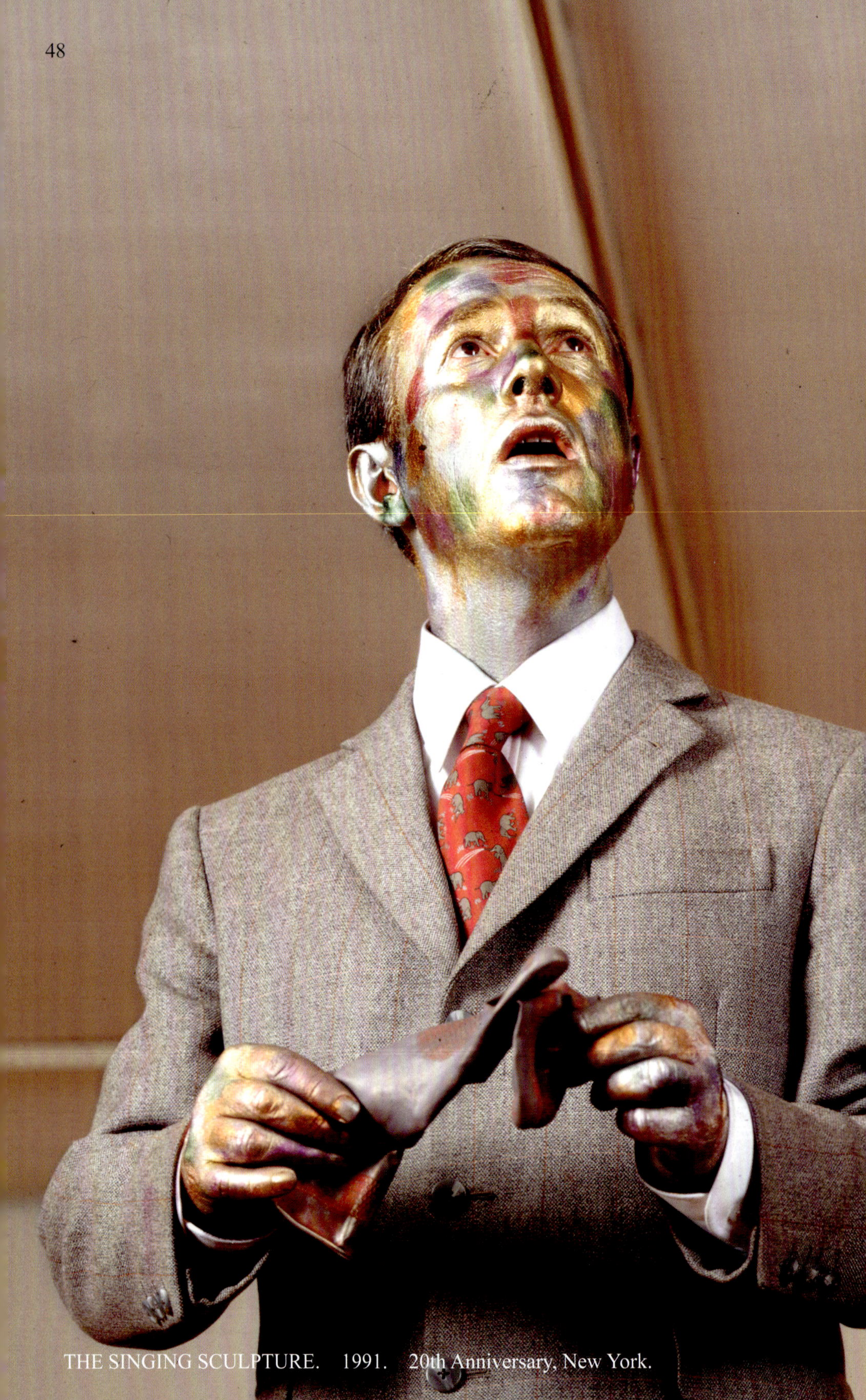

THE SINGING SCULPTURE. 1991. 20th Anniversary, New York.

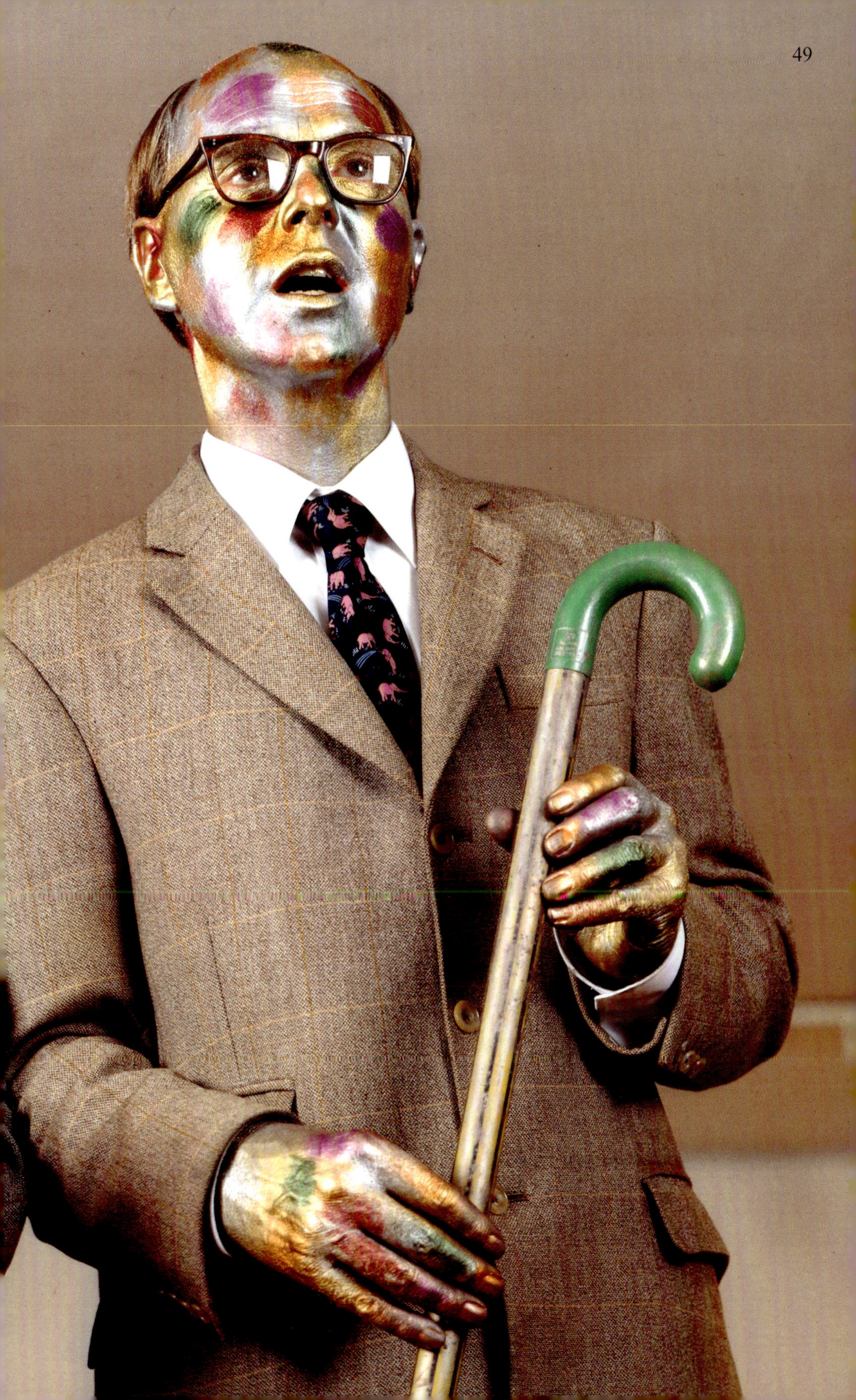

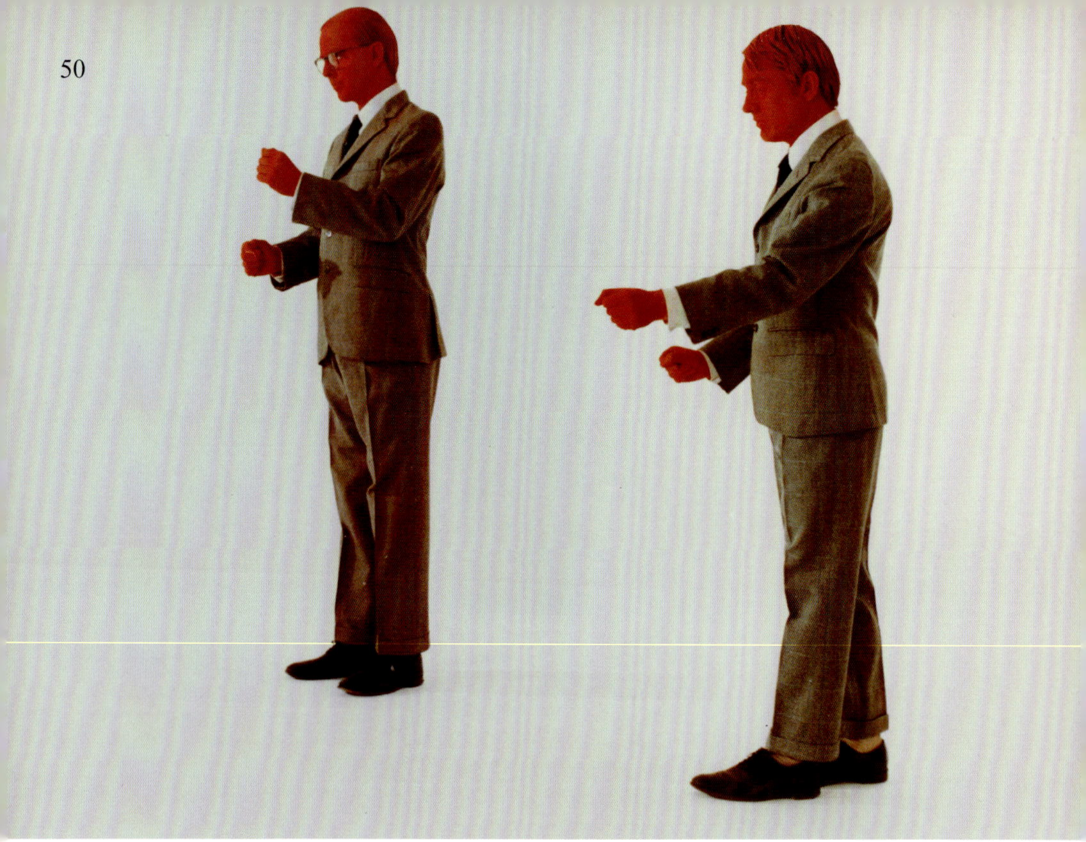

THE RED SCULPTURE

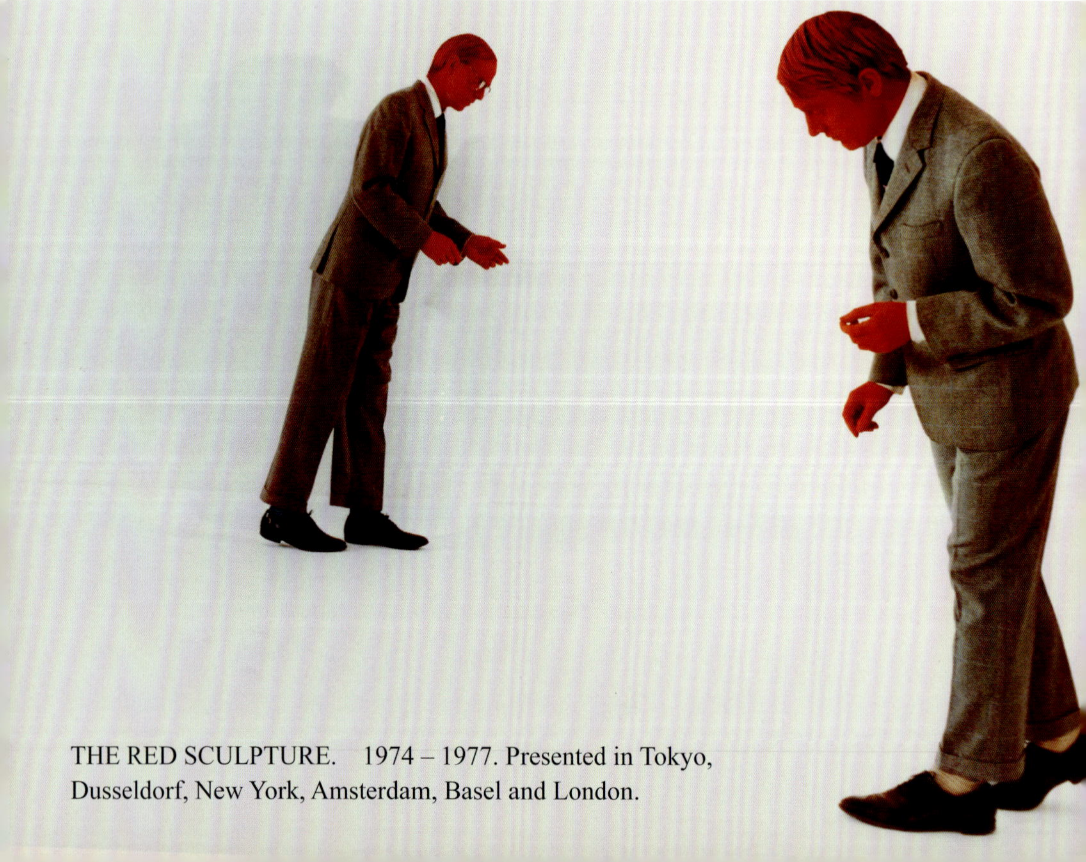

THE RED SCULPTURE. 1974 – 1977. Presented in Tokyo, Dusseldorf, New York, Amsterdam, Basel and London.

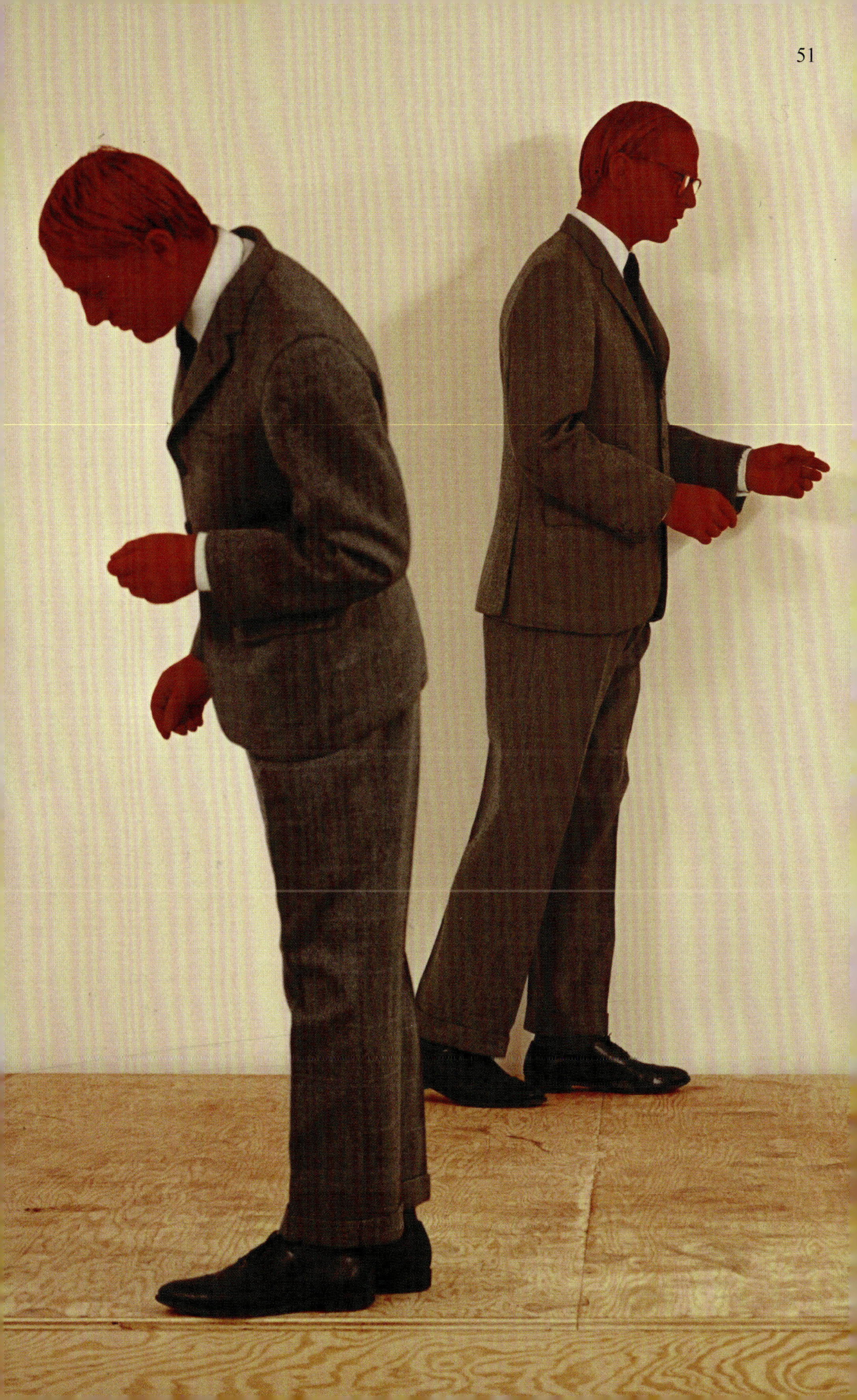

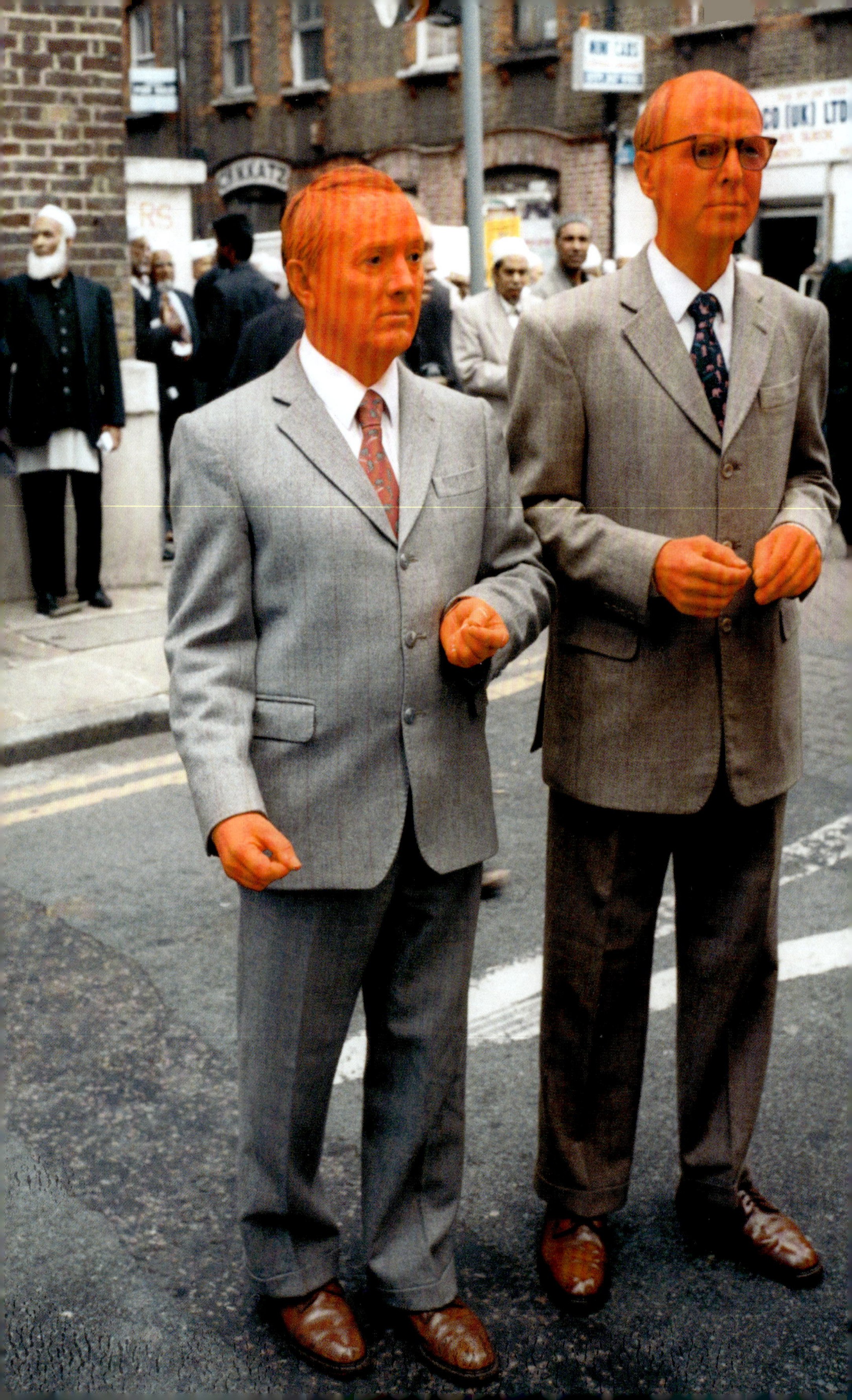
CO (UK) LTD

Fourteen
THE SINGING SCULPTURE: A Visionary Declaration of Intent

THE LIVING SCULPTURE of Gilbert & George was so arresting and so compelling that it soon caught the attention of the world. This was first achieved internationally with THE SINGING SCULPTURE made by Gilbert & George.

With their heads and hands coated in multi-coloured metalised powders, Gilbert & George stand on a table and sing along to an old recording of a sad but uplifting music hall song about happy tramps. They have a glove and a walking stick which they exchange each time the song ends. They move robotically on the table in a circular manner, looking upwards, looking outwards, but always seeming to see beyond their surroundings, as though in a parallel reality to the viewers. They repeat this for seven hours, day after day.

As evidenced by THE SINGING SCULPTURE, the art of Gilbert & George was mesmeric, disciplined, celebratory of the individual and of life, in praise of the outcast and the discarded, carefully conceived and planned, gruelling to create, outward looking to the world,

← THE RED SCULPTURE. 1998.
On the corner of Fournier Street and Brick Lane.

open-handed to the widest possible audience, British, charismatic, formal, empowered by time and history, romantic, friendly, detached, conservative, strange, enfolding, catchy, sympathetic, deeply emotional, glamorous, immediate and un-aesthetic.

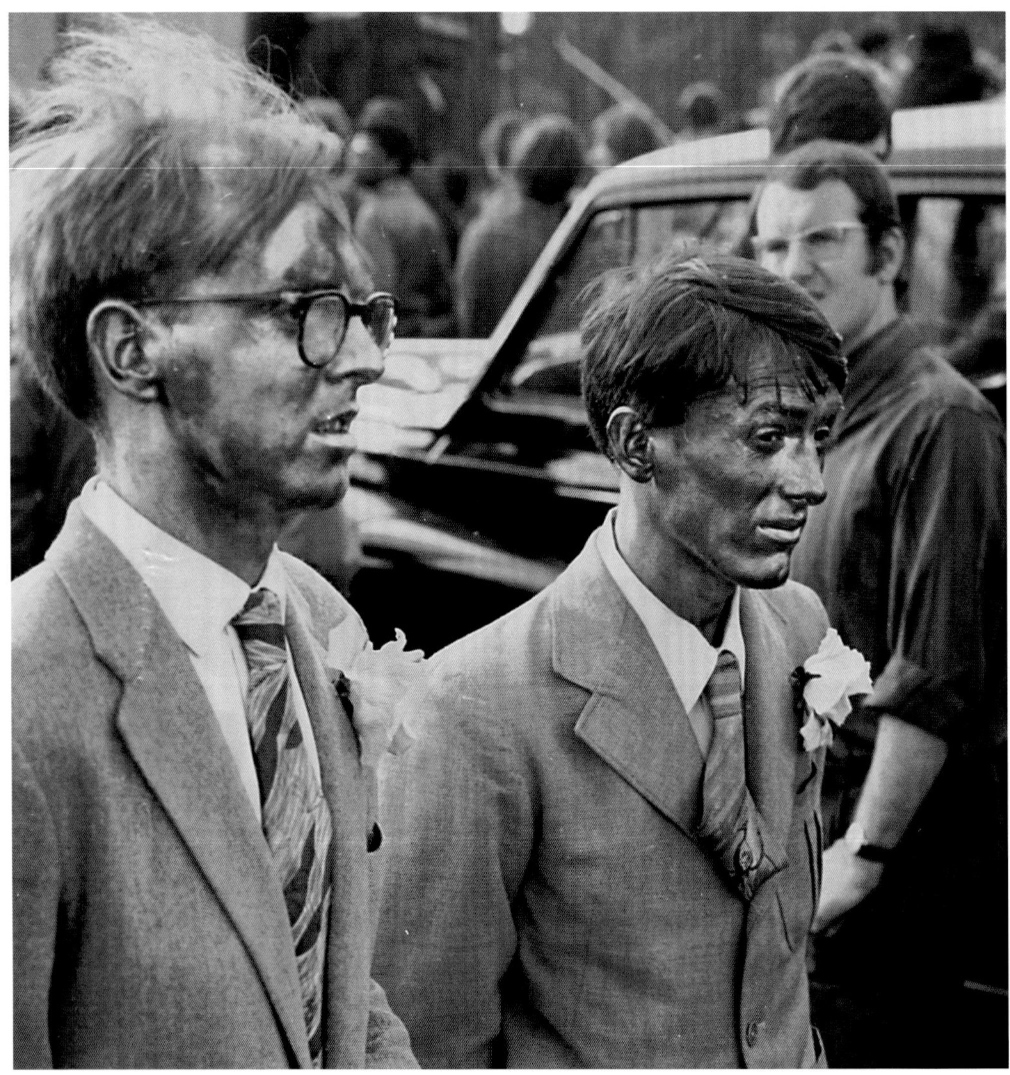

THE LIVING SCULPTURE. 1969. Hyde Park. Photo: Mirrorpix

Fifteen

Populism not Pop: 'There were two young men who did laugh'

One day in 1970, Gilbert and George sit in the Wimpy Bar at Liverpool Street station and write limericks.

These limericks are part of their vision and their art.

They write limericks because such vulgar, archaic, cheerful, simple, traditionally bawdy verses are the aesthetic and cultural opposite to the language of contemporary art as it exists in 1970.

The limerick they are writing is part of a CHARCOAL ON PAPER SCULPTURE, and will also be published in *Studio International's* survey of the British avant-garde (May, 1971) as a MAGAZINE SCULPTURE, accompanied by a picture of Gilbert & George standing quietly on the Thames embankment, facing the Houses of Parliament. The effect is arresting and poetic.

'Low', popular, populist forms communicate efficiently and directly to large numbers of people. When used to convey 'high' ideas, these low forms articulate complexity, radicalism and strangeness with a particular verve and charisma. Indeed, the 'lower' the form, when skilfully handled, the more intense and persuasive its communication of 'high' ideas can be. (Hence the power of pop music.)

This afternoon, Gilbert & George write:

There were two young men who did laugh
They laughed at the people's unrest.
They stuck their sticks in the air
And turned them around with the best.
Then in time they began to feel strange
For no longer it swung in their way,
So to capture again that old thrill
They started to take the life-pill.

This strange limerick, a psycho-nursery rhyme, recounts how a pair of jubilantly mocking young outsiders, high on heroics, become gradually disconcerted and out of step. Then, sensing around themselves some form of opposition, they take a fantastical pharmaceutical – a kind of spiritual Viagra, which may simply be life energy itself – in order to regain their high spirits.

This ambiguous, cryptic nonsense rhyme – one of many such Gilbert & George would write, utilising the form – enforces the mythology of Gilbert & George and more specifically their place of self-reinvention between the words 'serious' and 'jest'.

From the tension between those forces derives their founding identity and calling, described by THE SINGING SCULPTURE, as isolated vaudevillians and miserable comedians.

In these roles – those of a variety show or music hall double act – Gilbert & George can communicate their vision of the modern world, in which frozen seriousness combines with violence, disorder, spiritual journeying and extreme emotional states. They pursue this compulsion, unwaveringly, from THE SINGING SCULPTURE to their JACK FREAK PICTURES, THE SCAPEGOATING PICTURES and beyond.

Although they have been claimed many times over as 'honorary rock stars' by successive generations and possess pop celebrity, Gilbert & George have no interest in, or affiliation to, either Pop art or pop music.

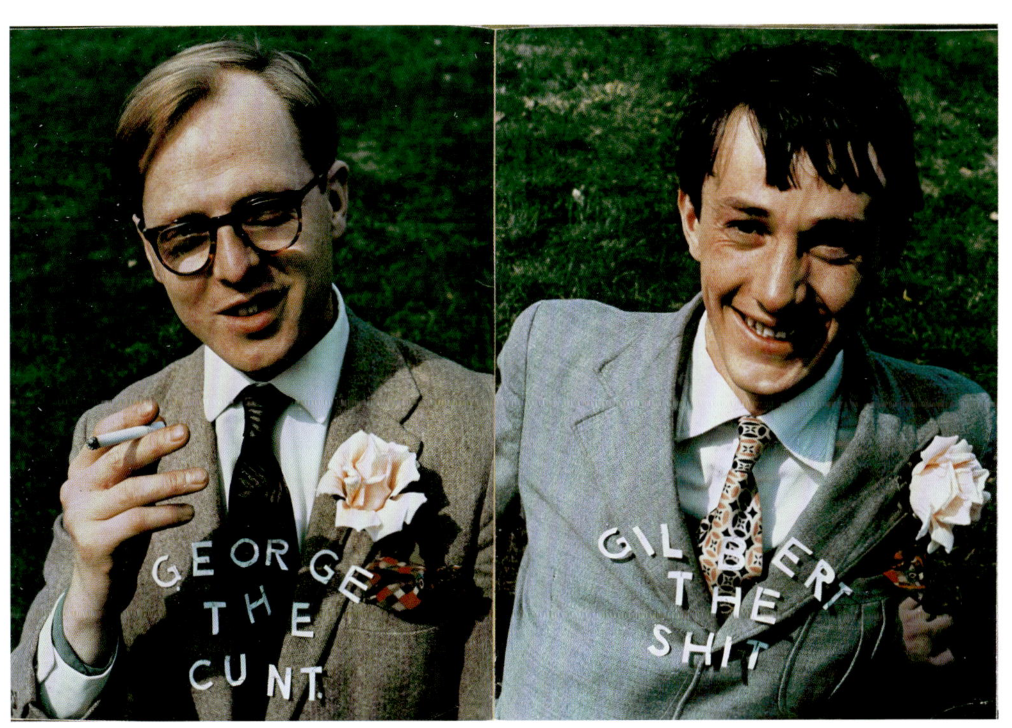

A MAGAZINE SCULPTURE. 1969.

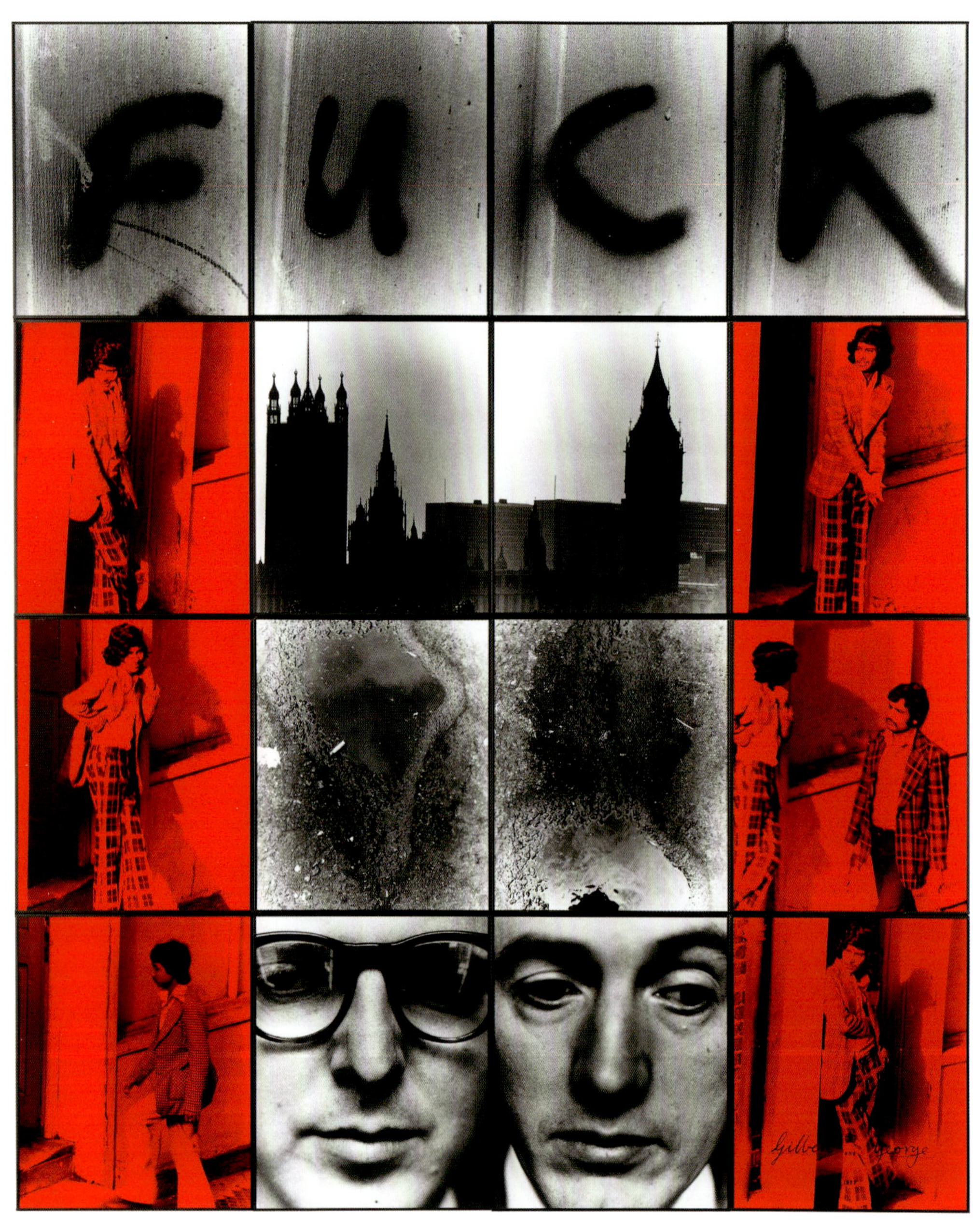

FUCK. 1977. 241 x 201 cm

Sixteen
Formality not Formalism

Larvatus Prodeo – (I advance masked). (Descartes)

Gilbert & George see the world with heightened feeling. They look at the friendless, the thrown out, the miserable and remote; at the immensity of the city as a thoroughfare of life and death. Their street fighting men are aimless, closed-featured, cocky, friendly, shy or heroic local youths. Luxuriant nature, trees, leaves and flowers echo their love and desire. Systems of belief proliferate from Theosophy to boy bands. Evidence for the search for oblivion is constant: drugs, sex, alcohol, craze or ideology. The corporeal (shit and body fluids) addresses the physical (youth and beauty).

For Gilbert & George, the modern world is always in broiling volatile restlessness: sexual, moody, intent, transgressive, clamouring and screaming to the senses. In the art of Gilbert & George, that is their vision, the modern world looks accordingly brooding, lonely, disrupted, portentous, mad, cosmic, melancholy, monumental, chaotic, ordinary, desolate, dream-like, dull, monstrous, violent, blasphemous, infinite.

In conveying the intensity of this vision to the viewer, the art of Gilbert & George is empowered by formality rather than formalism.

The formality of Gilbert & George derives from their embodiment of their vision as LIVING SCULPTURES. Good manners, friendly politeness, respect for social convention, the genteel archaism of their names and conservatism of appearance and demeanour are the principle means. Paradoxically, by which they declare, expand and enhance the opposite of these qualities: the crazed visionary outsider manifesto passion of their artistic independence, beliefs and world view.

The more formal the demeanour and manner of Gilbert & George, the more intense and direct their communication of extreme emotional states, behaviour, landscape and ideology. It is a position once described by the writer Gustav Flaubert: 'You must be regular and natural in your habits like a bourgeois, that you may be violent and original in your work.' Meaning: personal constraint enables artistic liberation.

In the case of Gilbert & George, the formality of their appearance and demeanour, so contrasting to their art and their vision, yet also its basis, provides the strongest 'container', artistically, personally and ideologically, for the violence and separatism of their feelings.

Discipline, rigour, convention, restraint, quiet amiability, traditionalism, decorum, tea party manners, the world-view and language of polite respectability: the tauter the formality of Gilbert & George becomes, the more deafening the amplification of their vision. Thus, two naked middle-aged men surf through space on giant turds, closing in on a bland landscape traversed by a commuter train; before which, the same middle-aged men, now red suited, calm, with expressions of impassive politeness, their hands on their knees, sit with neat posture on the arms of a chair made out of shit. This abuttal of extremes triggers the communication of their vision.

The untameable extremism of Gilbert & George lies within themselves; their suits and ties have accordingly the function of bomb casing. The art of Gilbert & George reveals this interior violence and intensity, like magic bringing to view a hidden world. The formality of Gilbert & George is therefore mask, armour, protocol, vessel, weapon, protective clothing, charm, glamour and language – an entire arsenal.

Here are young Gilbert & George, charming and smiling in the sunshine. With their suits and neat haircuts, they look like shy students on an innocent jaunt. Pinned to their clothes are carefully cut-out letters that spell, respectively, 'George The Cunt' and 'Gilbert The Shit'. If some long haired, wildly dressed freak screamed out these words, declaiming his stance of otherness, his demeanour would cancel them out.

It is the well-mannered conservatism of Gilbert & George that re-arms these statements: the creation of a precisely balanced paradox, a collision of appearance and reality, converting prank into provocation, innocence into insolence – unsettling, unforgettable, blurring the reactionary and the radical to declare an autonomous position, at once hilarious and combative.

Artistic formalism, such as that studied or practiced by many of their contemporaries at the art school, is the antithesis of the deployed formality of Gilbert & George.

Formality frames, contains and concentrates their independent anti-art celebration of life's mysteries and wonders. Suited and impassive, Gilbert & George take their places in the visionary landscapes of their art as both participants and witnesses.

Unchanging, they have the appearance and countenance of sober-minded, anonymous citizens, respectable, conscientious (see them, for example, in their NEW HORNY PICTURES, severe and straight-laced) but embarked on the astral journey of their own *Divine Comedy*: purgatory, heaven and hell as they find it and perceive it in the streets of London, in nature and in themselves.

Formality carries the ferocity and determination of this journey, their feelings and beliefs, soaring spire-high into the visionary world, taking the fight to the enemy.

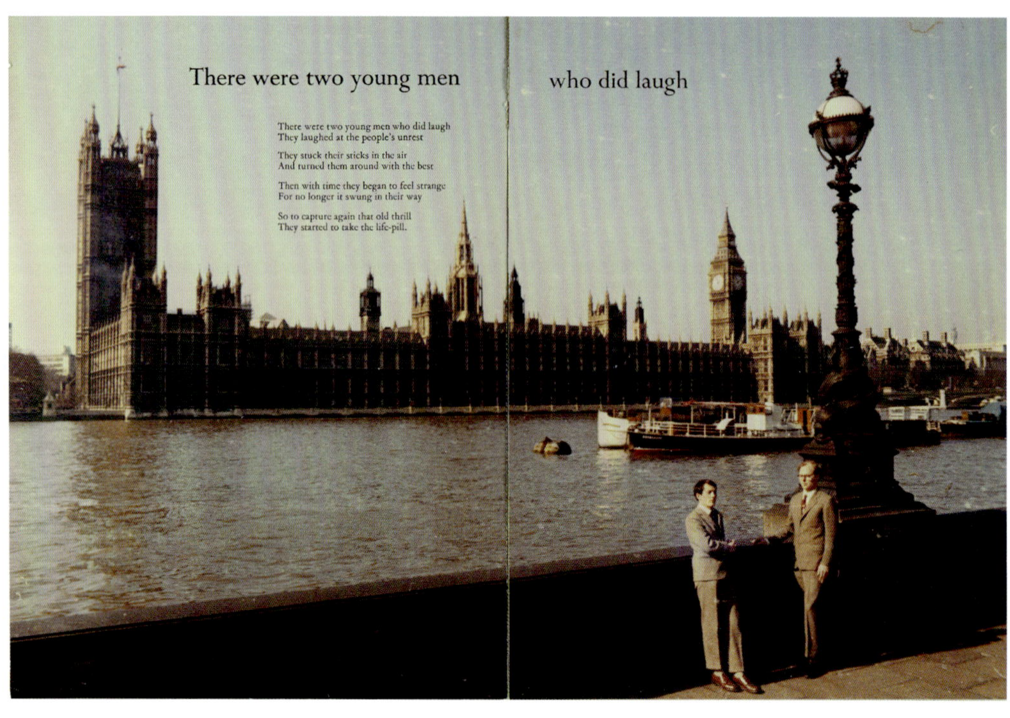

A MAGAZINE SCULPTURE. 1969.

Seventeen
Gilbert & George: Existential and Libertarian

If there were no eternal consciousness in a man, if at the bottom of everything there were only a wild ferment, a power that twisting in dark passions produced everything great or inconsequential; if an unfathomable, insatiable emptiness lay hid beneath everything, what would life be but despair?
Soren Kierkegaard

'Facticity (throwness)': We find ourselves existing in a world not of our own making and indifferent to our concerns. We are not the source of our existence, but find ourselves thrown into a world we don't control and didn't choose.

The refusal to belong to any school of thought, the repudiation of the adequacy of any body of beliefs whatever, and especially of systems, and a marked dissatisfaction with traditional philosophy as superficial, academic and remote from life – that is the heart of existentialism.
Walter Kaufmann (1956)

The art of Gilbert & George is libertarian and existential in its assertion of autonomy, personal responsibility and freedom of choice.

The art of Gilbert & George conveys expressions and representations of individual decisions and belief systems of all kinds. As acts and ideologies define humankind, so these acts and ideologies appear in the art of Gilbert & George, at times isolated and particular, conjuring their own mood; at others, resembling a deafening cacophony of beliefs and statements, or an index of human consciousness and directory of events.

As they take their place in their art, Gilbert & George appear either impassive, spectral, monstrous, respectable, fearful or possessed. They are witness-participants within the visionary world of their art; they become agents of the scenes they traverse. They channel atmospheres rather than make pronouncements. In this they resemble the indwelling 'spirits' of each of their pictures and sculptures.

If there is a unifying 'temper' to the art of Gilbert & George, it derives from their moral vision, in which the modern condition is seen as chaotic, poetic, indifferent to fate in its vastness, without meaning save that which the individual creates for himself and for which he alone is responsible.

In the art of Gilbert & George, 'meaning' derives more from atmosphere – the psychic traces left by time, reanimated by the light or the weather – than from the immediacy of event. The art of Gilbert & George therefore conveys an array of feelings and atmospheres, from liberated soaring wonder to isolation, facticity and angst.

The art of Gilbert & George could therefore be seen to share aspects of libertarian and existential thinking. The common-denominator of these positions is active engagement with the nature of freedom and choice; with the volatility, alienation and randomness of modern life, as it is bounded by technology, borderlines and beliefs.

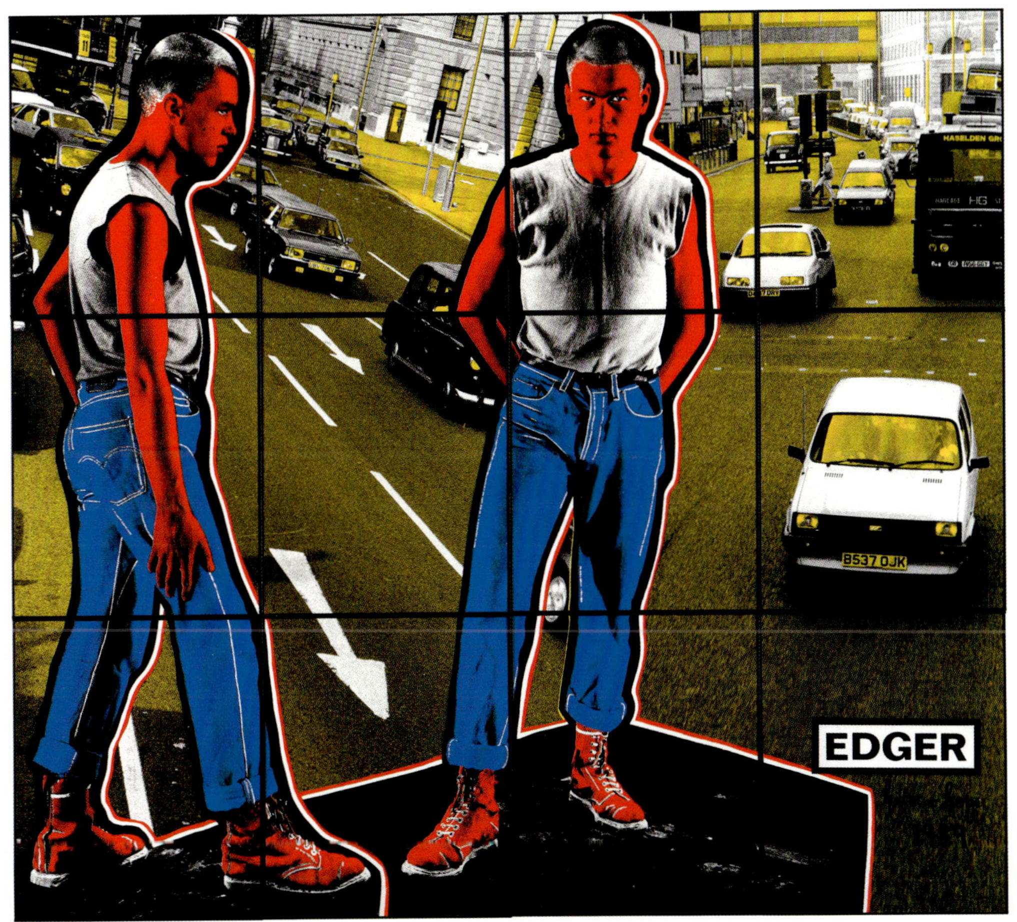

EDGER. 1989. 226 x 254 cm

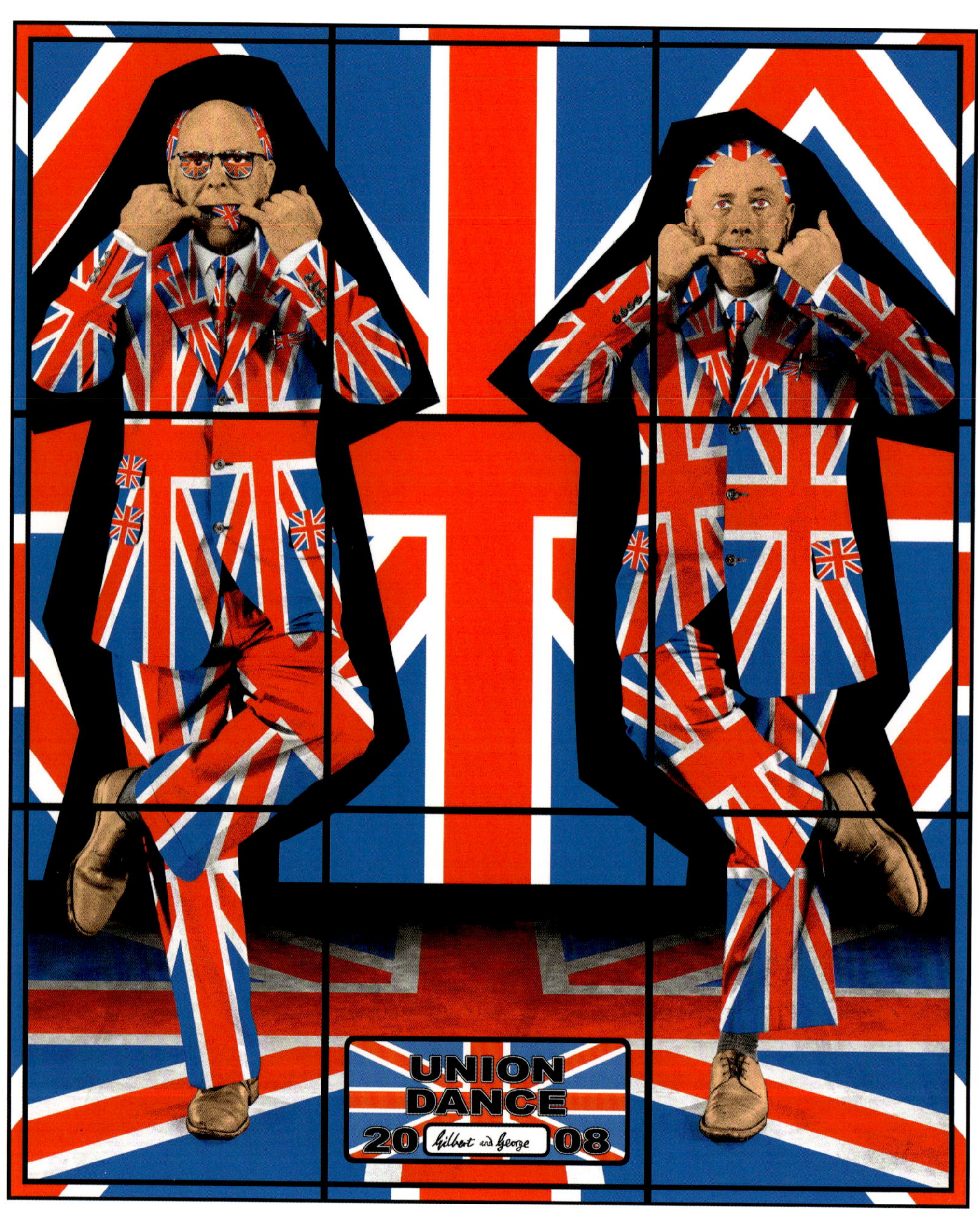

UNION DANCE. 2008. 226 x 190 cm
One of the JACK FREAK PICTURES.

Eighteen
Nationhood and Nationalism

The vision of Gilbert & George espouses the symbolism and iconography of monarchic, imperial and Commonwealth Britain, in many forms: flags (Union Jack and St George's Cross), medals, coins, statues, royal insignia, the Royal Crest, the Royal Family. Gilbert & George also represent the subjects and the auras of patriotism, nationalism and jingoism in their art; from early reference to imperial pageantry, emblems of Englishness and the National Front, to the epic group of JACK FREAK PICTURES, dominated by mutated Union Jack designs, with titles such as BRITAINERS, BRITAIN, INGERLAND, HM & HRH and BRITICISM.

It is up to the viewer how they see the representation of these subjects: as insinuations or celebrations of nationalist ideals, a depiction of modern nationhood, or sociologically, as an idea and state of mind.

In their art, Gilbert & George also represent class war, anarchism, vandalism, street and shop signage, religious, agitprop or sub-cult stickers, ripped posters and sexual advertisements. Like 'nationhood', these are subjects, sets of values and systems of belief – often confused, abbreviated and inchoate, but fervent and emotive – that have been largely either abandoned, ignored or demonised by the deeds and discourse of contemporary art. Concentration on such vernacular and discarded phenomena, as subjects for art, would therefore challenge a mind-set determined to occlude them.

Do Gilbert & George befriend the ungainly, culturally sensitive subjects of nationhood or ultra-patriotism – their picture GOD GUARD THEE defines the mood – in the same way that they befriend other ignored subjects, such as litter, ruins, leaves, graffiti and gum? Or are they declaiming their own nationalism? Or, are they challenging the complacencies of a cultural faction who regard such subject matter as antithetical and antagonistic to their beliefs? Or none of these things; but rather communicating the blizzard of modern phenomena, that is as indifferent to the complexities of individual and collective opinion as the natural world?

The viewer must decide for himself. But a further suggestion might be that Gilbert & George are representing the spirit and temper of nationalism and nationhood – as an atmosphere and a mood; as an emotion, and an individual and social value.

Here are their KNIGHTS and COCKY PATRIOTS and British Lion and Max Miller style suits emblazoned with a pattern of medals; and here are young Gilbert & George, shoulders back, tensed, unsmiling in aggressive stance, fists clenched, stares fixed. The pageantry, insignia and sad old statues of long forgotten generals and soldiers in mourning; pictures of The Queen, Elgar, Jack Buchanan. The postcard views of parks and piers, music hall stars, chancels, soldiers, barracks and Big Ben, seen as though by the fading light of a last imperial summer, prior to total war. Nationhood, after all, can be melancholy too.

Likewise, might Gilbert & George not assert 'British' or 'English' subject matter, repeatedly and forcibly, in defiance of, and as a corrective to, the early modernist championing of non-British art as the basis of artistic relevance?

The art of Gilbert & George communicates and 'tests' the feeling – the consciousness – of its subjects, as Gilbert & George experience those subjects and feelings. In their art and as their vision, Gilbert & George occupy, explore and embody phenomena as moods: as though possessed, taken up into the temper of a common feeling.

Nationhood and nationalism, fundamental to modern society, is likewise a moody, psychic climate – bracing, humid, exhilarating, oppressive, storm-driven. And so, the mood of the JACK FREAK PICTURES, for instance (saturated with the design and 'mood' of British insignia) is one of monstrosity, vacuity, hysteria and madness: a gaga-senile-zombie world of cheerless pageantry; a music-hall spirit world, sinister and malign, virtually cartoon-like.

In many of the JACK FREAK PICTURES the figures of Gilbert & George, their surroundings of bricks or leaves or flags are mutated into near abstraction or serial meaninglessness: monstrous absurd grotesques, fat and leering, symmetrically sub-divided into circular patterns or reduced to squinting spheres suspended in leafless trees. Some science fiction underclass. In others, dressed in crazy Union Jack or 'medal' suits, Gilbert & George perform an empty-headed ghost dance – a zombie music hall double-act.

But the art of Gilbert & George has always been of the spirit world, as the spirit world may be perceived to exist as atmosphere and symbol within human feeling and perception: the living archetype, the numinous locale, the infinite transferability of overt and covert meaning. It is a perception, as communicated by the art of Gilbert & George, that acknowledges the truths, pleasant or unpleasant, to be discerned within the shadows of ambiguity.

Skinheads recast as a race of stricken Jobs. Nationhood and nationalism: the subject of country, home, belonging, pride, disaffection, exile, race. Histories swept away by ideologies, vanished worlds and their romance. The eventual exhaustion of strength and muscle, old age, stiffening limbs, lost fights, the coming colder weather: 'David, the wind blows – bits of your life away… Your friends all say, "Where is our boy? Ah, we've lost our boy…."'

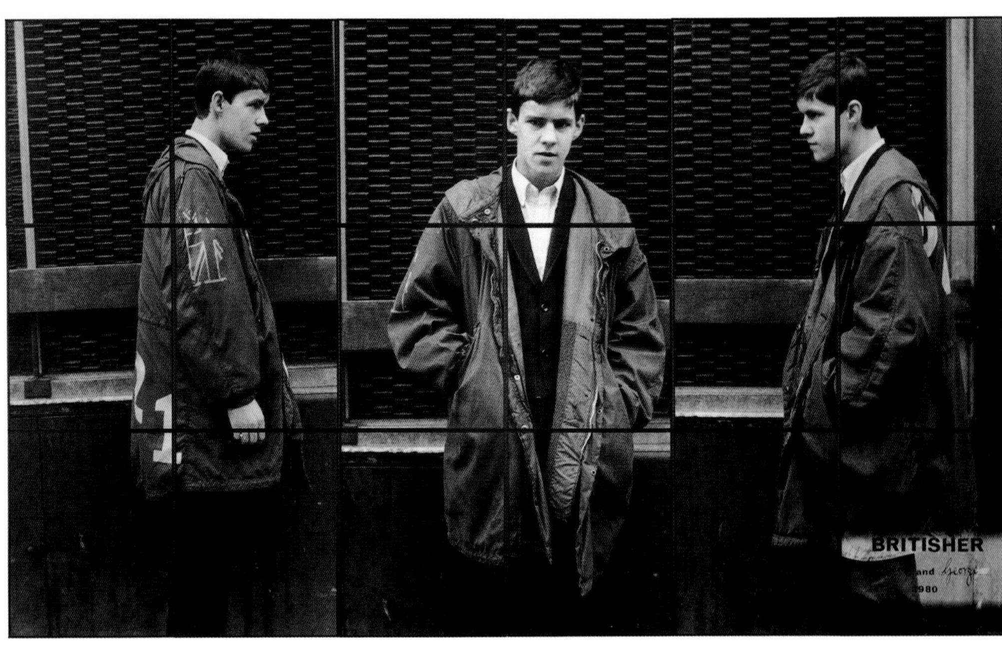

BRITISHER. 1980. 181 x 300 cm

Views of Exhibitions

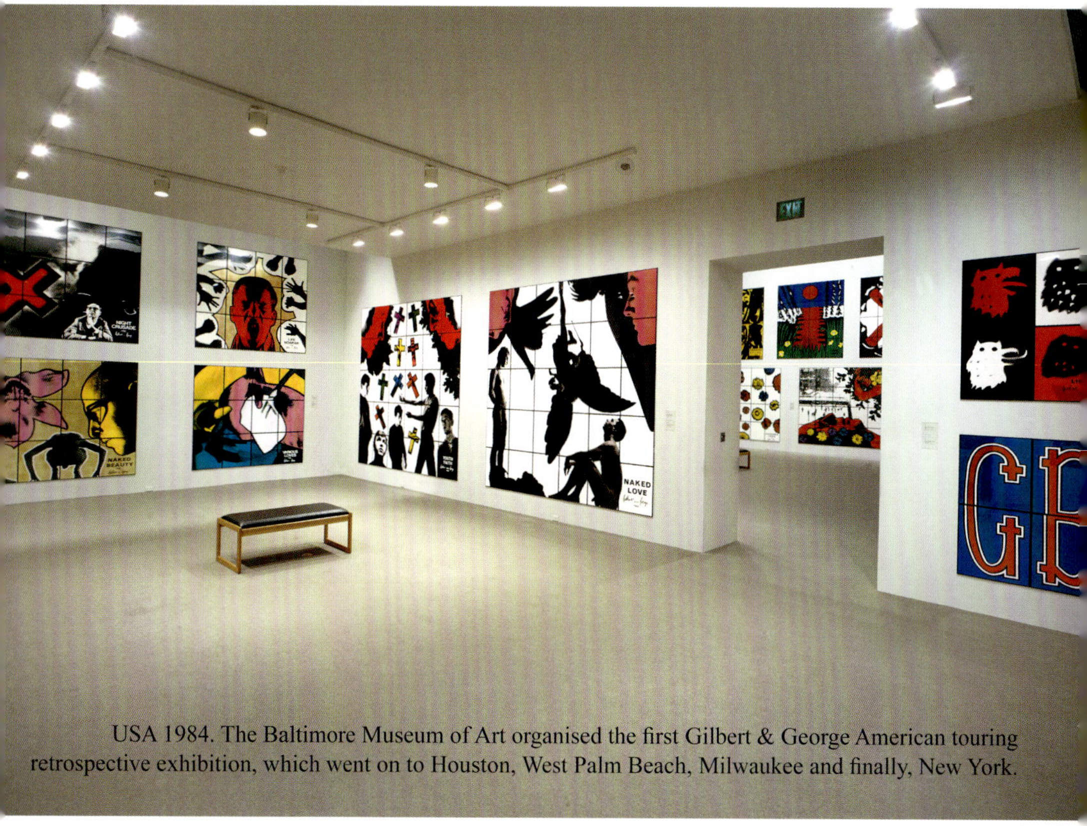

USA 1984. The Baltimore Museum of Art organised the first Gilbert & George American touring retrospective exhibition, which went on to Houston, West Palm Beach, Milwaukee and finally, New York.

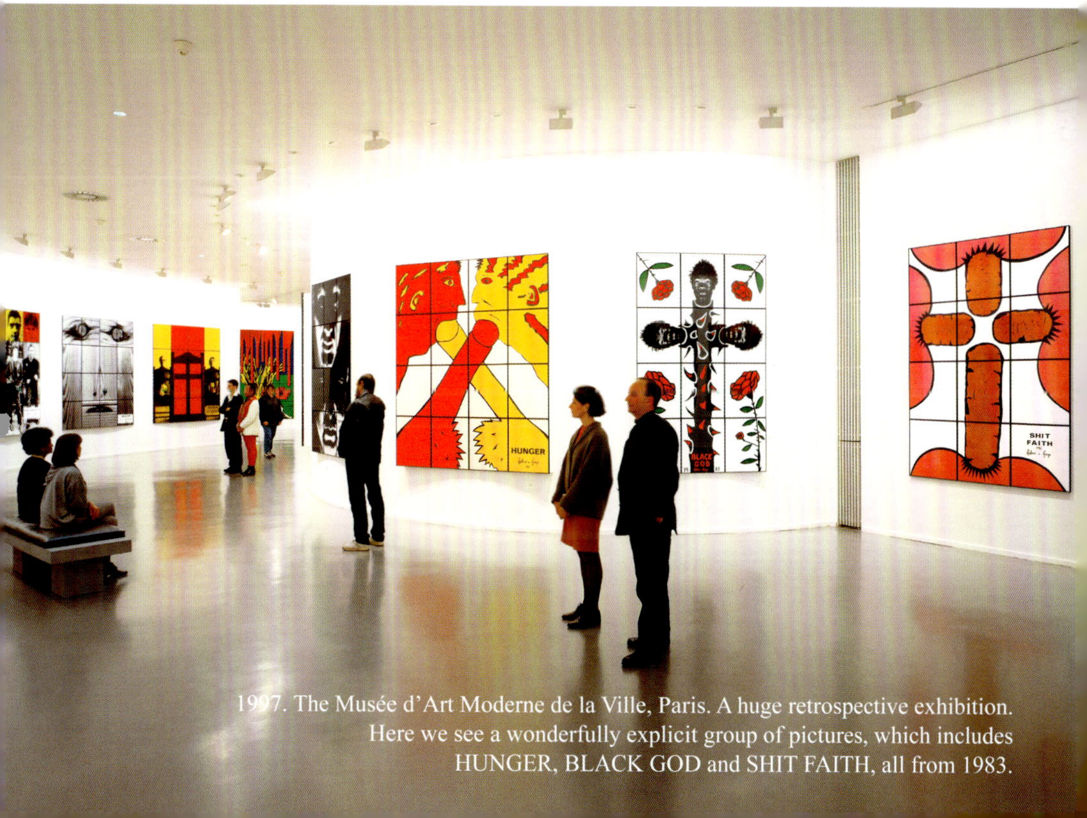

1997. The Musée d'Art Moderne de la Ville, Paris. A huge retrospective exhibition. Here we see a wonderfully explicit group of pictures, which includes HUNGER, BLACK GOD and SHIT FAITH, all from 1983.

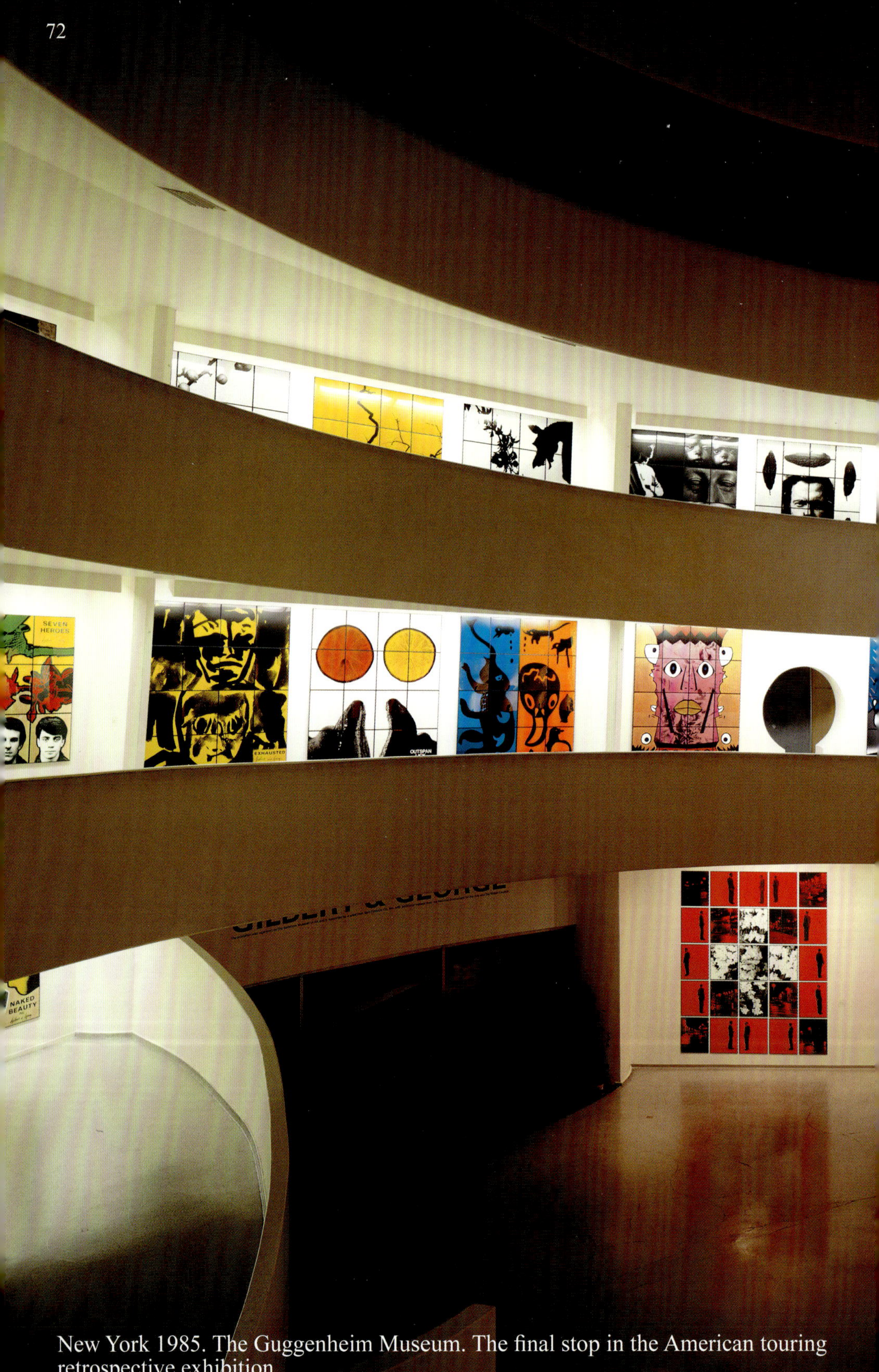

New York 1985. The Guggenheim Museum. The final stop in the American touring retrospective exhibition.

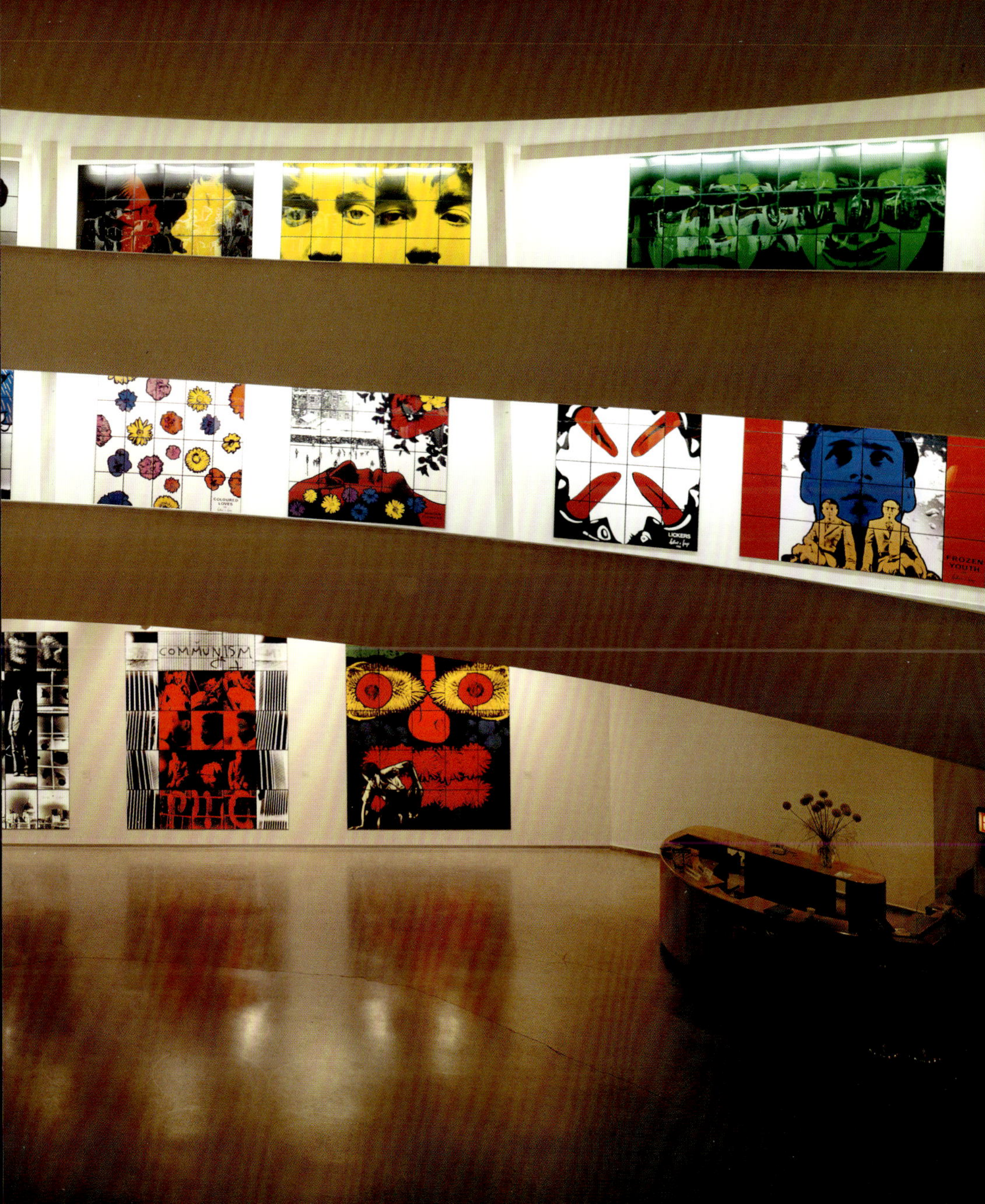
COLOURED LOVES
LICKERS
FROZEN YOUTH
COMMUNISM

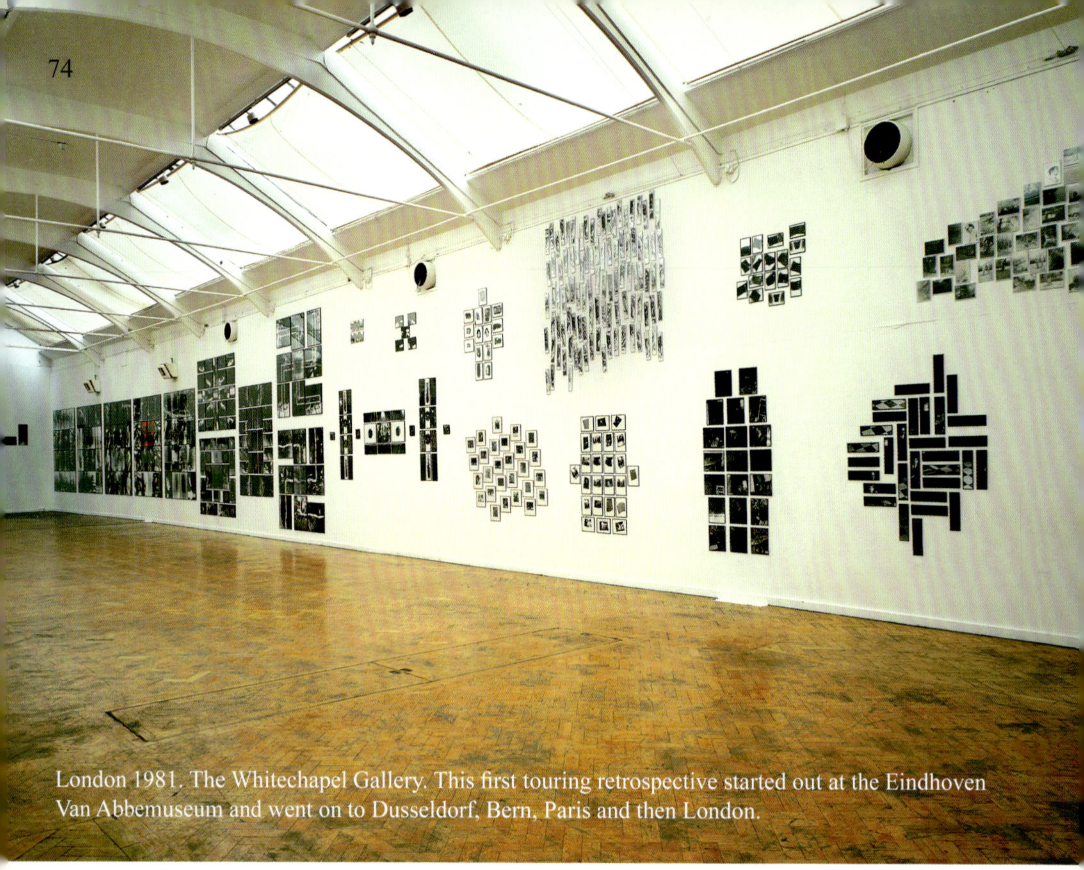

London 1981. The Whitechapel Gallery. This first touring retrospective started out at the Eindhoven Van Abbemuseum and went on to Dusseldorf, Bern, Paris and then London.

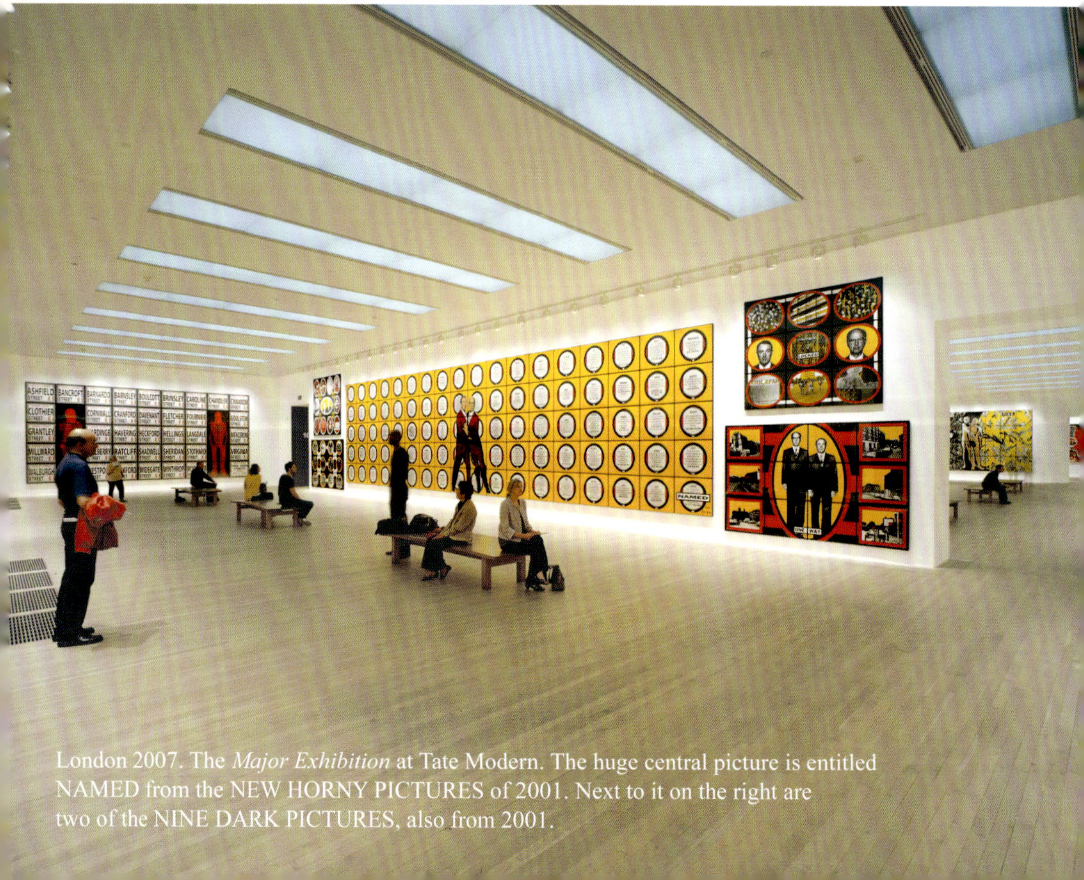

London 2007. The *Major Exhibition* at Tate Modern. The huge central picture is entitled NAMED from the NEW HORNY PICTURES of 2001. Next to it on the right are two of the NINE DARK PICTURES, also from 2001.

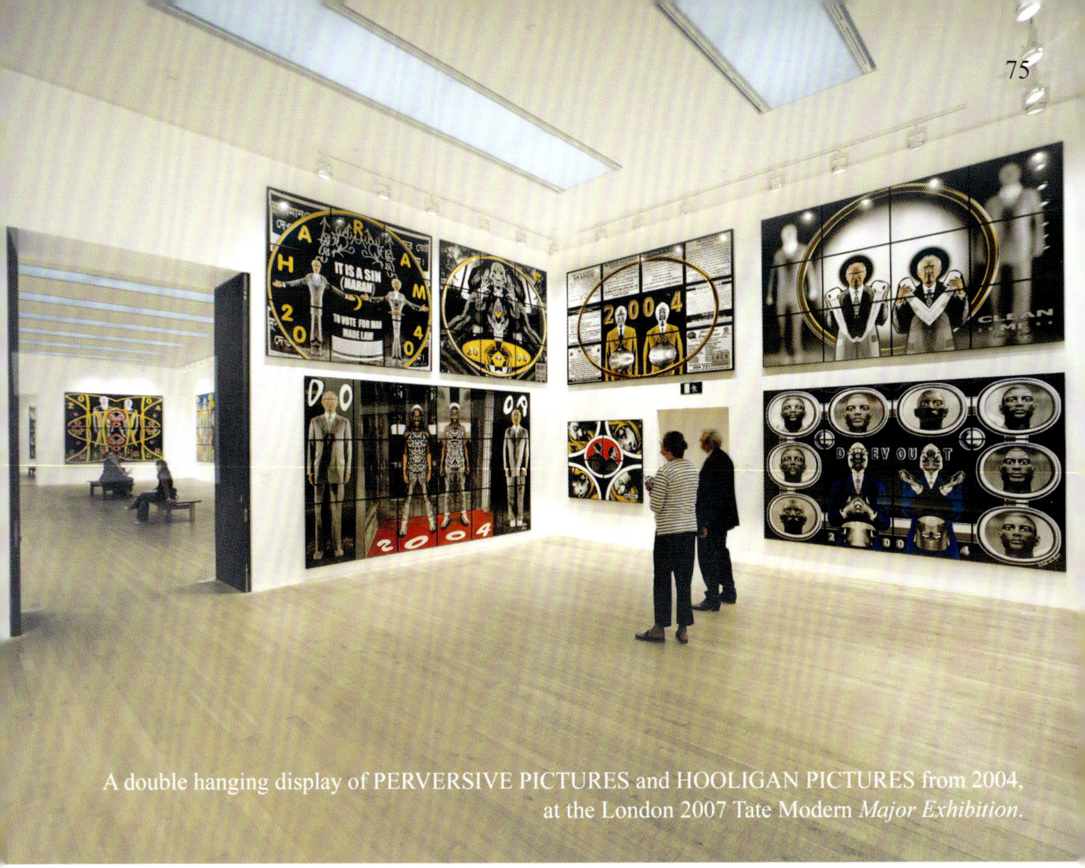

A double hanging display of PERVERSIVE PICTURES and HOOLIGAN PICTURES from 2004, at the London 2007 Tate Modern *Major Exhibition*.

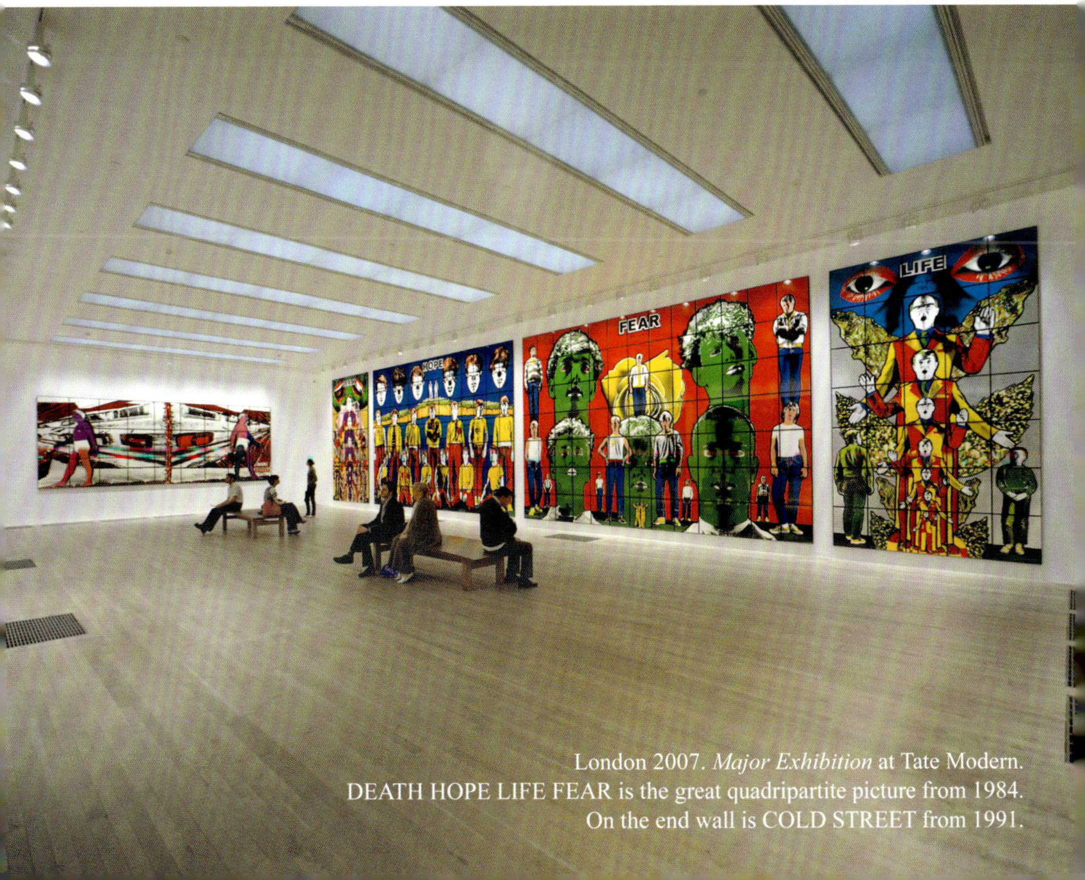

London 2007. *Major Exhibition* at Tate Modern.
DEATH HOPE LIFE FEAR is the great quadripartite picture from 1984.
On the end wall is COLD STREET from 1991.

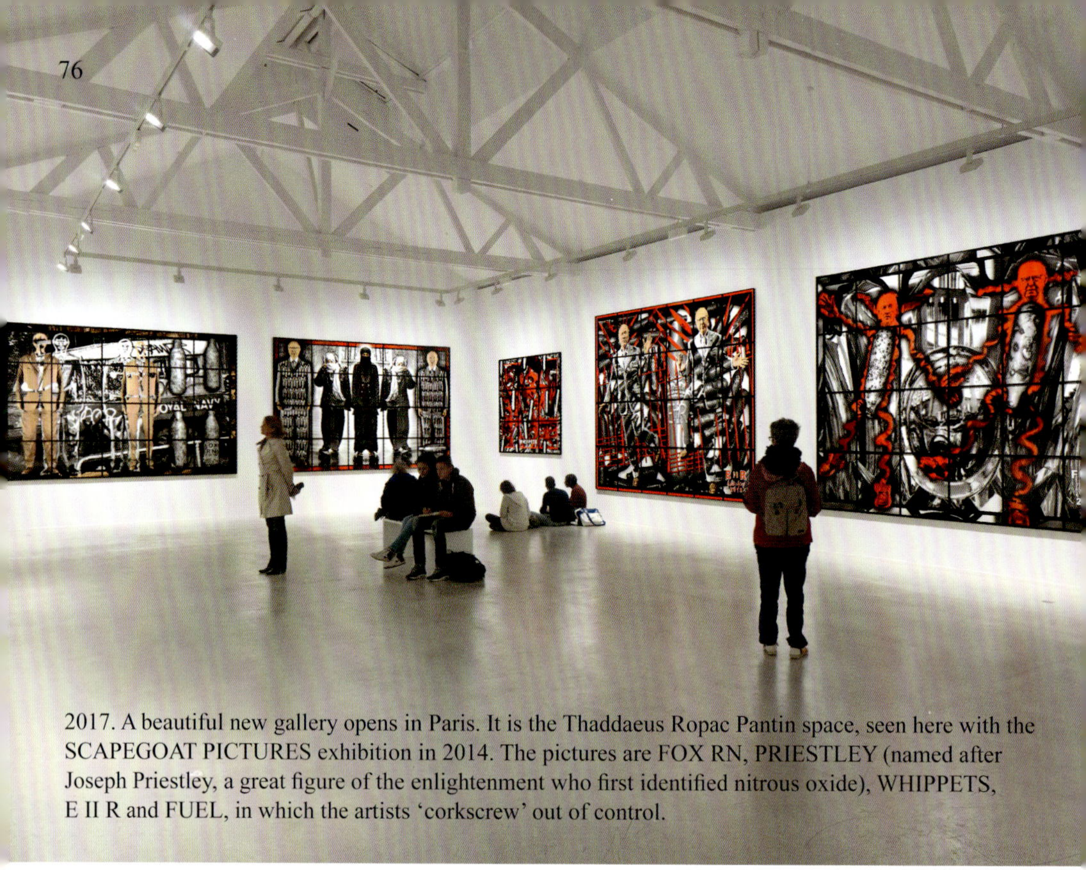

2017. A beautiful new gallery opens in Paris. It is the Thaddaeus Ropac Pantin space, seen here with the SCAPEGOAT PICTURES exhibition in 2014. The pictures are FOX RN, PRIESTLEY (named after Joseph Priestley, a great figure of the enlightenment who first identified nitrous oxide), WHIPPETS, E II R and FUEL, in which the artists 'corkscrew' out of control.

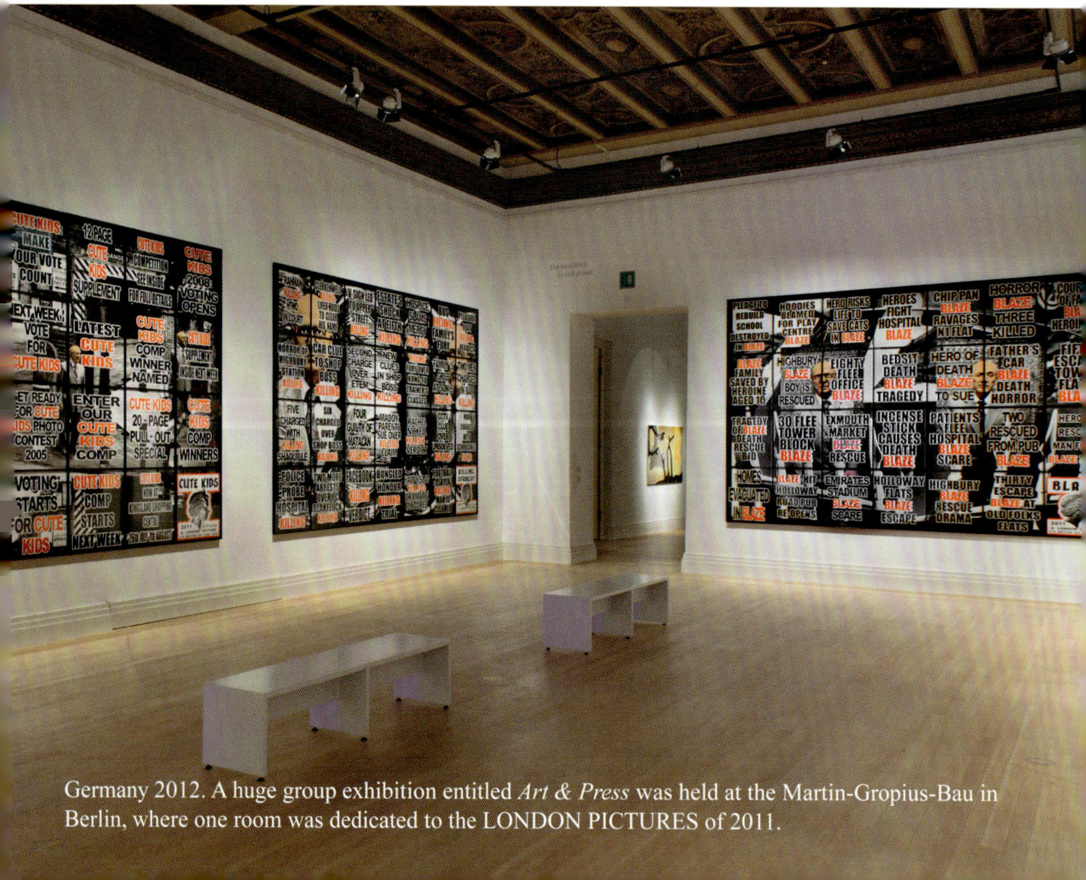

Germany 2012. A huge group exhibition entitled *Art & Press* was held at the Martin-Gropius-Bau in Berlin, where one room was dedicated to the LONDON PICTURES of 2011.

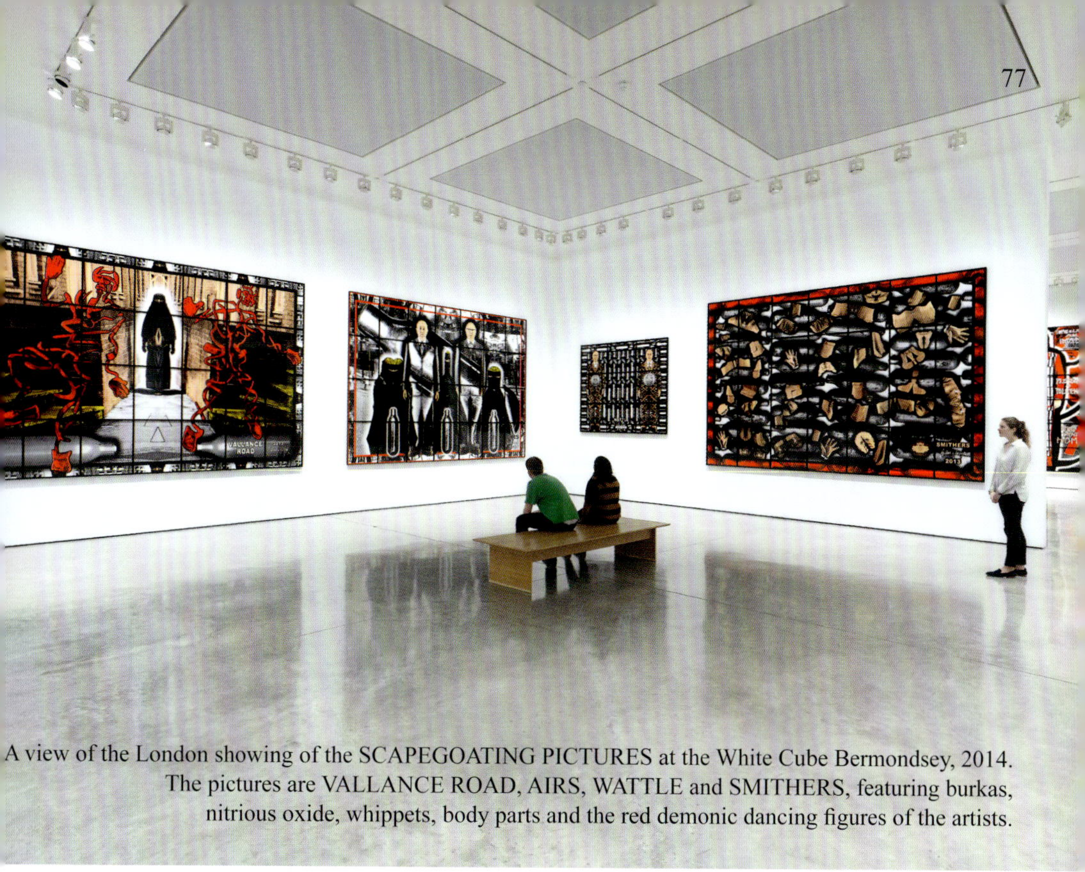

A view of the London showing of the SCAPEGOATING PICTURES at the White Cube Bermondsey, 2014. The pictures are VALLANCE ROAD, AIRS, WATTLE and SMITHERS, featuring burkas, nitrious oxide, whippets, body parts and the red demonic dancing figures of the artists.

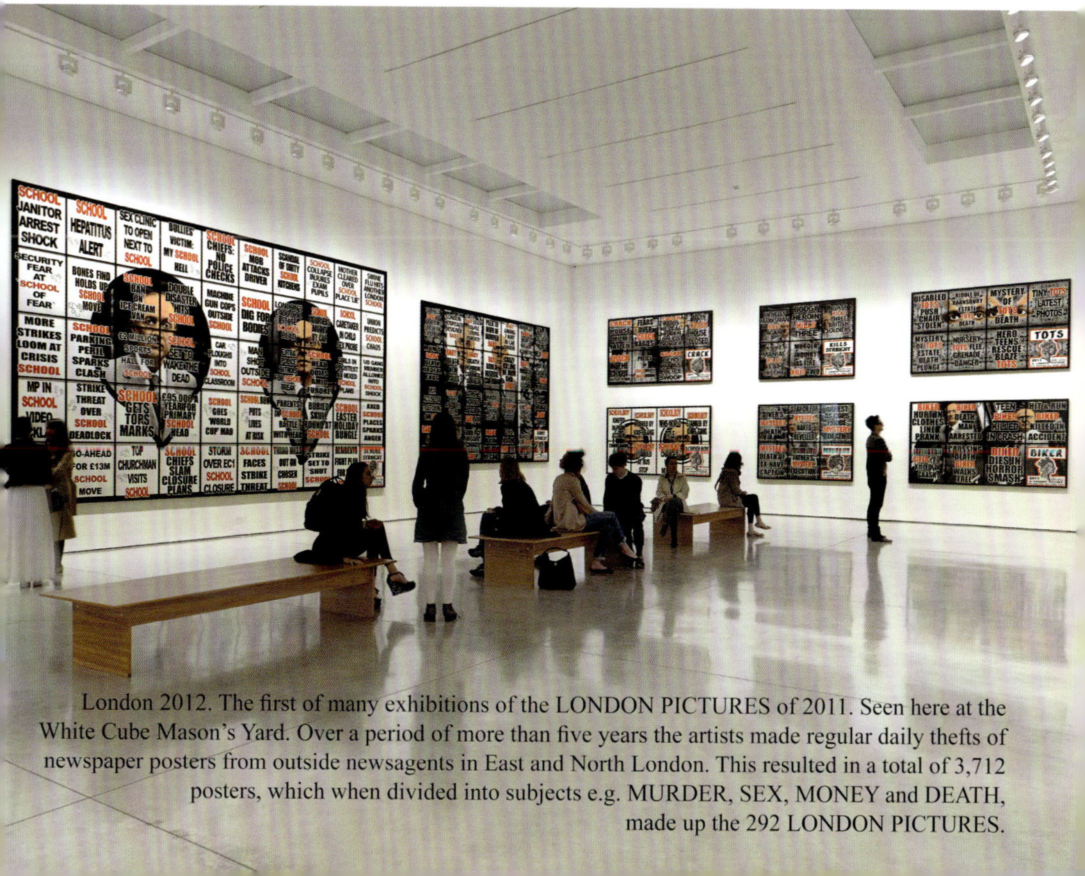

London 2012. The first of many exhibitions of the LONDON PICTURES of 2011. Seen here at the White Cube Mason's Yard. Over a period of more than five years the artists made regular daily thefts of newspaper posters from outside newsagents in East and North London. This resulted in a total of 3,712 posters, which when divided into subjects e.g. MURDER, SEX, MONEY and DEATH, made up the 292 LONDON PICTURES.

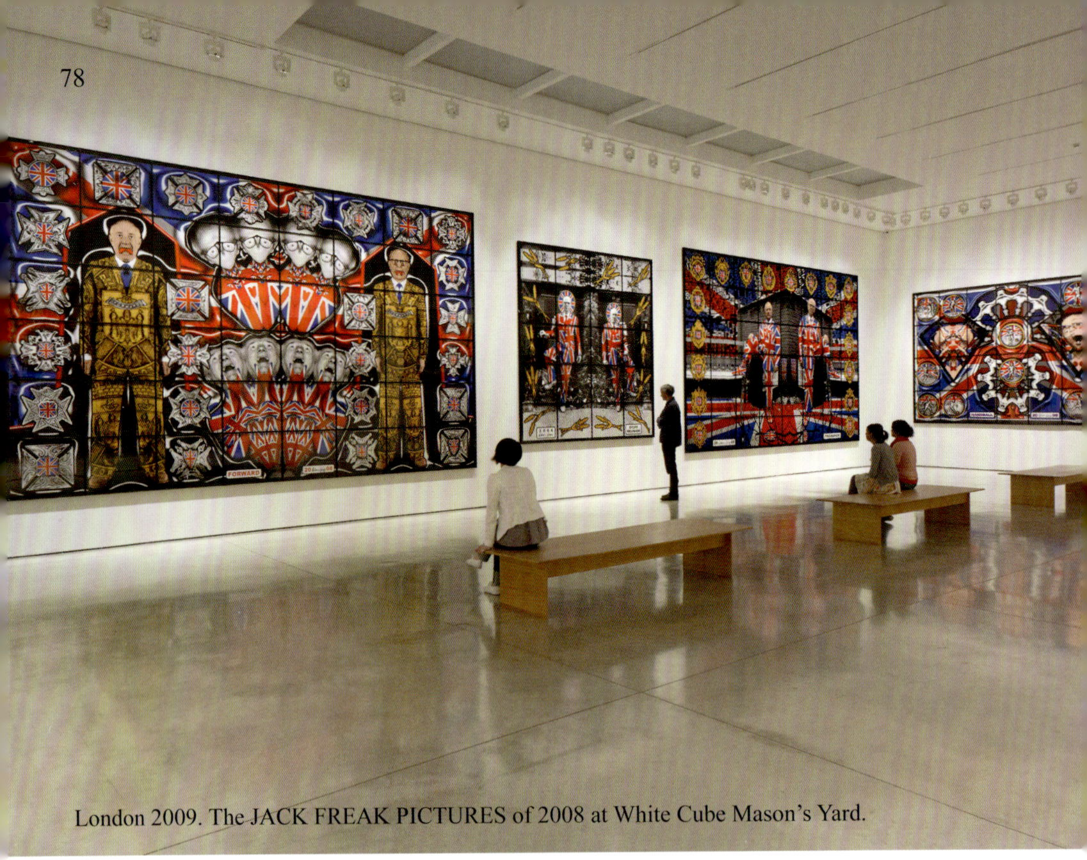

London 2009. The JACK FREAK PICTURES of 2008 at White Cube Mason's Yard.

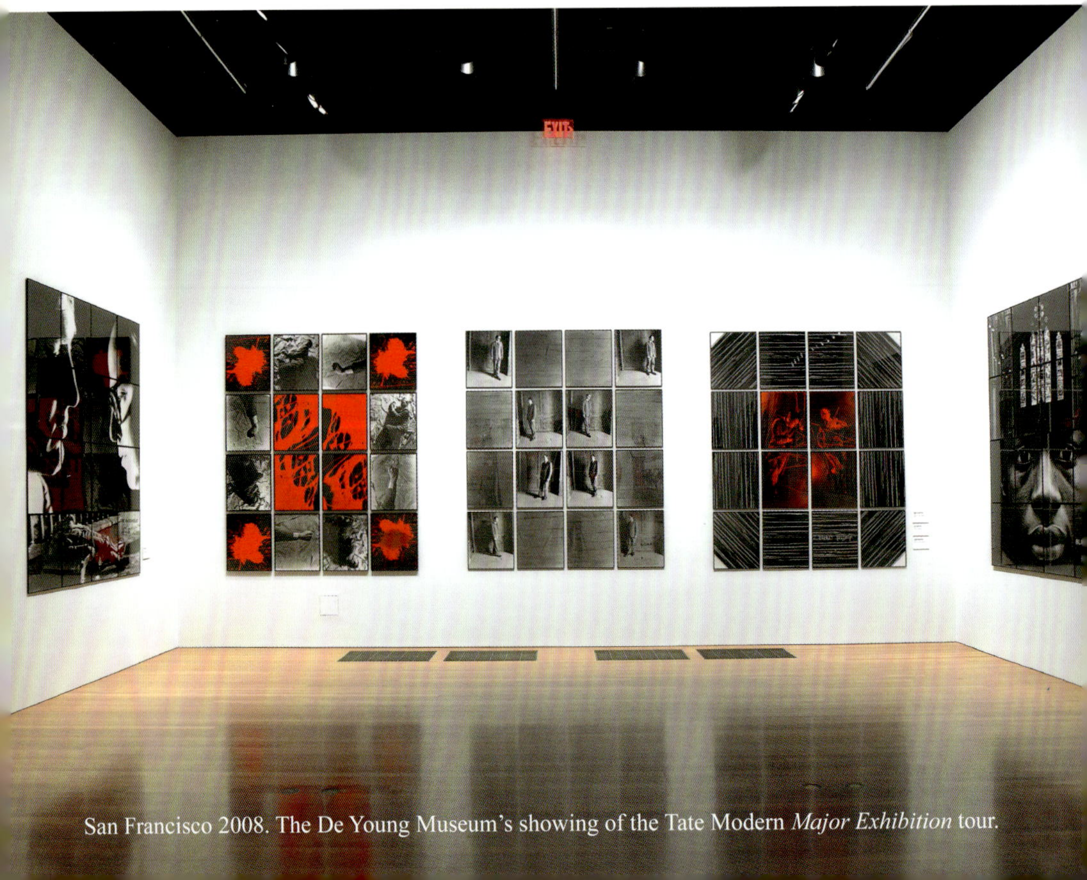

San Francisco 2008. The De Young Museum's showing of the Tate Modern *Major Exhibition* tour.

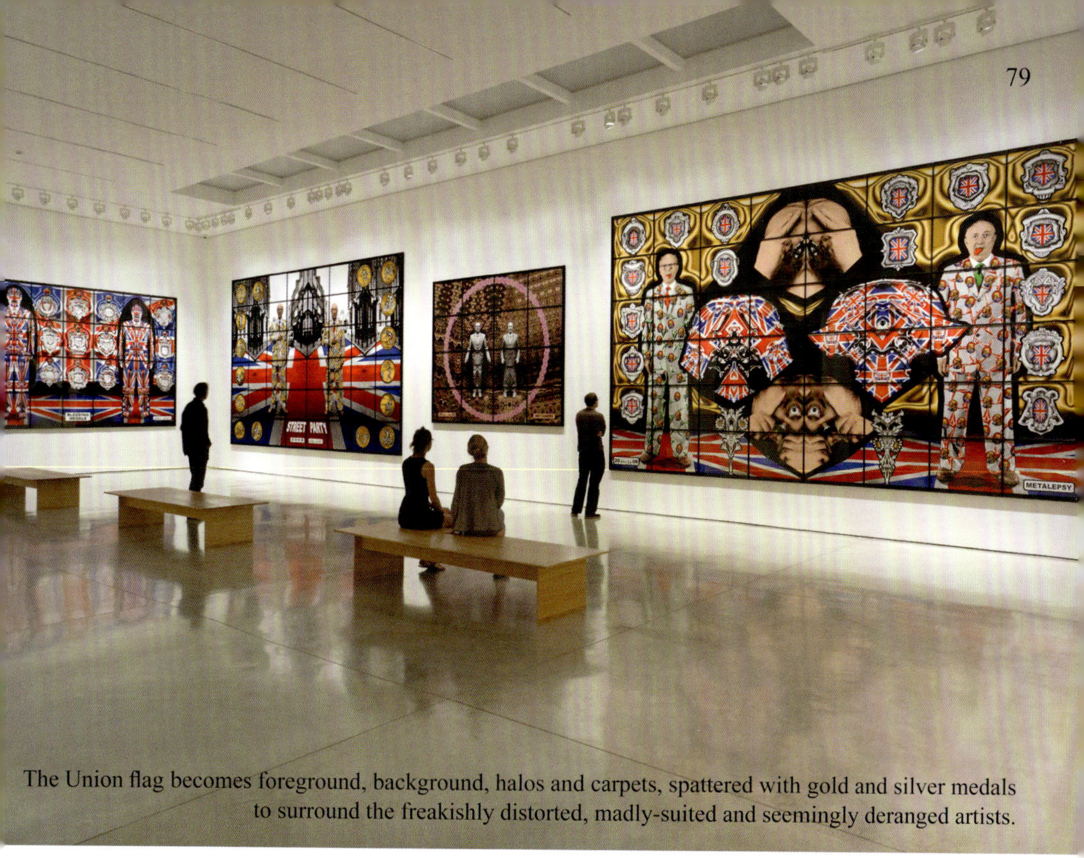

The Union flag becomes foreground, background, halos and carpets, spattered with gold and silver medals to surround the freakishly distorted, madly-suited and seemingly deranged artists.

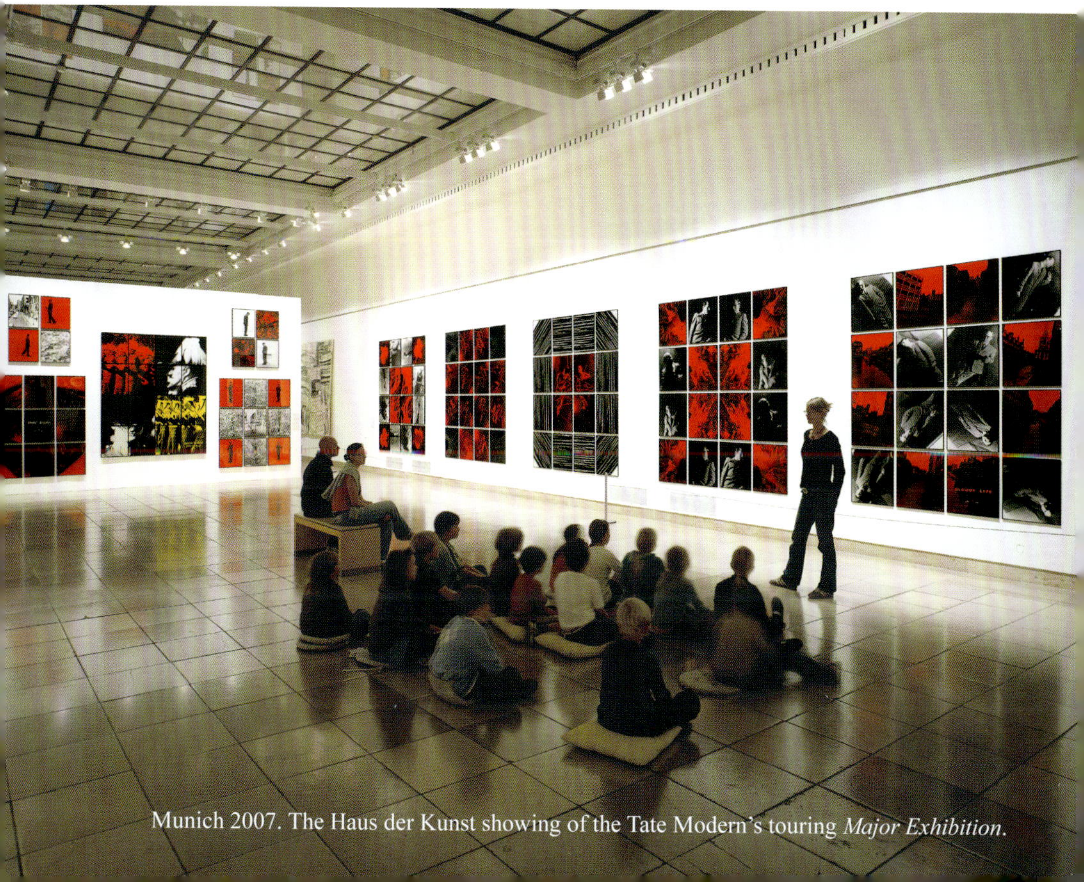

Munich 2007. The Haus der Kunst showing of the Tate Modern's touring *Major Exhibition*.

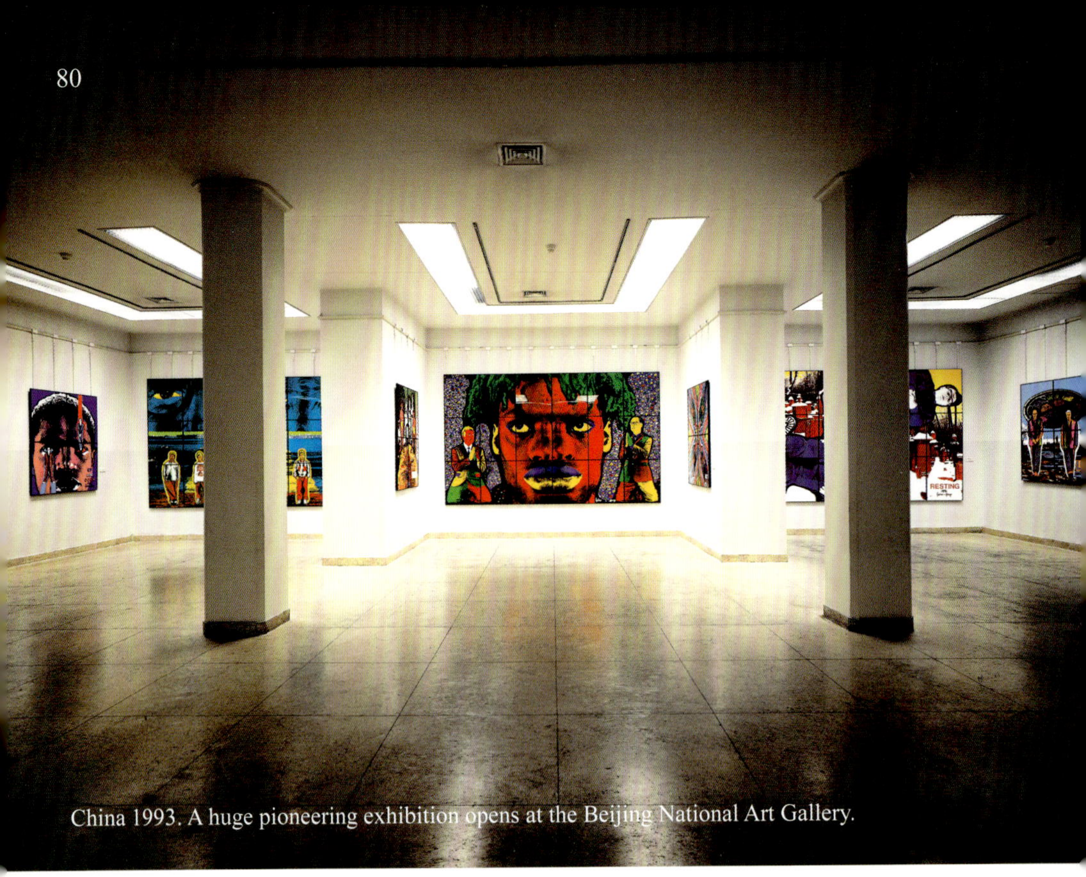

China 1993. A huge pioneering exhibition opens at the Beijing National Art Gallery.

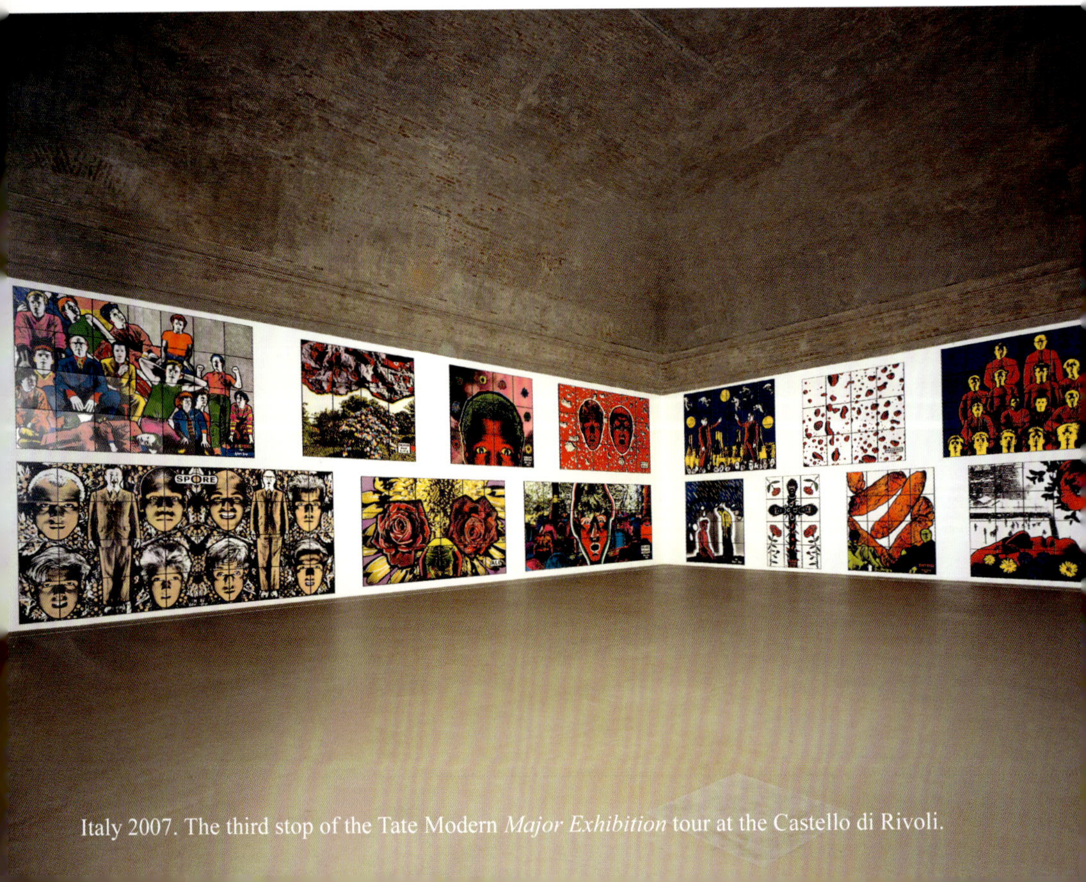

Italy 2007. The third stop of the Tate Modern *Major Exhibition* tour at the Castello di Rivoli.

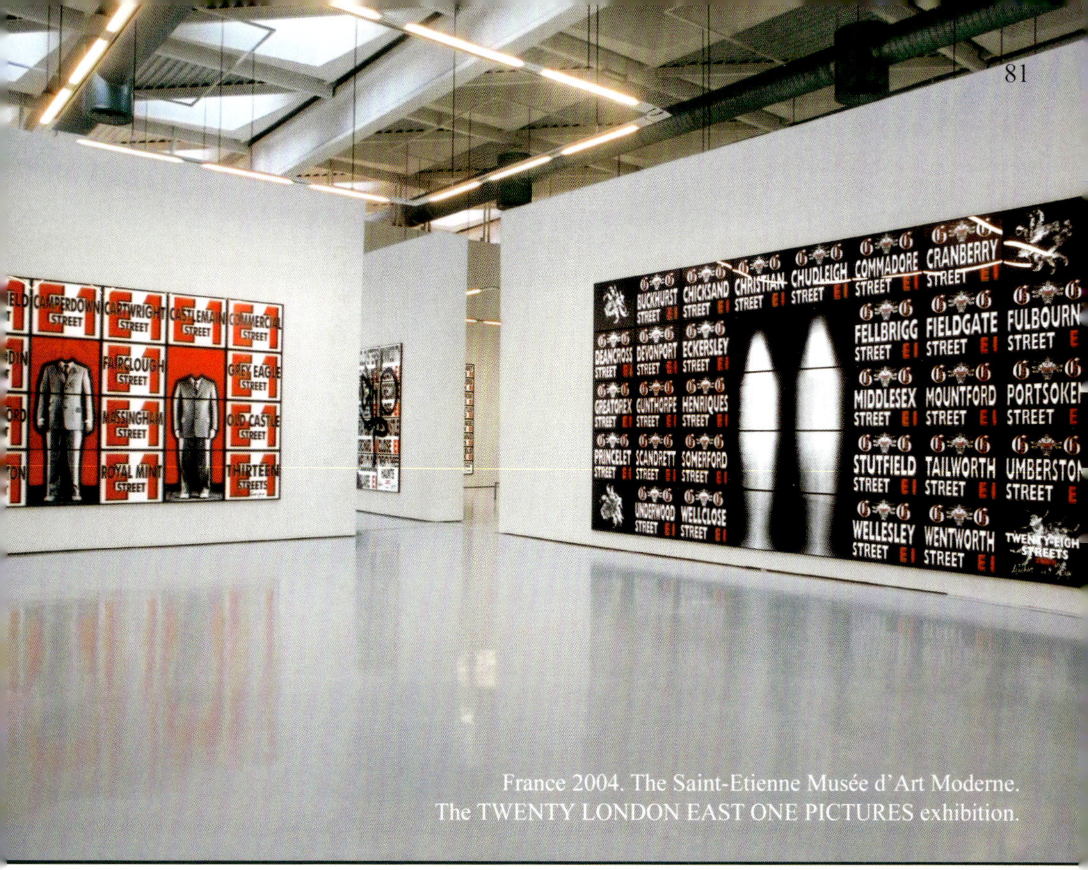

France 2004. The Saint-Etienne Musée d'Art Moderne.
The TWENTY LONDON EAST ONE PICTURES exhibition.

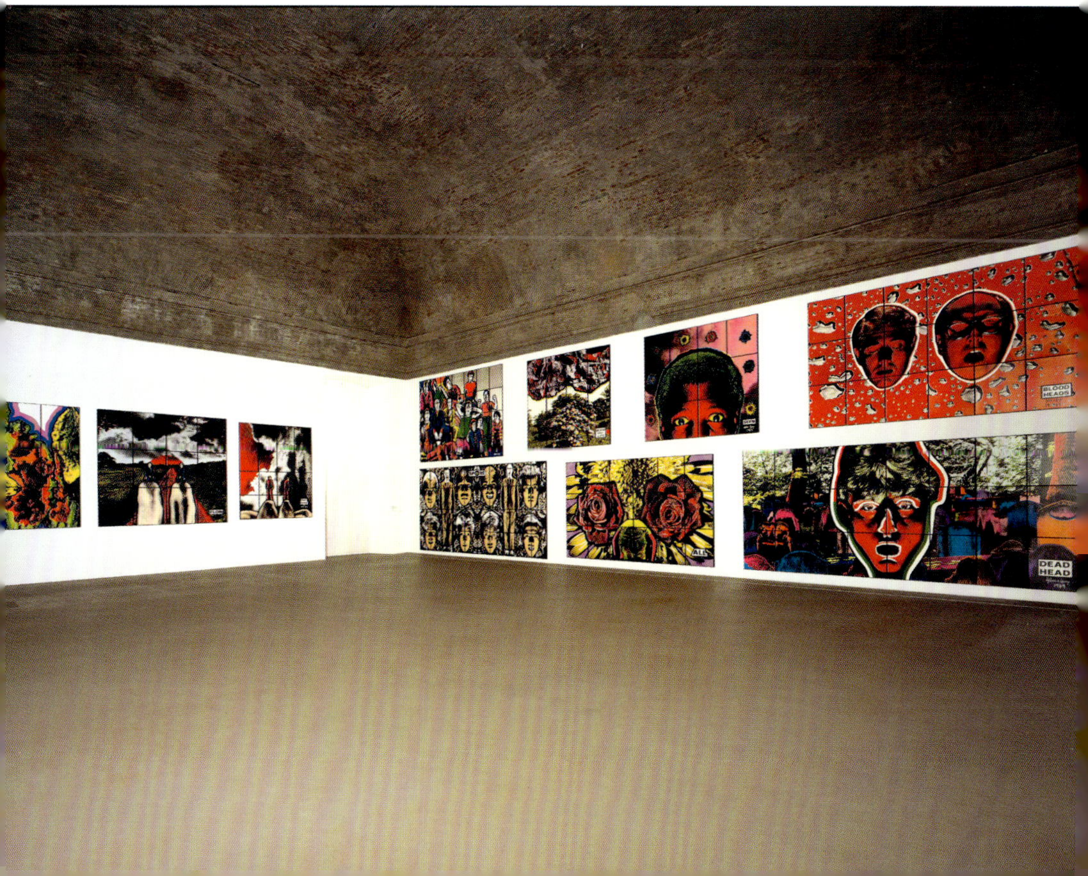

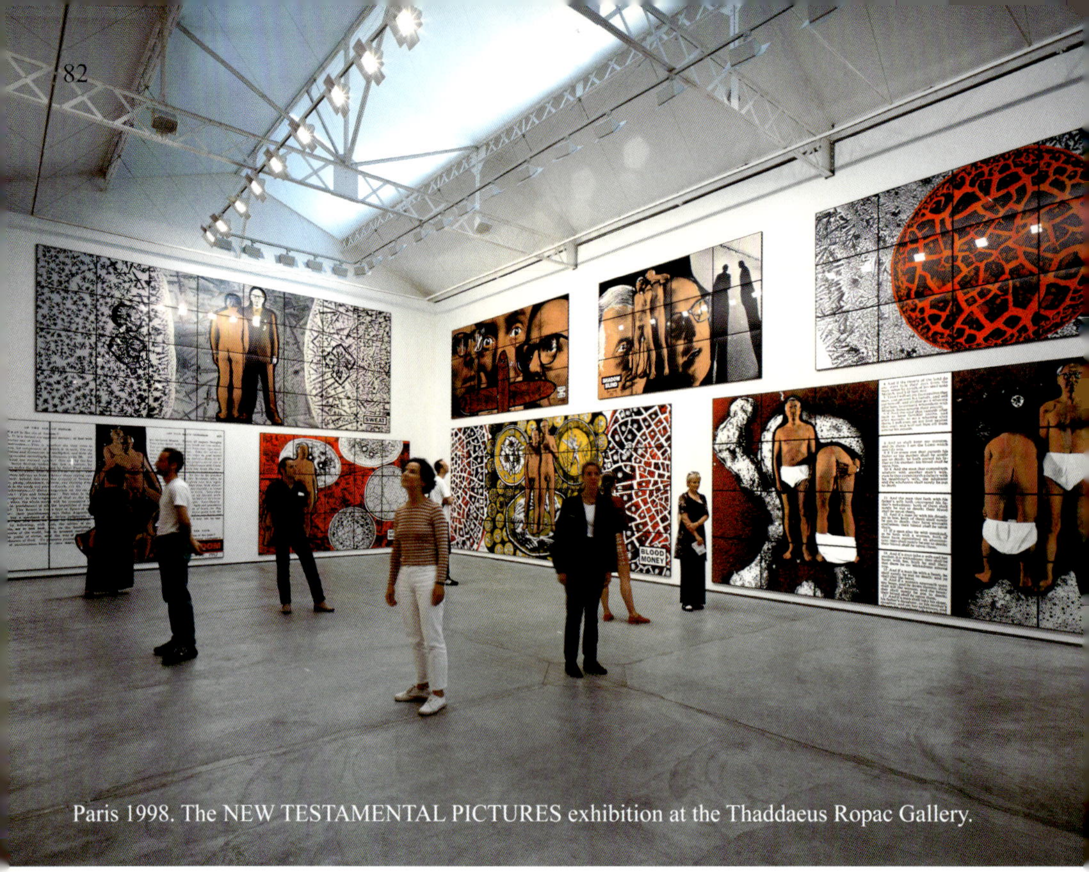

Paris 1998. The NEW TESTAMENTAL PICTURES exhibition at the Thaddaeus Ropac Gallery.

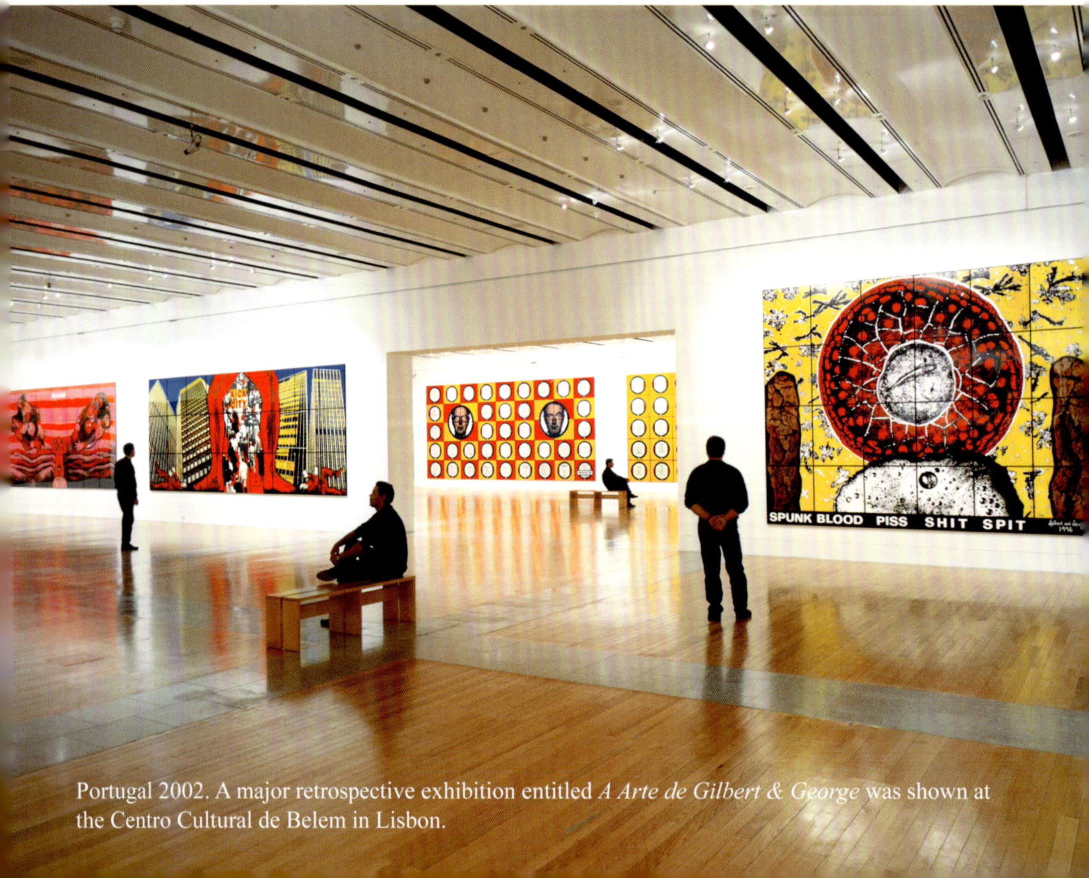

Portugal 2002. A major retrospective exhibition entitled *A Arte de Gilbert & George* was shown at the Centro Cultural de Belem in Lisbon.

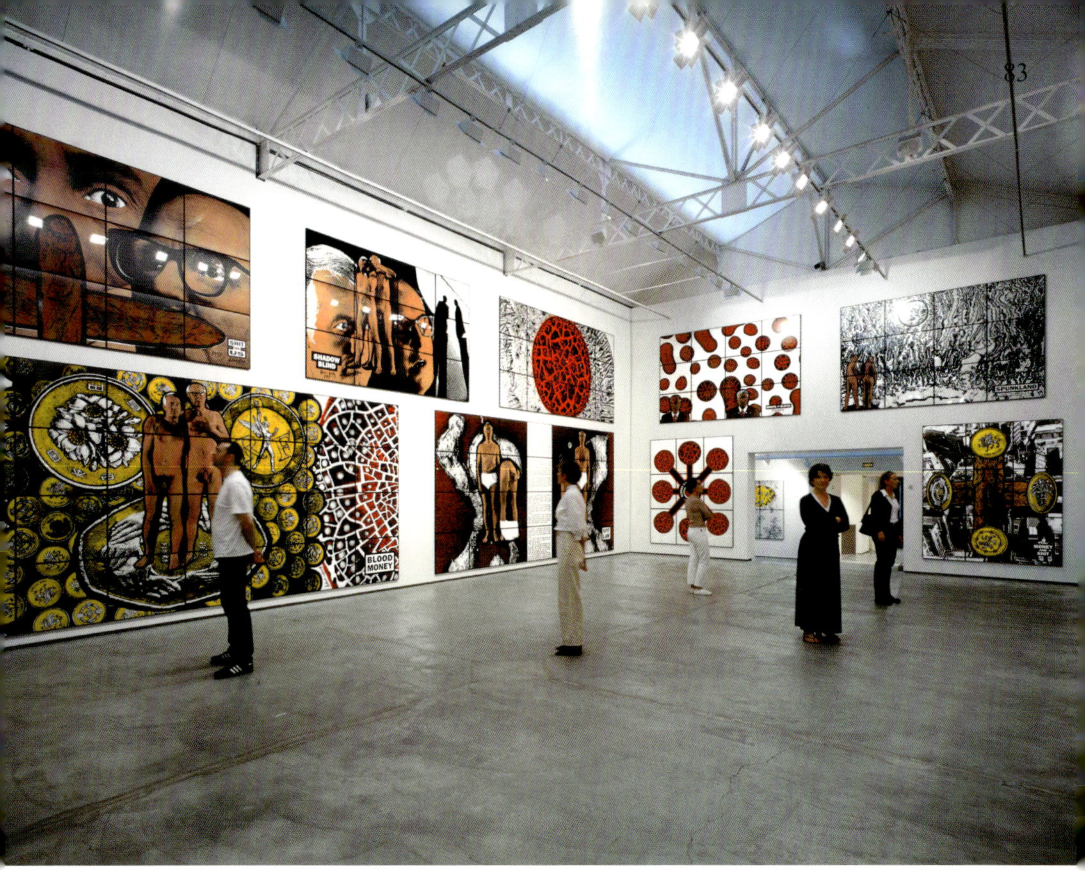

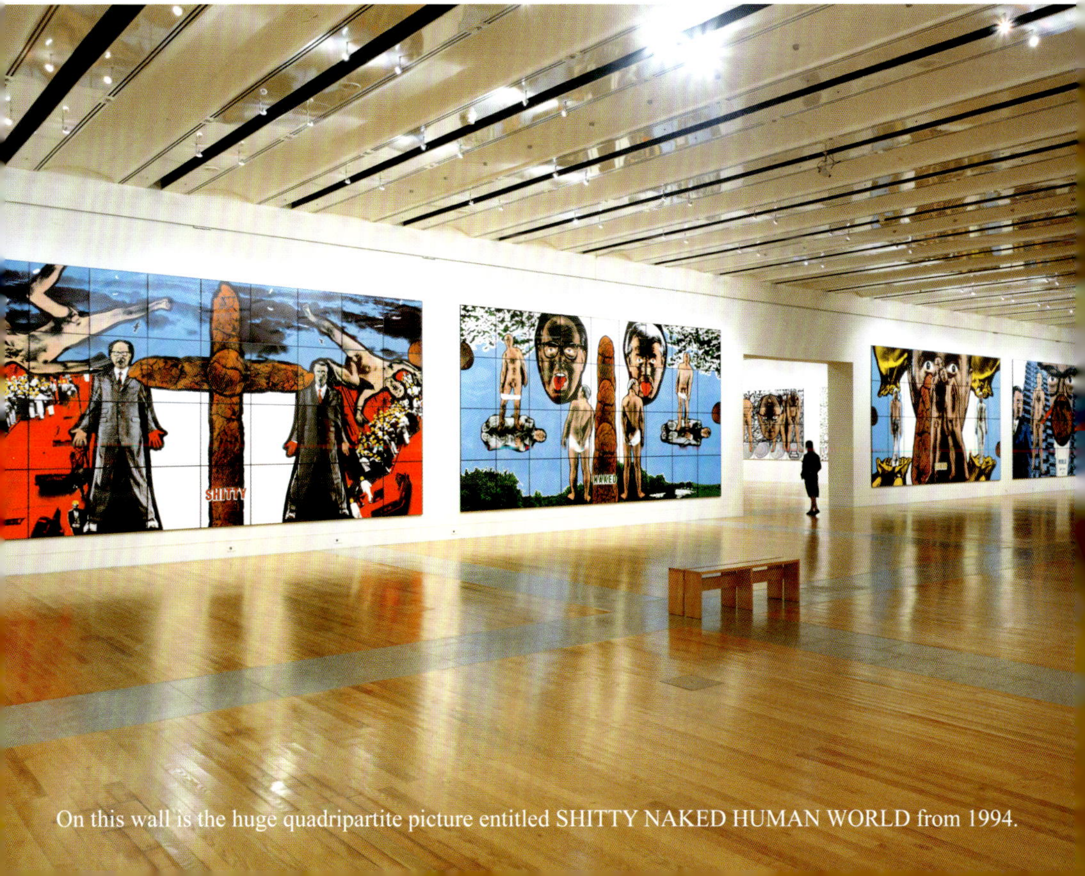

On this wall is the huge quadripartite picture entitled SHITTY NAKED HUMAN WORLD from 1994.

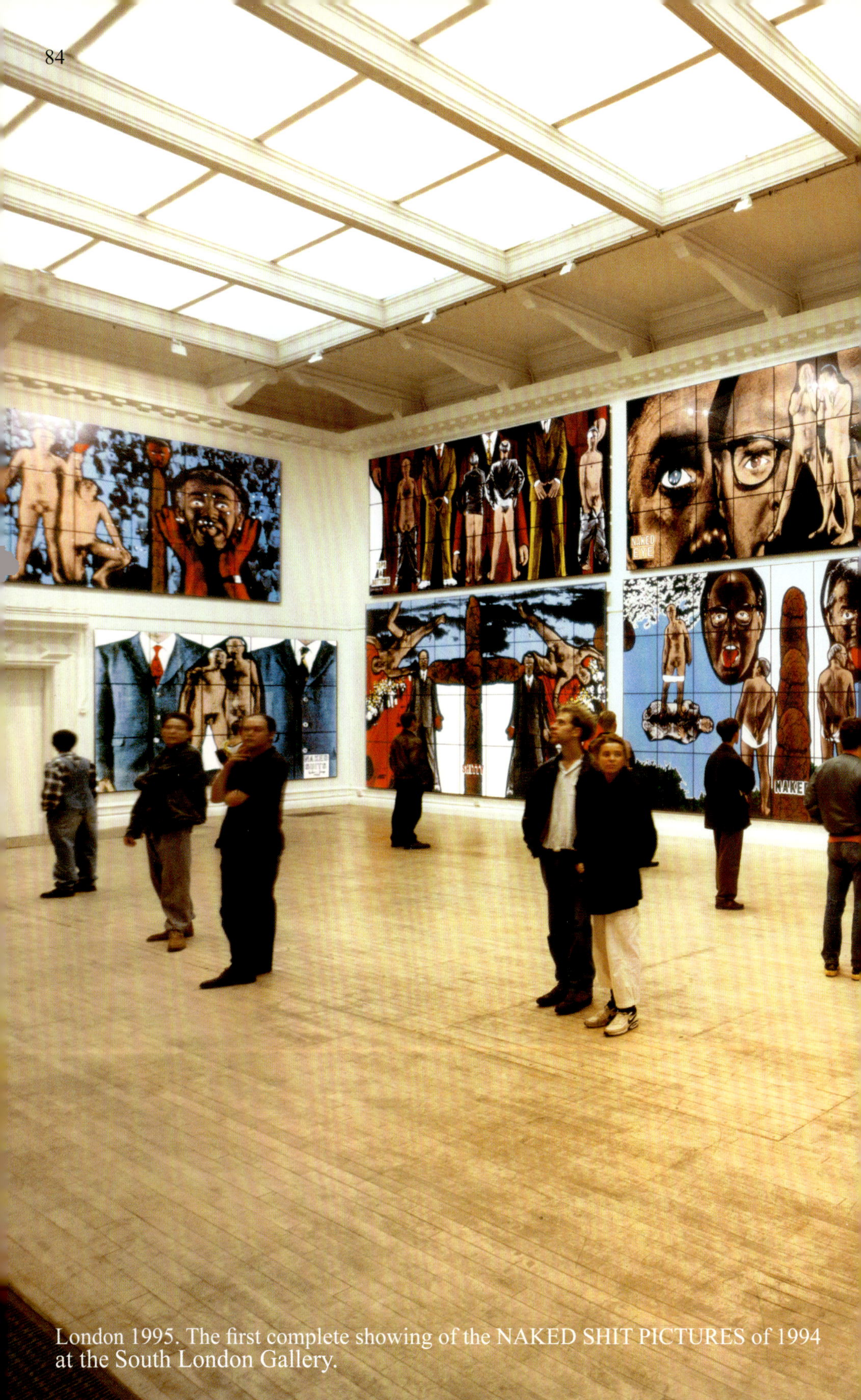

London 1995. The first complete showing of the NAKED SHIT PICTURES of 1994 at the South London Gallery.

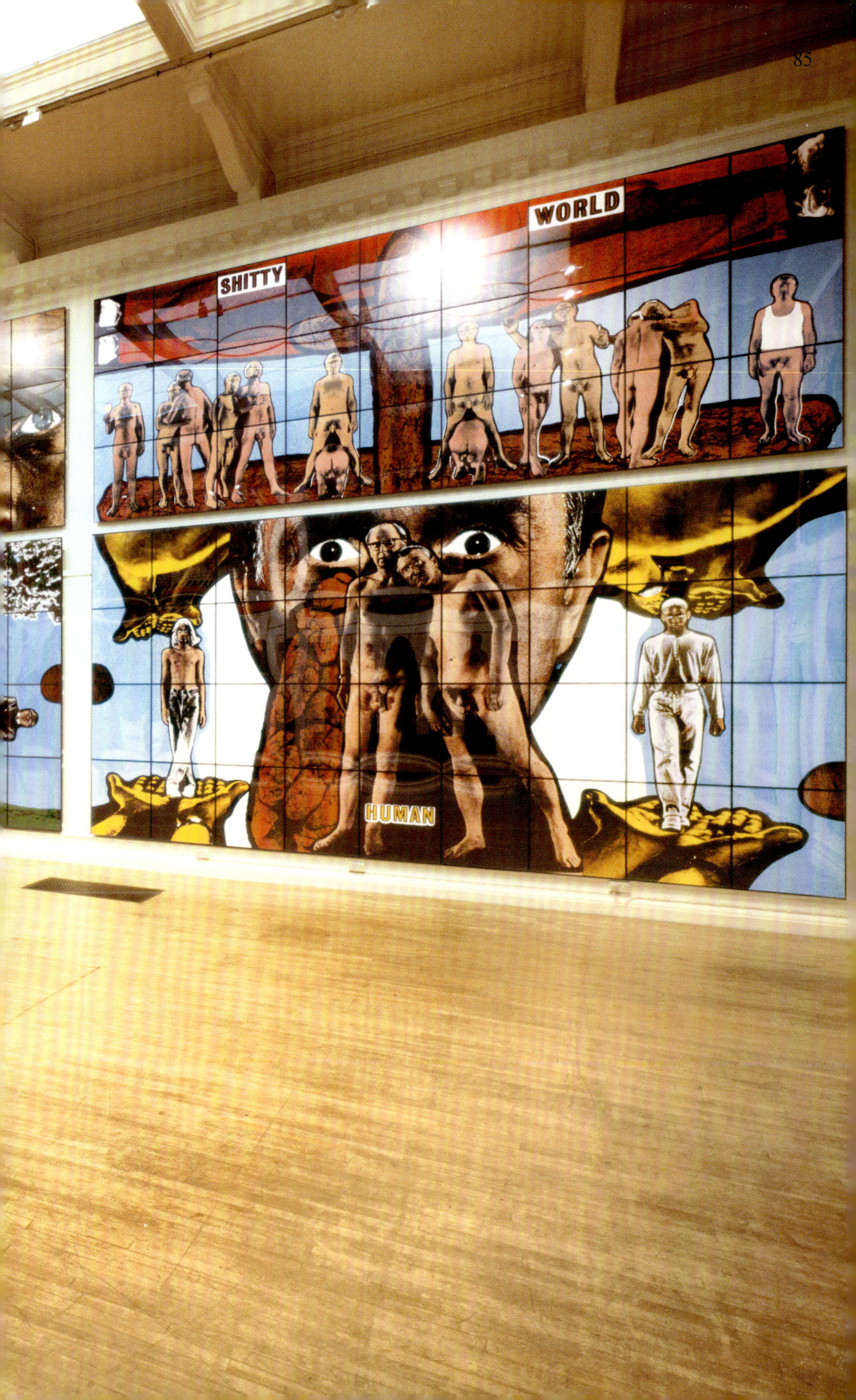
SHITTY
WORLD
HUMAN

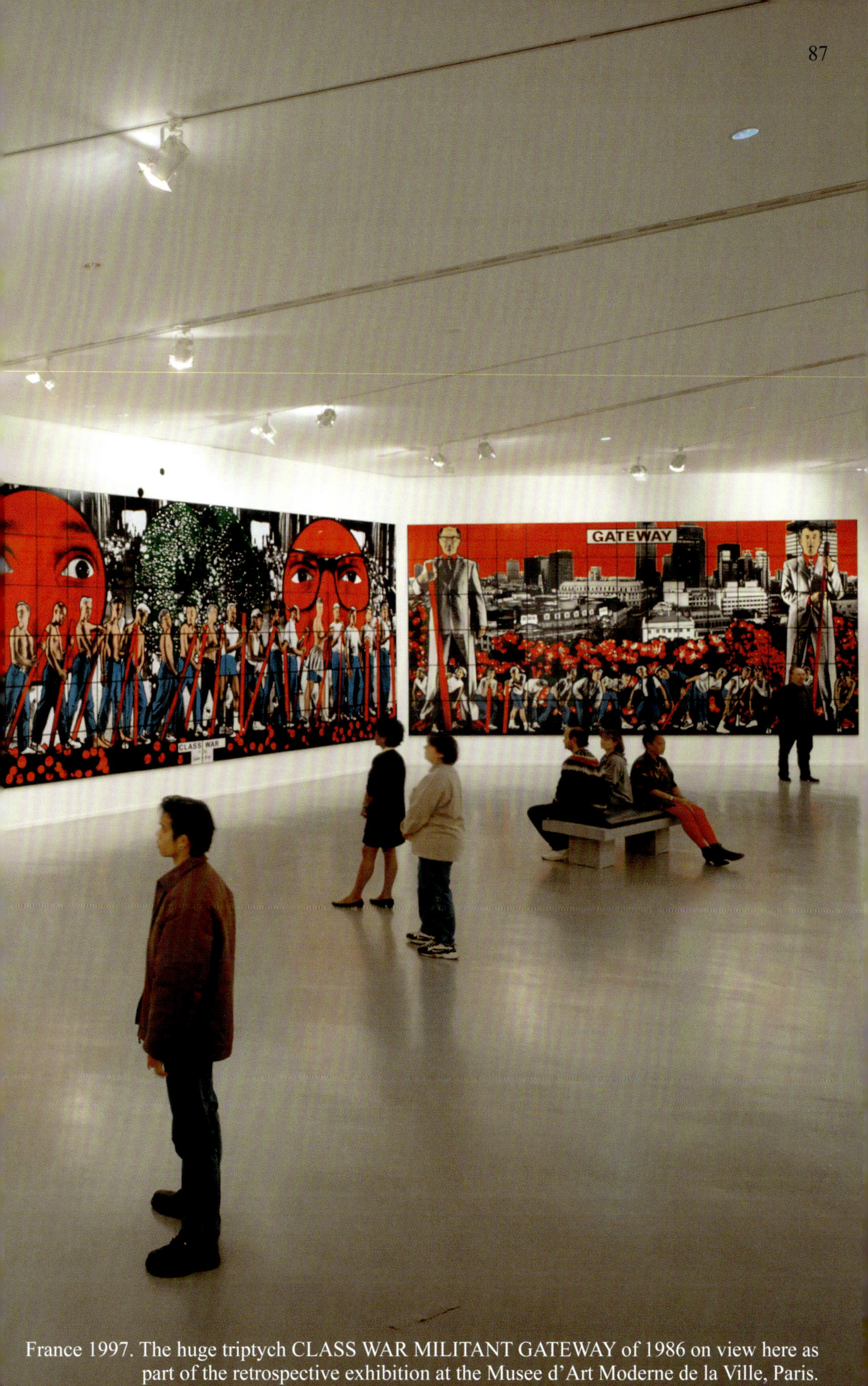

France 1997. The huge triptych CLASS WAR MILITANT GATEWAY of 1986 on view here as part of the retrospective exhibition at the Musee d'Art Moderne de la Ville, Paris.

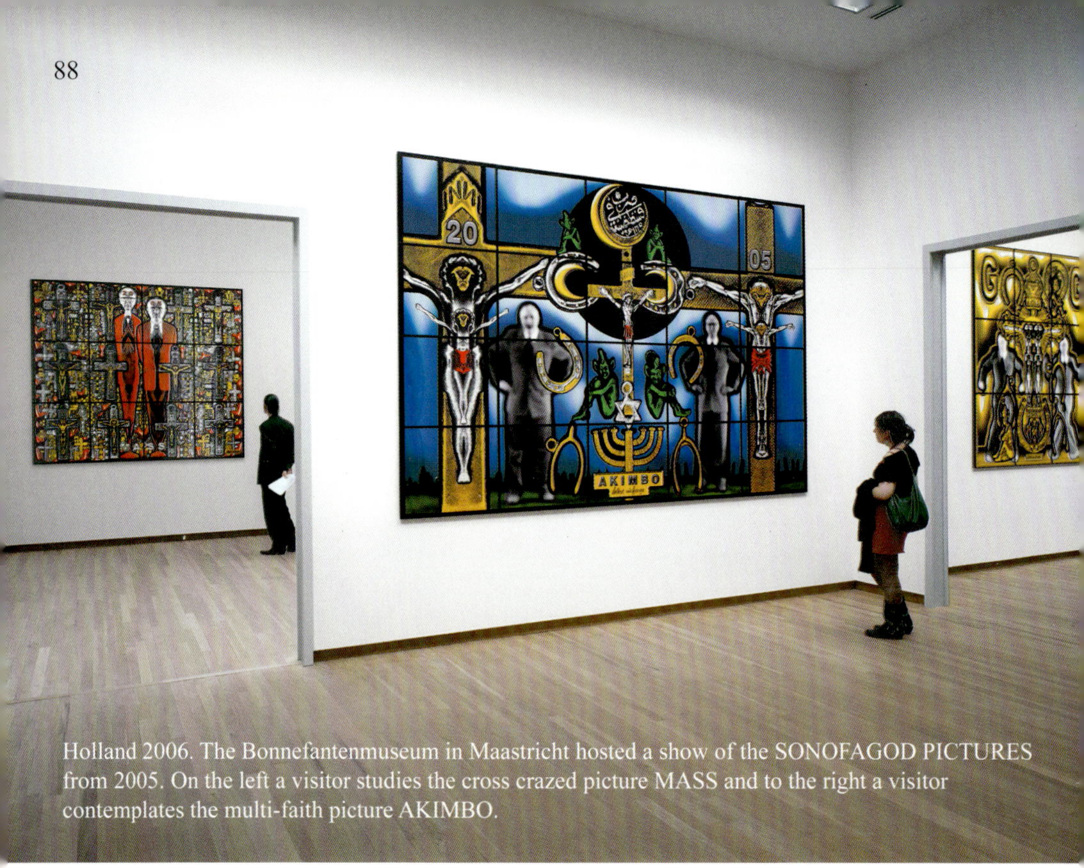

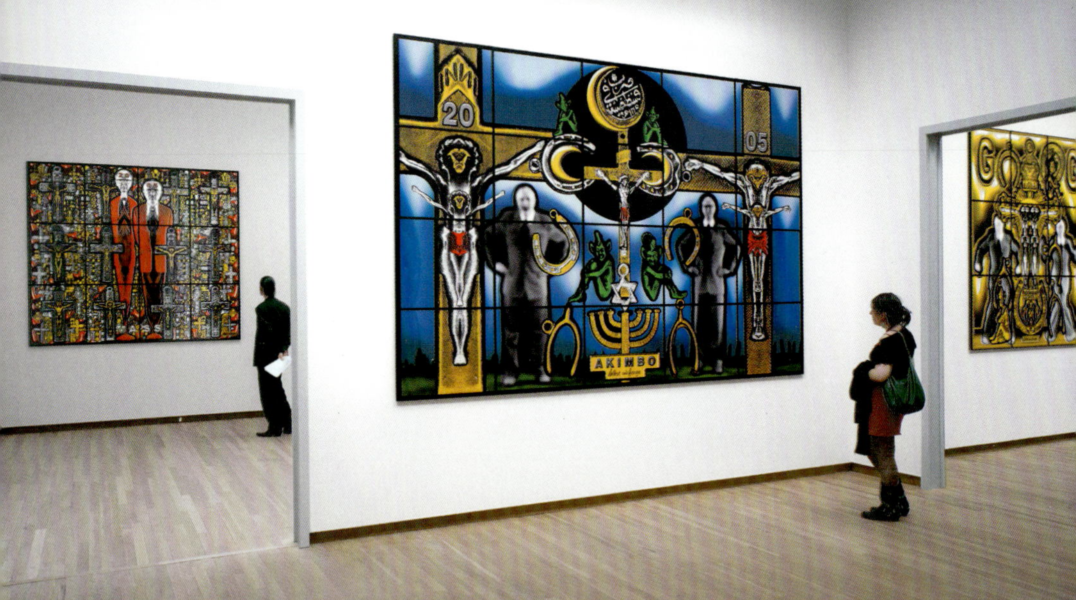

Holland 2006. The Bonnefantenmuseum in Maastricht hosted a show of the SONOFAGOD PICTURES from 2005. On the left a visitor studies the cross crazed picture MASS and to the right a visitor contemplates the multi-faith picture AKIMBO.

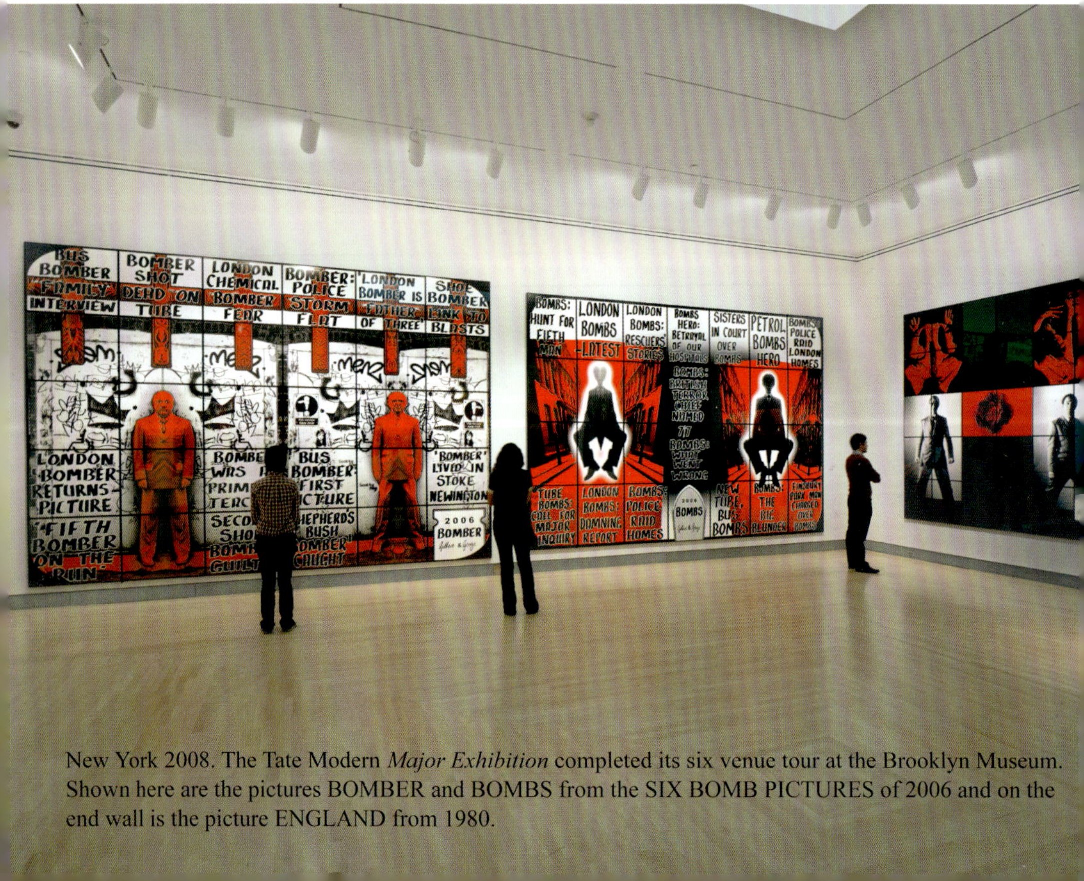

New York 2008. The Tate Modern *Major Exhibition* completed its six venue tour at the Brooklyn Museum. Shown here are the pictures BOMBER and BOMBS from the SIX BOMB PICTURES of 2006 and on the end wall is the picture ENGLAND from 1980.

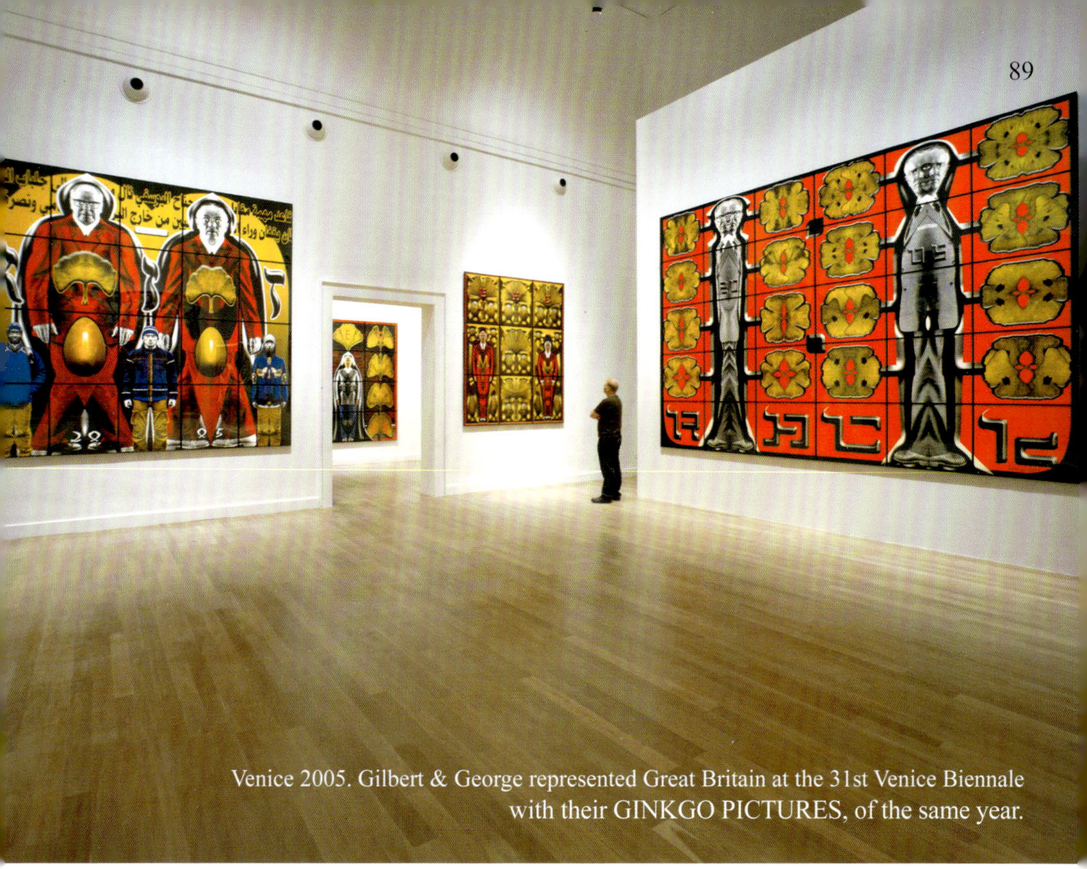

Venice 2005. Gilbert & George represented Great Britain at the 31st Venice Biennale with their GINKGO PICTURES, of the same year.

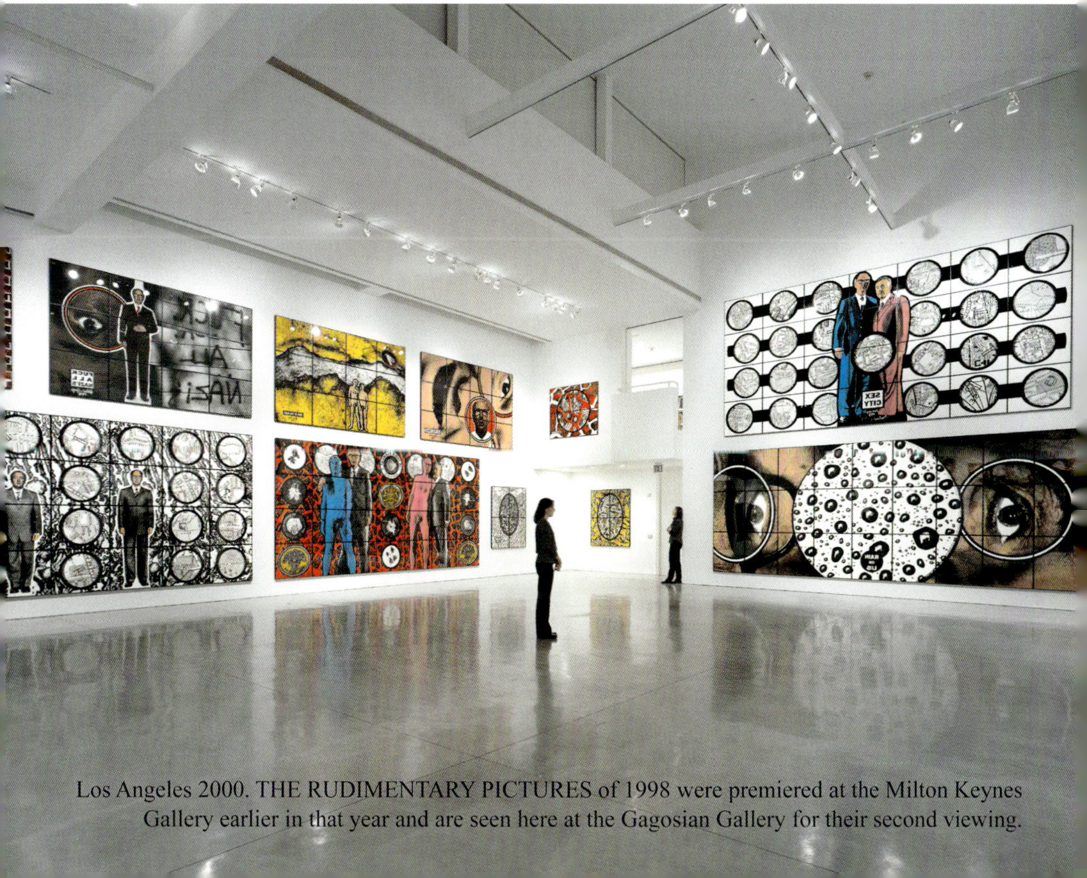

Los Angeles 2000. THE RUDIMENTARY PICTURES of 1998 were premiered at the Milton Keynes Gallery earlier in that year and are seen here at the Gagosian Gallery for their second viewing.

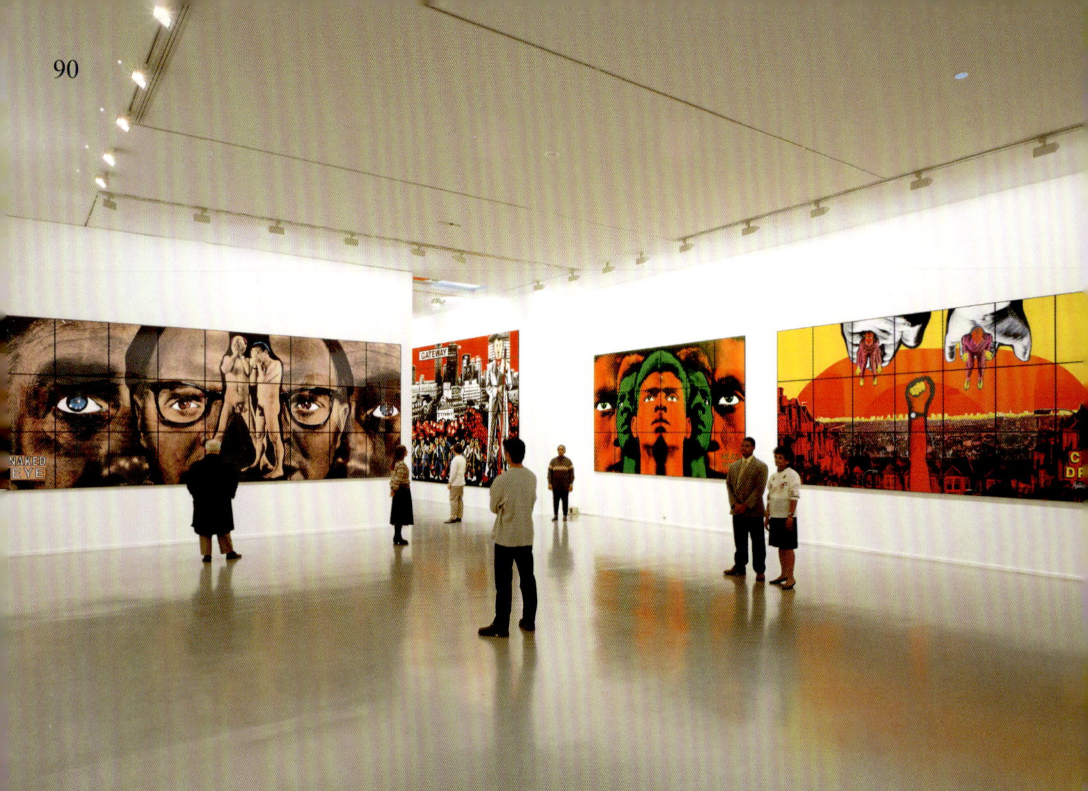

France 1997. The artists' retrospective exhibition at the Musee d'Art Moderne de la Ville, Paris.

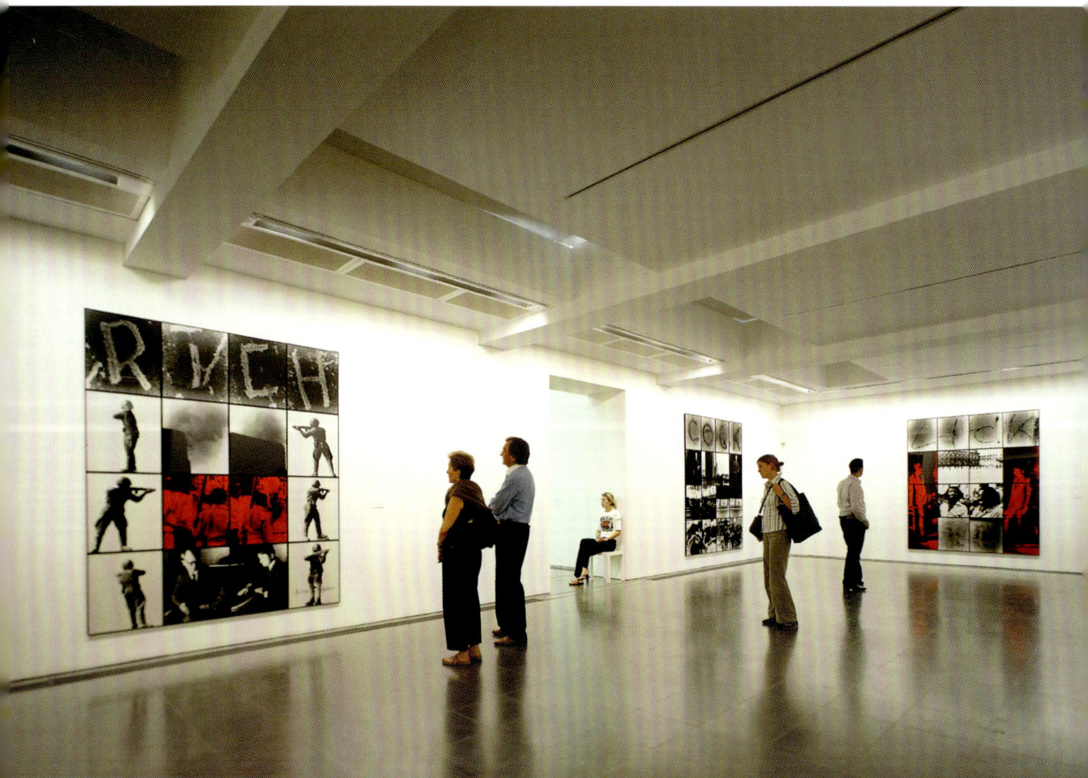

London 2002. The Serpentine Gallery. The 26 DIRTY WORDS PICTURES of 1977 were shown here in their entirety for the first time, on the twenty-fifth anniversary of their creation.

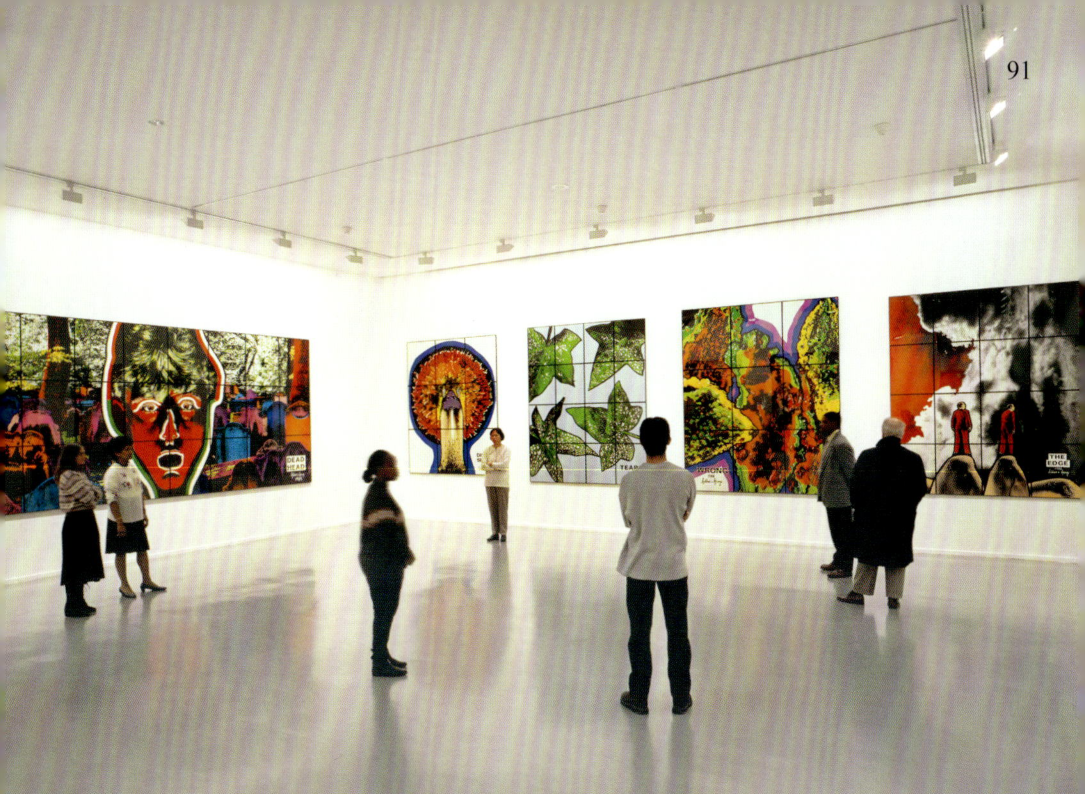

Another view of the artists' retrospective exhibition at the Musee d'Art Moderne de la Ville, Paris.

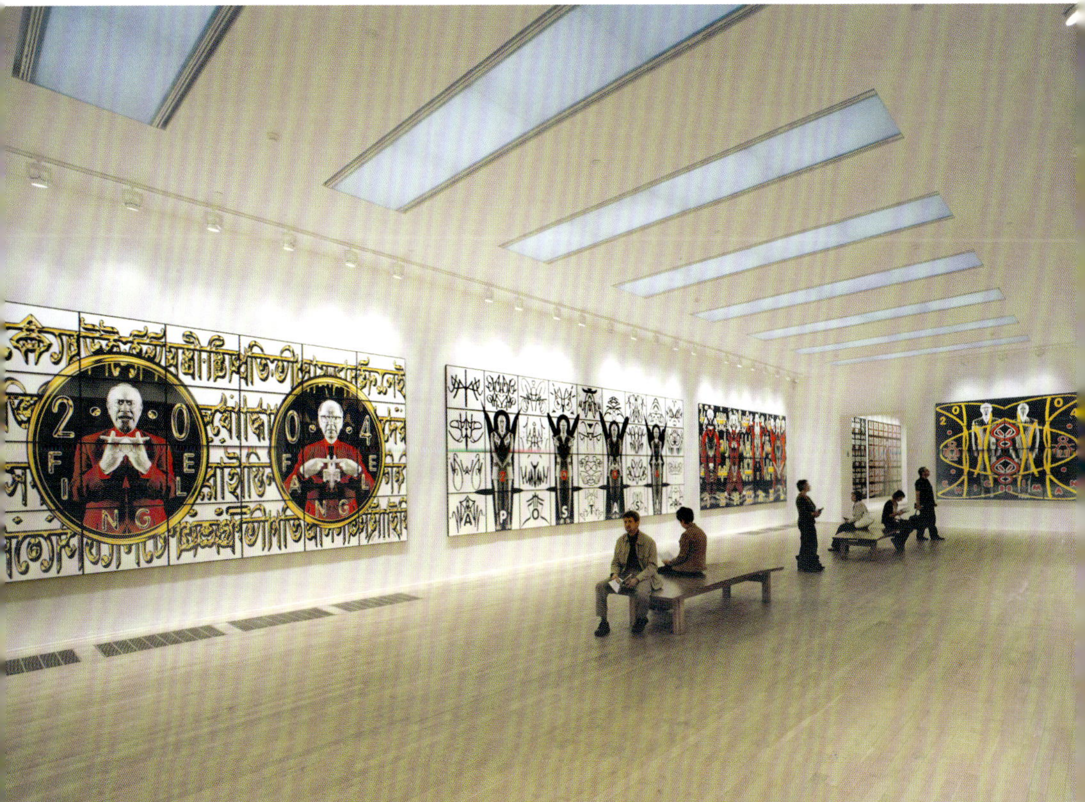

London 2007. A view of the PERVERSIVE PICTURES of 2004 at the Tate Modern *Major Exhibition*.

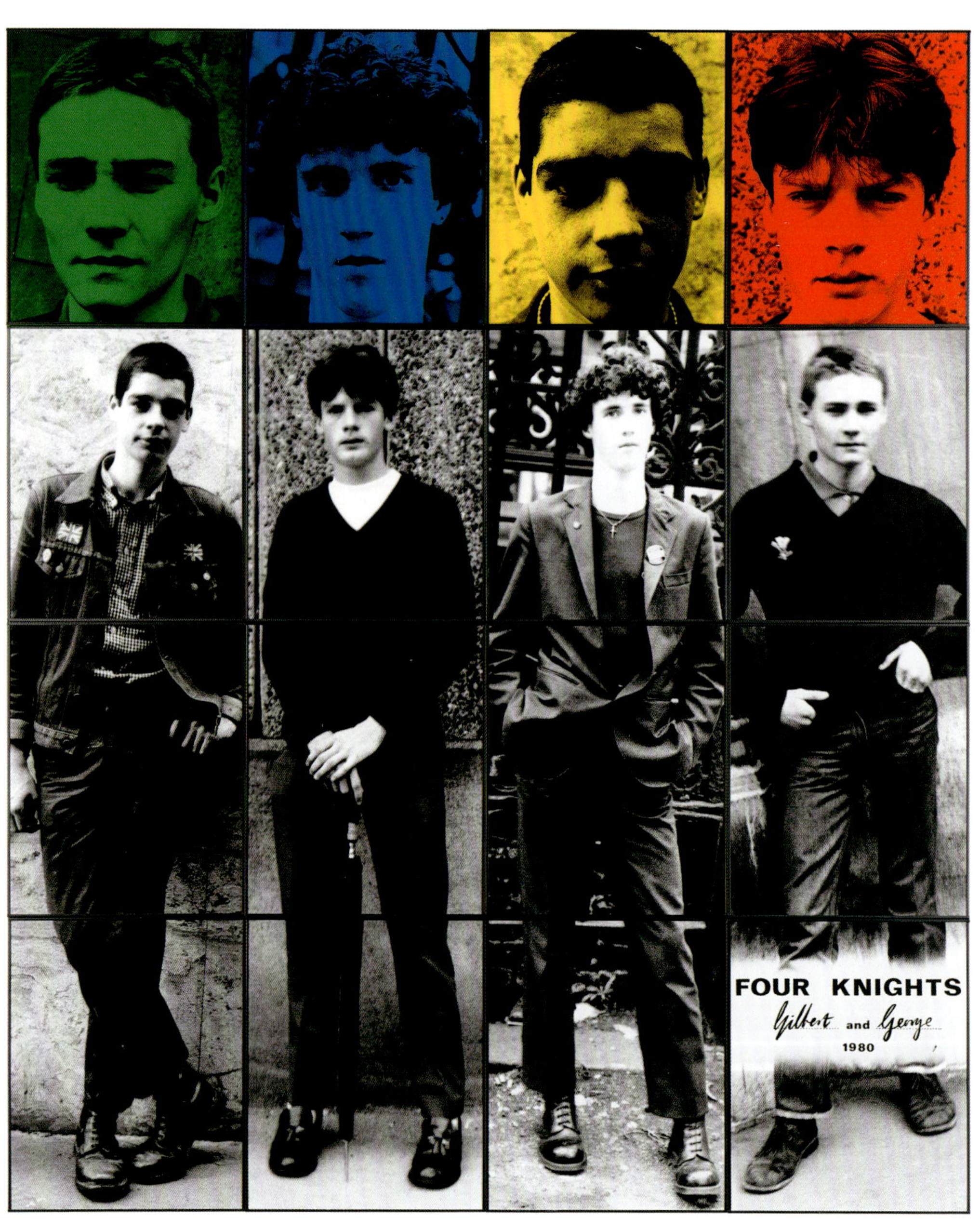

FOUR KNIGHTS. 1980. 241 x 201 cm

Nineteen
Punks, Teds, National Front, Rastas, New Romantics, Mods, Rockers, Hippies, Gangs, Hipsters, Lads and Skinheads

Gilbert & George have always recognised and represented in their art the vigour and glamour of youth and the tribal energy of youth sub-cultures.

For Gilbert & George, youth itself, energy, pride, passion, strength and extremism are intense and heightened conditions. Sub-cultures provide new, alternative realities for the youths who join them and feel empowered by them. The dedication of youth to these alternative realities, and the lengths they will go to maintain their commitment to their renewed identity within a sub-culture, comprises an emotional bond that Gilbert & George represent in their art as a life force, in different ways.

Uncertain youths, wary teenagers, youths who shut the world out, youths as a youth army, postmodern acolytes; youths as sex, desire and love; doomed youth; anonymous youth; tagging, graffiti, advertisement, vandalism.

Since 1968, Gilbert & George have seen the procession of youth in a visionary manner. Sub-cultures change while the need for individualism and belonging, the resentment of authority and the desire for excitement remains constant. The processional of youth is represented in the art of Gilbert & George, as in a vast, visionary, ageless picture.

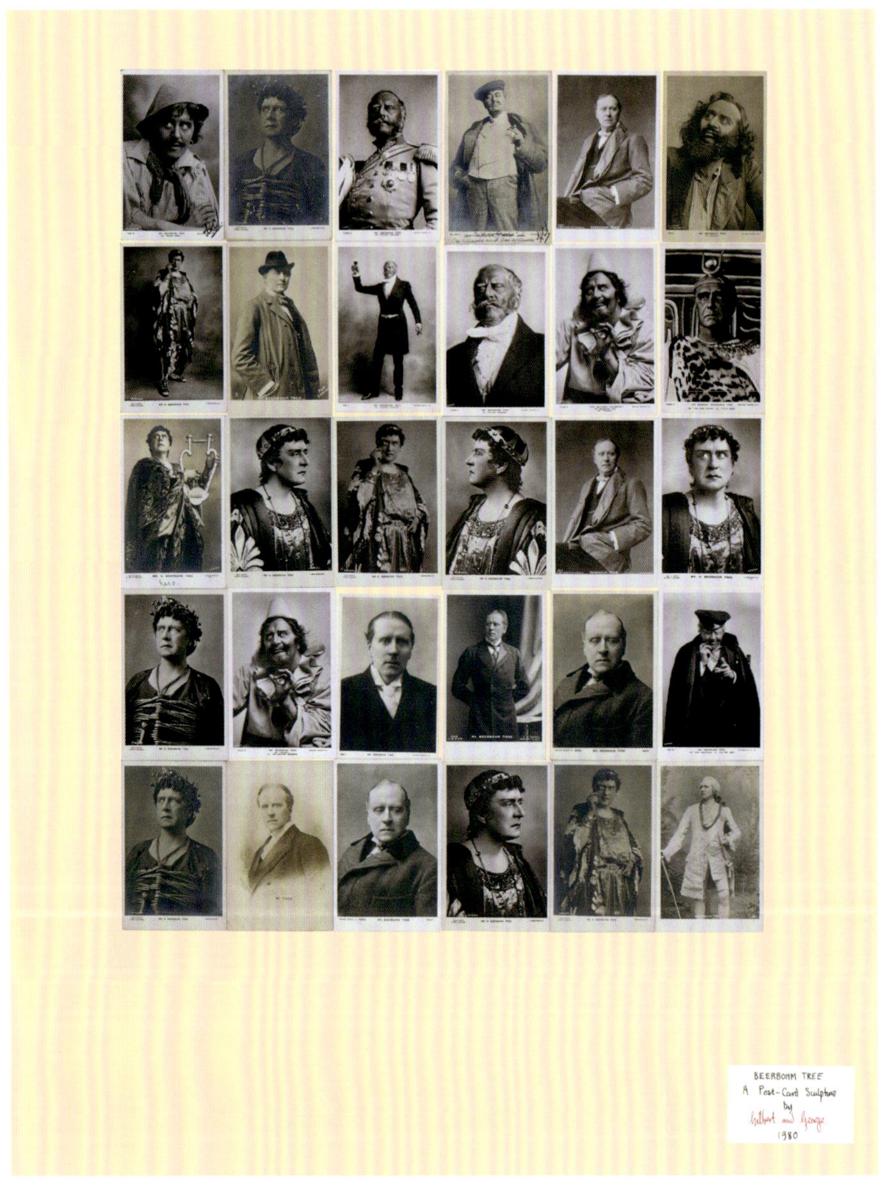

BEERBOHM TREE. 1980. 113 x 81 cm A POST-CARD SCULPTURE.

Twenty
Gilbert & George and the Victorians

The art of Gilbert & George extends into the science-fiction-seeming present day, the zeal, radicalism and imagination of certain British non-conformist and rebel artists, writers and thinkers of the Victorian period.

These include: William Blake, for whom the mystical, religious and supernatural worlds were real and apparent, ecstatic, fearsome; their representation in his art and writing, challenging orthodoxy and convention.

The painter John Martin, snubbed by the Royal Academy of Art and many critics of his day, but whose spectacular, visionary depictions of Biblical catastrophe and apocalypse proved hugely popular with the general public.

Likewise, the commitment of the Pre-Raphaelite Brotherhood, in its earlier period, to creating a new, super-vivid hyper-realism: a mimetic rendition of nature that results in a dream-like, intensely atmospheric overlay of actuality and vibrancy. Their art and vision was also disdained by critics (throughout the ages) as first 'ugly', 'depraved' and ‘insulting’ to the genius of Raphael, and later as ‘sentimental’, ‘unsophisticated’, ‘kitsch’ and by insinuation ‘reactionary’ and ‘anti-modern’.

Blake, Martin and the Pre-Raphaelite Brotherhood pursued vision and principle over in-house formalist debates and artistic respectability. Similarly, the art criticism of John Ruskin – early champion of the Pre-Raphaelites – is melded with his social criticism and extravagant imagery to comprise a vision and principle in its own right.

This adherence to vision, principle, anti-formalist and pro-realist modern art is the basis of the art and ideology of Gilbert & George, which shares also the role of ‘outsider’ and fierce artistic and personal independence. Likewise, a commitment to pursuing the furthest reaches of imagination and visualisation.

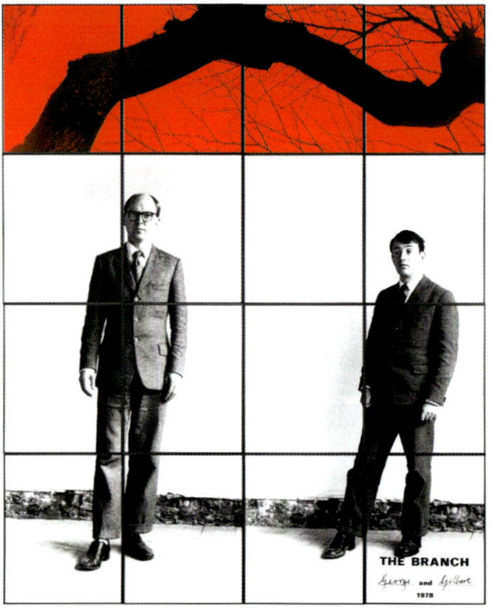

THE BRANCH. 1978. 241 x 201 cm

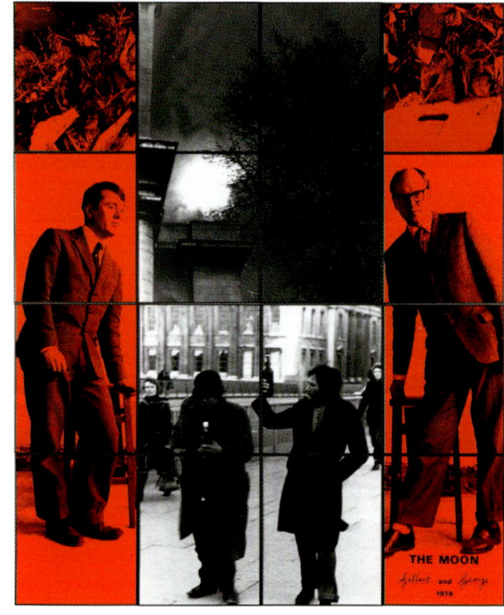

THE MOON. 1978. 241 x 201 cm

Twenty-One
Like Something out of Dickens

As the nineteenth century progressed towards its artistically febrile *fin-de-siècle*, the Victorians created forms, images and ideas of extraordinary extravagance and innovation, across all media. The aesthetic sensibility ripened into the visionary weirdness of British Symbolism – an art imbued, pictorially, with a curious luminosity that might be that of either dusk or dawn and suggests the interplay of terrestrial and supernatural atmospheres. It is a vision in close proximity to, but in its narratives distinct from, the irrational mindscapes and dream motifs of surrealism.

Gilbert & George communicate scenes and tableaux of atmospheric intensity, rendering actuality supernatural in mood and tension; whether the emptiness of rooms or the emptiness of modern days against concrete coloured skies; the dark streets, the rising moon, the high-rise vista; the fluorescent toxic cosmos; Gilbert & George as slab-faced sentinels, bomb-suited amidst dizzily divided and reflected digital-multi-faith weekday streets.

This confluence of the visionary, the disturbed and disoriented, and cold realism, creates a compression of time and feeling, taking a depiction of events into a place between the fantastical and the factual, in which fact and fantasy inform one another. Gilbert & George have described each of their pictures as a 'particular view' – a view into a subject, its mood, reality and mystery.

The writings of Charles Dickens contain many passages of such strangeness, the opening of *Bleak House* for example:

London. Michaelmas term lately over, and the Lord Chancellor sitting in Lincoln's Inn Hall. Implacable November weather. As much mud in the streets as if the waters had but newly retired from the face of the earth, and it would not be wonderful to meet a Megalosaurus, forty-feet long or so, waddling like an elephantine lizard up Holborn Hill. Smoke lowering down from chimney-pots, making a soft black drizzle, with flakes of soot in it as big as full-grown snowflakes – gone into mourning, one might imagine, for the death of the sun....

Such evocation of time and place and mood, in which experience and feeling access strangeness, which in turn opens new perceptions, shares with the art and vision of Gilbert & George the enchantment, drama and portent of phantasmagorical realism.

Blake, Ruskin, Martin, Pre-Raphaelitism, Dickens – add Samuel Palmer, artist, Christopher Dresser, artist-designer, and Augustus Welby Pugin, architect – established a pre-modernist British avant-garde, in which vision, art and principle combine and interrelate. The art of Gilbert & George, their vision and commitment to ideological principle are the postmodern continuation.

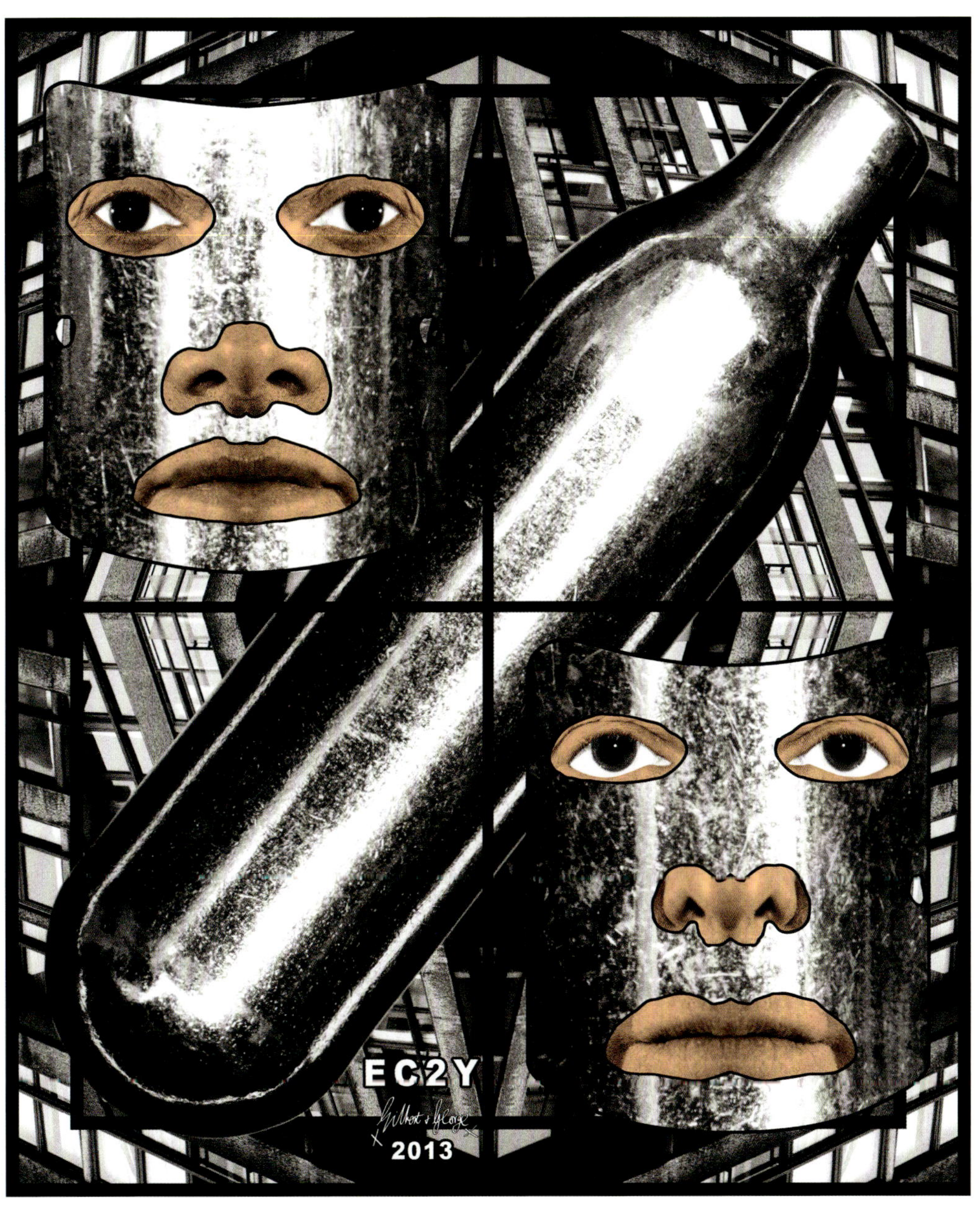

The curiously entitled picture EC2Y. 2013. 151 x 127 cm
A SCAPEGOATING PICTURE.

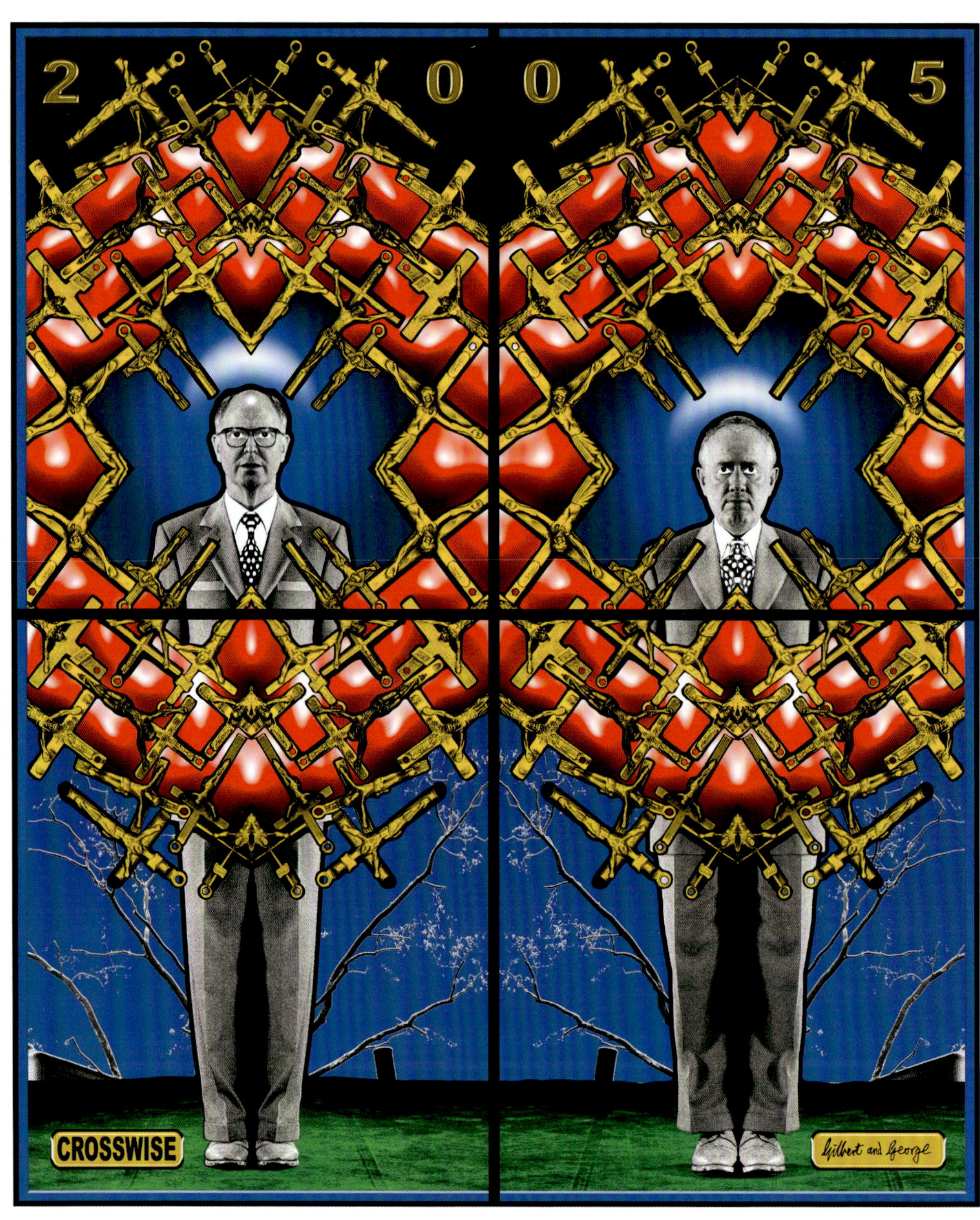

CROSSWISE. 2005. 150 x 126 cm
One of the SONOFAGOD PICTURES.

Twenty-Two
Provocation

Gilbert & George stick two fingers into each other's mouths; Gilbert & George flick 'V' signs at the viewer; Gilbert & George, naked, bend over and expose their anuses to the viewer; Gilbert & George hold banners proclaiming 'Burn That Book' and 'Fuck The Planet'; Gilbert & George, sombre, un-reacting or remote, look at scenes of dereliction and abjection, framed by graffiti of violent swear words; Gilbert & George compile a list of thousands of terms and expressions including the word 'Fuck'; Gilbert & George show crucifixes and effigies of Christ visually mutated; 'GOD LOVES FUCKING ENJOY'; the art of Gilbert & George can comprise grotesque, crude and absurd visual language that mocks formalism and curdles aesthetics; Gilbert & George show a directory of violence, trauma and tragedy in pictures made of newspaper headlines; Gilbert & George take their places full-frontally naked, at times comically posed, surrounded by magnified body-fluids, shit and extracts from the Bible.

Since becoming Gilbert & George, their art has been provocative and often fixated on abjection (noun: that which is cast off;

degradation, desolation; also, in post-structural theory: disrupter of convention.)

Armoured and armed by its fundamental dualism, Gilbert & George make art to challenge and oppose all other art and philosophies of art, including those art forms and schools of art that profess, overtly or in ironical silence, to be doing the same thing. Gilbert & George make art to vandalise all codes of artistic good conduct. The art of Gilbert & George makes the viewer think about art from first principles and primal responses: What does this make me feel and why?

The art of Gilbert & George can also be seen as the Jungian 'shadow' of modern art. This term refers to: the unconscious aspect of personality, often suppressed; all that is outside the light of consciousness; a link to primitive animal instincts, usually superseded by the development of the conscious mind; 'a reservoir for human darkness, and also – perhaps because of this – the seat of creativity…'; and '…the dark side of his being, his sinister shadow, represents the true spirit of life as against the arid scholar.' [Wikipedia entry for 'Shadow (Psychology)']

While other art could be seen to correspond in other ways to these definitions and proposals, the provocative art of Gilbert & George explores and expresses such subject-matter directly, specifically and aggressively – as though such exploration and such expression were one of its founding principles and its unflinching purpose.

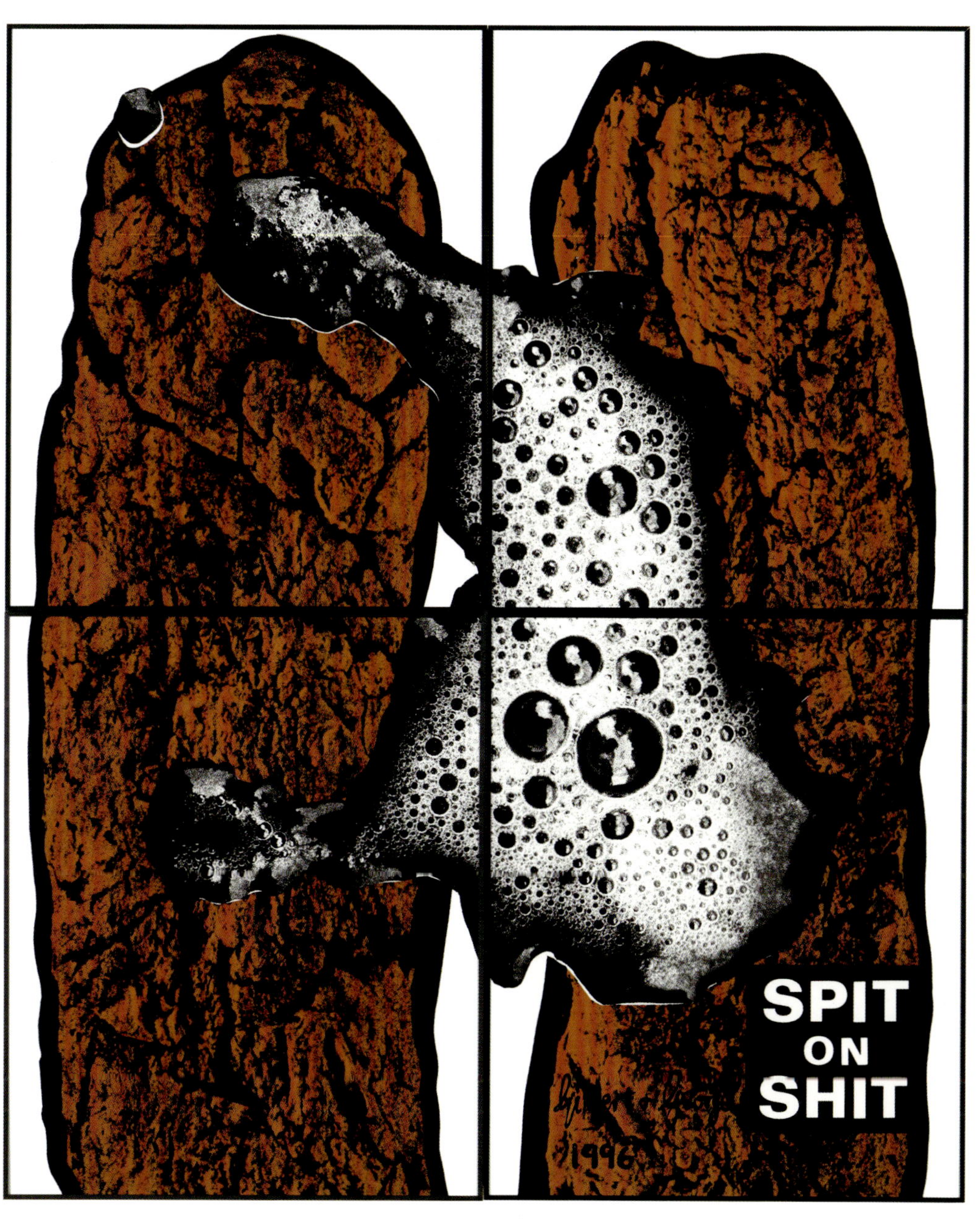

SPIT ON SHIT. 1996. 151 x 127 cm
One of the FUNDAMENTAL PICTURES.

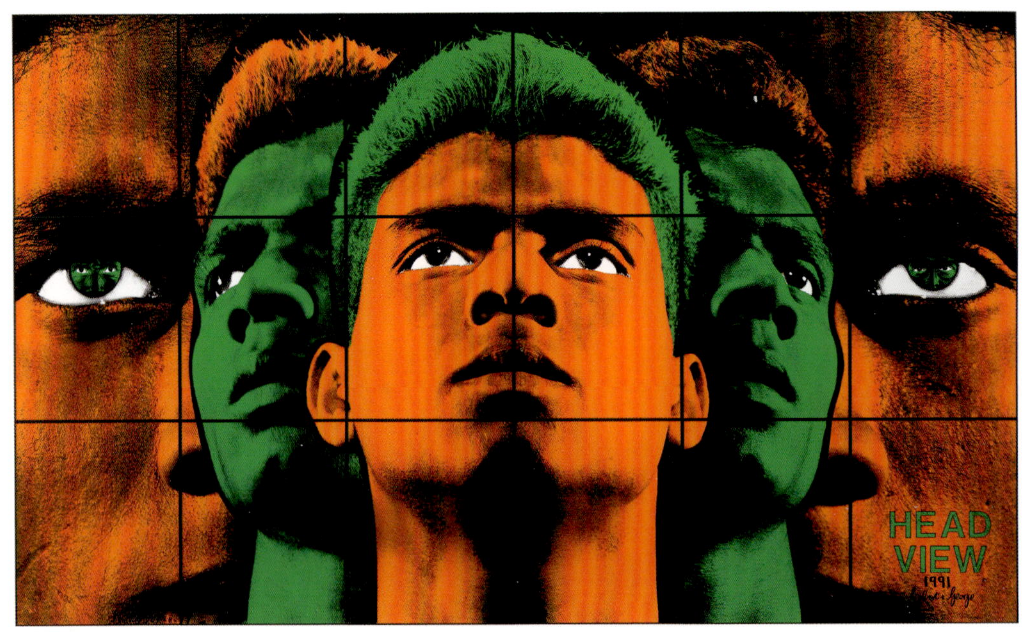

HEAD VIEW. 1991. 253 x 426 cm

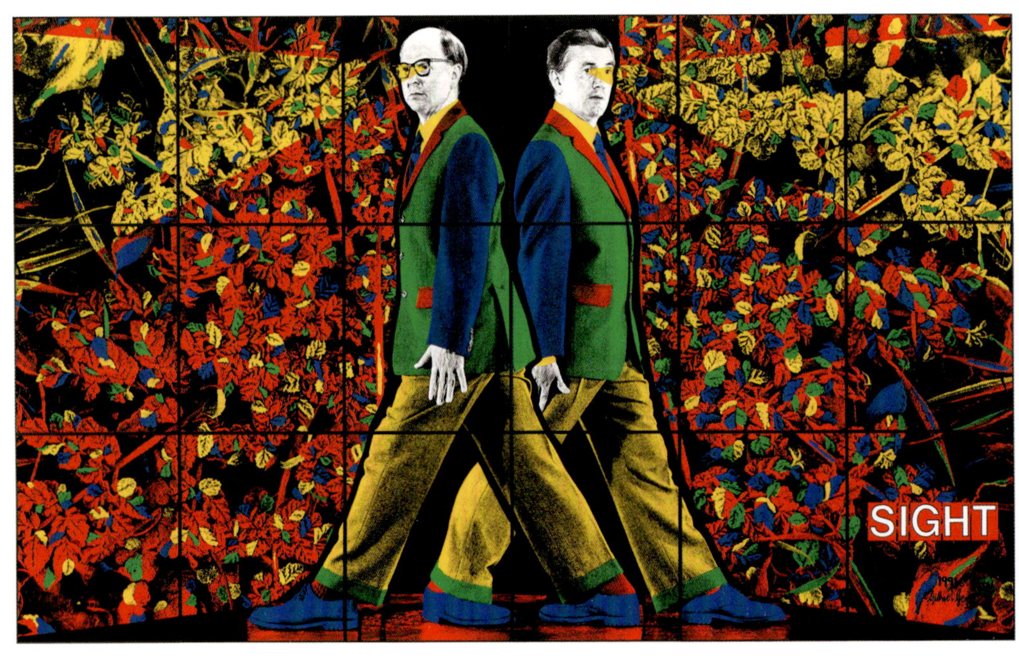

SIGHT. 1991. 253 x 426 cm

Twenty-Three
Celebration

A dark alley; a brisk pace. We hear the shoes of the walkers crunching on the pavement. Bells; ceremonial music. The world of Gilbert & George. Silence, light, relaxation. Sunrise and sunset. Verdant nature; strong young men; violent, vibrant colours. Togetherness; crazy calligraphy; glossy golden scarlet airbrushed plastic metal-looking curves and cowls and decorative panels. Stillness and the gentle indifference of the universe. Wonder and spectacle. The luxurious emotion of collapse. Epic visionary vistas, tower blocks and snow; symbol and procession; pictorial mood adventures close to home. The magic streets. Endless romance.

The art and vision of Gilbert & George contains as much celebration and energy as it does provocation and shadow.

The point in their art where shadow, provocation, energy and celebration meet is an other-worldly, ceremonial, possessed state, that is 'Gilbert & George'.

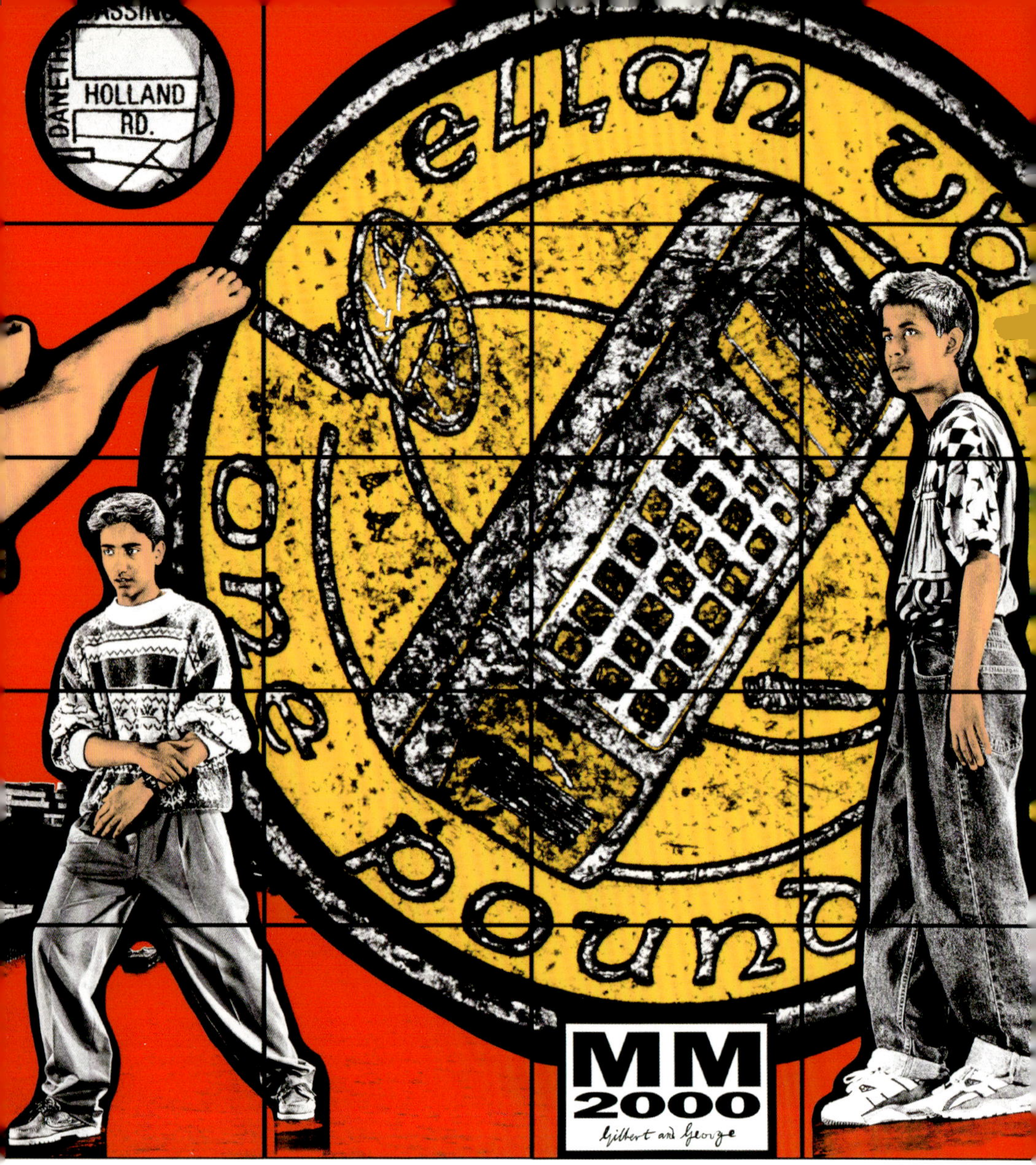

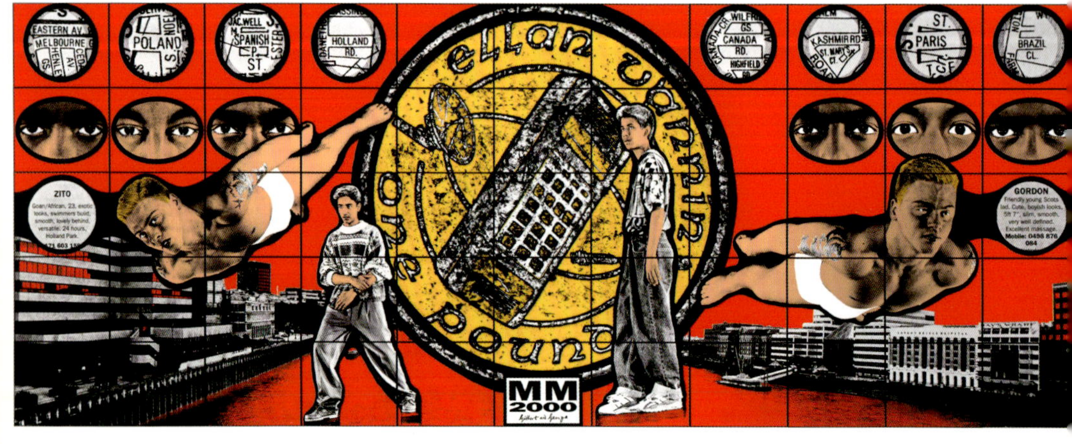
EASTERN AV
MELBOURNE
POLAND
SPANISH
ST.
HOLLAND
RD.
ellan vannin
one pound
CANADA
RD.
HIGHFIELD
KASHMIR RD
PARIS
BRAZIL
CL.
ZITO
GORDON
MM
2000
Gilbert and George

Twenty-Four
Premonition and Prediction in the Art of Gilbert & George

Seer, foresight, medium; those who have foresuffered all; those for whom the future is a memory.

Gilbert & George made a quadripartite picture in 1999 (titled NINETEEN NINETY NINE) and a triptych in 2000 (titled MM).

These monumental pictures summarise many of the subjects, atmospheres, atmospheres-as-subjects, beliefs, feelings and fundamental modern phenomena that have been expressed by the art and vision of Gilbert & George since the late 1960s.

The art of Gilbert & George – every picture, every sculpture, in any medium – always contains aspects, moods or presences that articulate and combine the past, the present and the future.

From the very beginning, therefore, Gilbert & George have imbued their art with atmospheric potency, subject matter and symbolism that are simultaneously archaic, contemporary, immediate and infused with a quality that feels drawn from the near or even distant future. A picture from 1985, such as WORLDS or MOONS, as much as a GINKGO PICTURE from 2005 or a RED MORNING picture from 1977, all exemplify this distinctive, constant and intoxicating quality.

← Central Panel of the Triptypch MM from 2000. 355 x 929 cm. Detail above.

Each picture may be viewed as a nexus of transmissions or psychic currents from the past, present and future, received by or conducted through the figures of Gilbert & George themselves.

In their CHARCOAL ON PAPER SCULPTURES, Gilbert & George seem to take their place in their art as time travellers, as much as a postmodern reprisal of Rousseau's 'reveries of the solitary walker'; and the drawings themselves – their material selves – might have been made in the future to be retrieved in the present, now looking 'weathered' by their journey through time.

It is this temporal aspect of the art of Gilbert & George that makes their vision so dense with premonition, as though predictive of psychic changes in the zeitgeist or the moral climate.

At the end of the twentieth century, in their triptych MM, Gilbert & George depict a multicultural city (London streets named after many countries), the eyes of strangers (of different nationalities), a mobile phone and communications satellite on a coin, classified advertisements for sex workers, prurient sexually abusive graffiti, bland riverside developments (seen from London Bridge) and a blonde 'superman' youth, as though soaring over the city in flight. There are also vivid yet indistinct knots of what seem like contorted physical contact: orifices, thumbs, tongues – but too closely observed to be comprehensible.

Such is the modern world at the end of the second millennium: sex, money, mobile phones, multiculturalism. Suited, serious, dignified, embodiments of middle-aged respectability, Gilbert & George take their place within this world to left and right, looking out to the viewer calm, stony-faced. They might be high ranking civil servants.

MM conveys a joyless, portentous vision – grubby, drear, forceful and sour-spirited. The light bland, the day, one imagines, dull and mild. Despite the airborne 'superman' youth (emissary of the new millennium?) the picture has less a feeling of historical event than of epochal *exhaustion*, which doubles as a faint but brooding overture of things to come.

The picture brings to mind first T. S. Eliot's oft-quoted pronouncement at the end of his poem, *The Hollow Men*, that the world will end 'Not with a bang but a whimper'. And more forcibly perhaps Eliot's later and more chilling comment (made in 1958) that he no longer believed either – bang or whimper – were right; for he had by then spoken to people who had been bombed out of their homes, and none of them could recall having heard anything.

MM, likewise, for all its violence and portent and sexual insinuation, feels above all heavy with silence – due in part to the authoritative yet reserved, severe yet anonymous officialdom of Gilbert & George themselves, coldly confronting the viewer. The modern world is seen as though suddenly stopped in its tracks, time suspended, all sound cosmically muted.

In 2001, the NINE DARK PICTURES delve suddenly deeper into this profound mood of closure, silence, farewell, abandonment, shutting-down, sleep and faith's end. Stark and visceral in their expression of finality and departure, coldly millennial in their intent, post-punk communication of a modern urban society approaching critical mass – violent protest the recent history of now deserted streets – these gold, red and monochrome chamber pieces feel monolithic, stilled, end of time, end of religion.

Their mood is summed up by a handwritten message left in the window of a local café (the famous Market Café) by the proprietors on their retirement:

We hate goodbyes so to save too many tears we have slipped out the back way to melt into the shadows. This is a very sad time for us. It has been great knowing you all and a pleasure serving you. Now the Market Café is no more. Farewell. Clyde. THE END.

The heartfelt message feels eternal. The NINE DARK PICTURES show locked doors, shuttered shop fronts, class war 'Fuck The Rich' stickers (old and scratched now, ideologically toothless, extinct, stuck to lamp posts), dead leaves, clouds, bland streets, local people. In CHAINED UP we see a secondary pair of head-and-shoulders portraits of Gilbert & George, in which their features are all but indiscernible in dark shadow, as though they are receding into the brilliant white light behind them. The mood of these two portraits seems to echo the message from Clyde at the Market Café – that Gilbert & George, too, are melting into the shadows, moving on....

Beyond the NINE DARK PICTURES, but already encoded in their still, sombre, tense, elegiac mood, lies a new epoch defined by technology and fundamentalism. And beyond the coldly diagrammatic impersonality of the NEW HORNY PICTURES, in 2001 (in which ranks of classified advertisements for escorts and sex workers, each listing their individual services and attributes, become bleakly synthetic, touchingly anonymous) Gilbert & George will re-appear first in 'ghost' form (in their TWENTY LONDON EAST ONE PICTURES), before transforming, like comic-book super-villains, into nightmare mutant versions of themselves: possessed, terrified, terrifying, spirit, guardian, sentinel, witness; avatars of an accelerating and increasingly dangerous world, biblical, medieval, random, terrorised, futuristic, now.

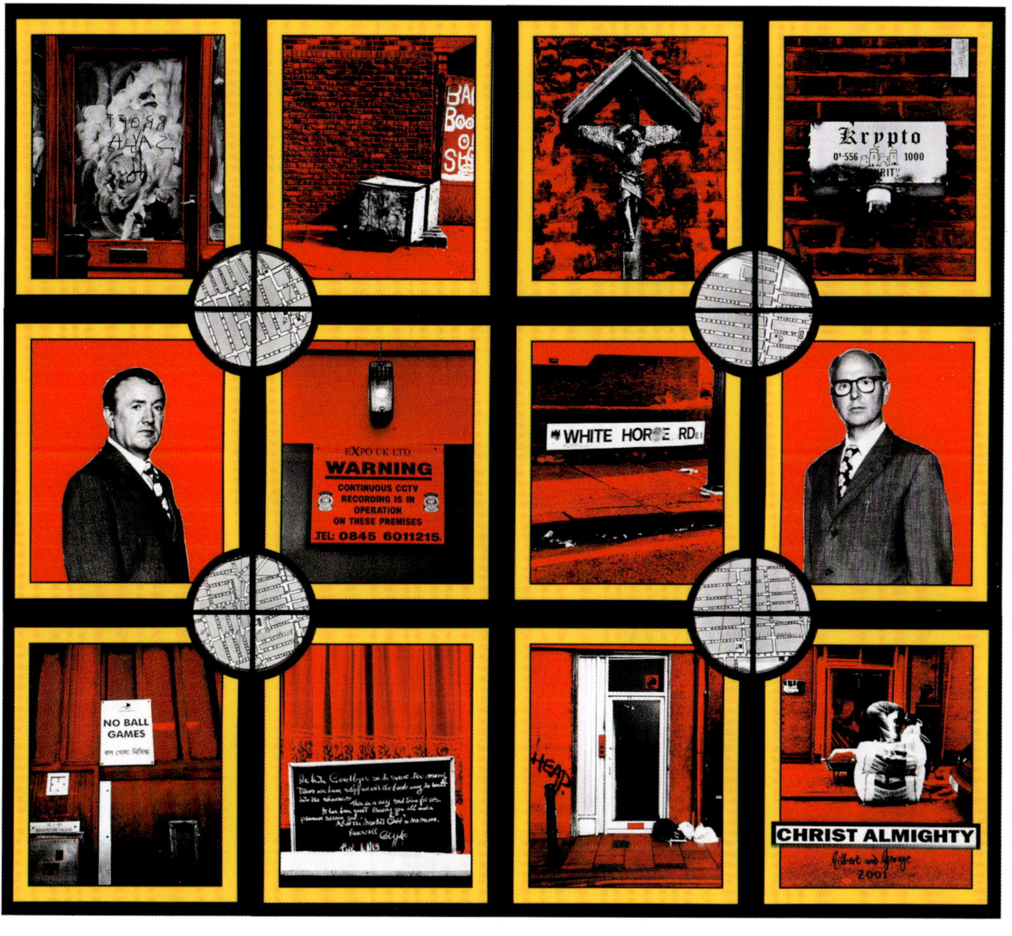

CHRIST ALMIGHTY. 2001. 226 x 254 cm
One of the NINE DARK PICTURES.

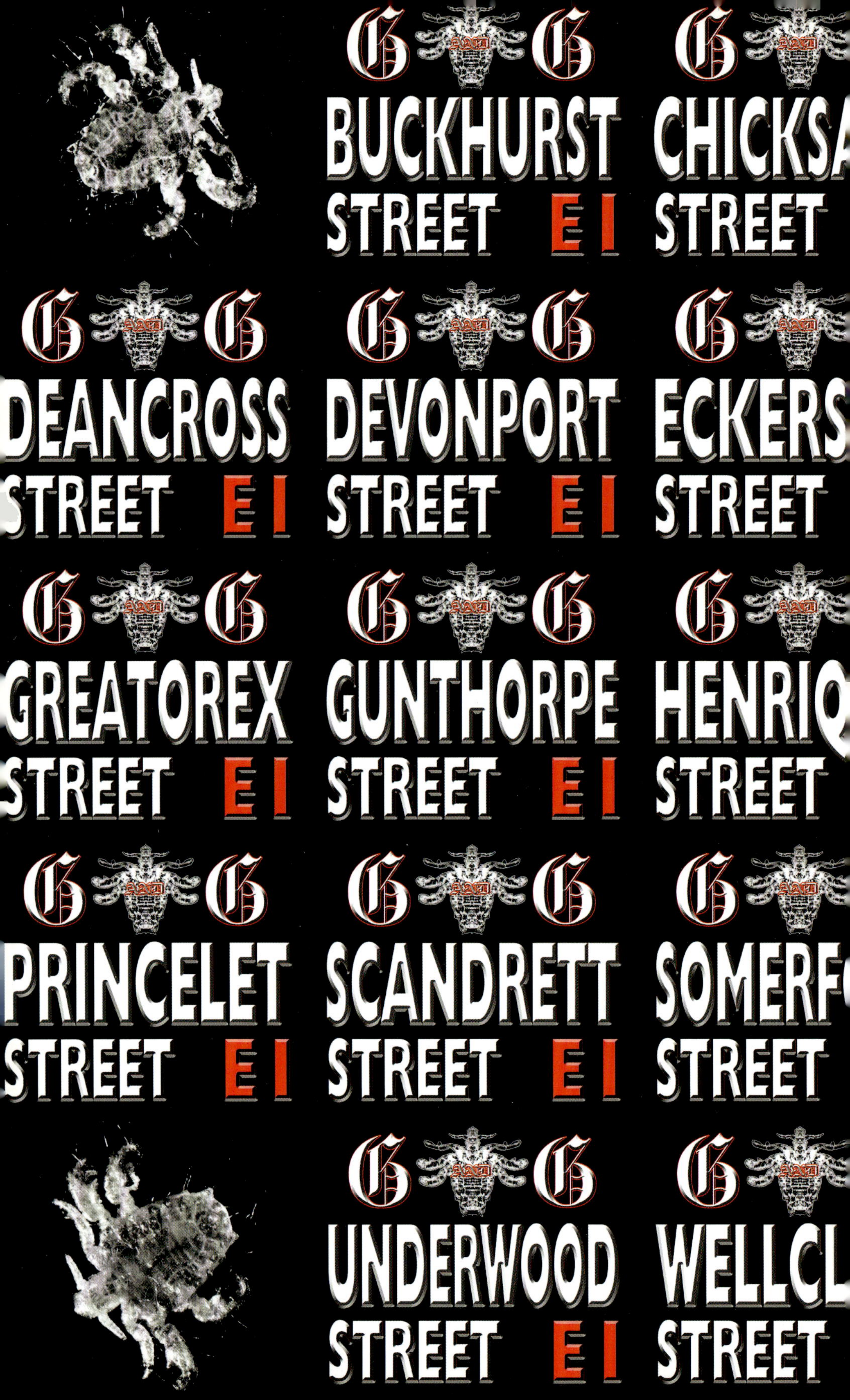
BUCKHURST STREET E1
DEANCROSS STREET E1
DEVONPORT STREET E1
GREATOREX STREET E1
GUNTHORPE STREET E1
PRINCELET STREET E1
SCANDRETT STREET E1
UNDERWOOD STREET E1

Twenty-Five
Ghosts

There is ghostly and spectral imagery in the art of Gilbert & George. Psychic phenomena are a part of their vision. The nature of these phenomena, as subjects and as images, is both allusive and literal in the art of Gilbert & George.

In the TWENTY LONDON EAST ONE PICTURES, for example, Gilbert & George shape-shift into vaporous, headless, transparent or diaphanous shroud-like outlines. Five of the location-based pictures are titled as HAUNTS. In the PERVERSIVE PICTURES the figures of Gilbert & George are vacant, zombie-like, contorted, poltergeist violent, blurred, remote, mutant. One picture is called HAUNTERS, another SPELL. These pictures are filled with the arcane and possibly meaningless coded calligraphy of 'tags' and 'tagging' – street name and gang signatures. Within the mood of the PERVERSIVE PICTURES this writing becomes sigil-like in mood and aura.

The moral vision of Gilbert & George – the imprint of time and event on objects, materials, atmospheres and places ('everything

← Detail from the picture TWENTY-EIGHT STREETS. 2003. 352.5 x 672 cm
Here the artists have used a pubic louse to form a coat of arms.

matters') – resembles a manifestation of the past as an anonymous memory, possessing its own sentience and character, a spirit or a ghost presence, communicated as feeling. The past haunts the present. The turn in the stairs, the mark on the wall, resonant emptiness, the light at this time of day, that vase.

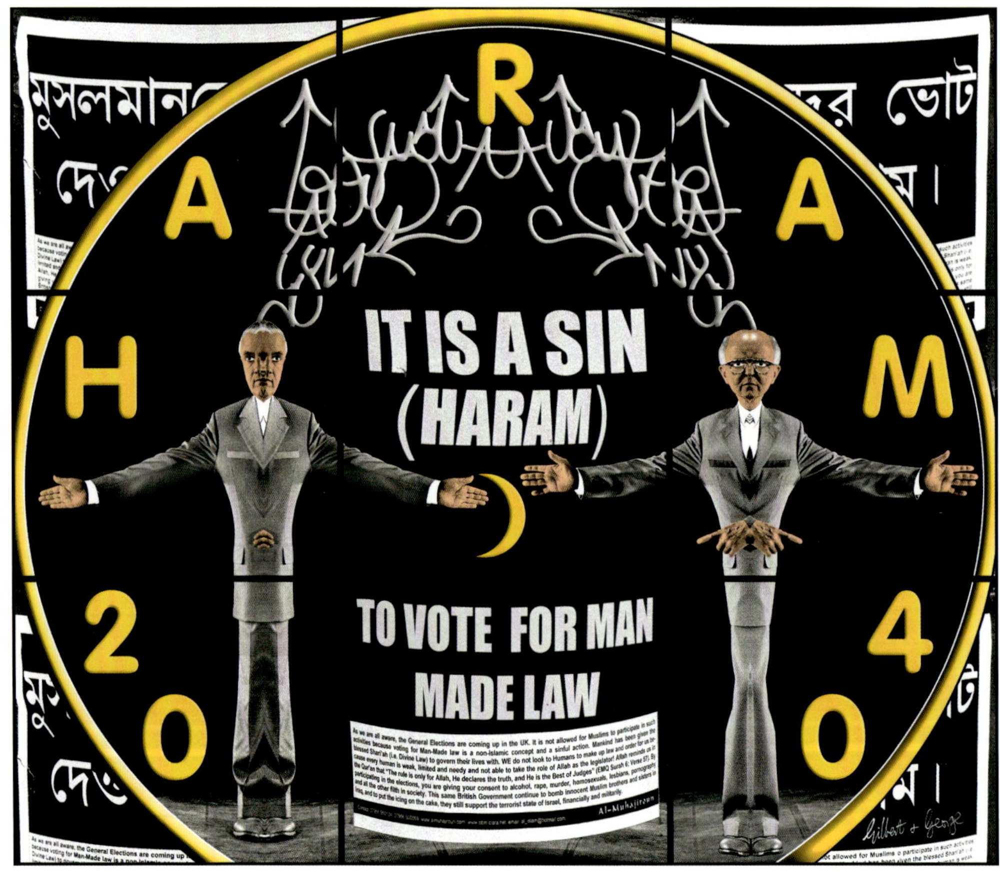

HARAM. 2004. 189 x 225 cm
A PERVERSIVE PICTURE.

Twenty-Six
Advance Through Friendship

Courtesy and friendliness are intrinsic to the vision of Gilbert & George. This has been demonstrated by the early correspondence and 'POST-CARD SCULPTURES' which Gilbert & George, having nothing, would first send as a means of sharing their art with viewers. The viewer feels that Gilbert & George are inviting them personally to experience their art. The art of Gilbert & George, however dramatic, confrontational, bizarre or spectacular, is always, also, intimate.

Amiability, politeness and formal courtesy create their own frame around the violent and visionary art of Gilbert & George, adding to its temper, whilst emphasising the aloneness of the artists themselves.

These qualities seem also to endorse the desire of Gilbert & George to create art which is open to everyone and regards each individual viewer – as if personally invited, as a friend – as rare, precious and extraordinary. It is an attitude that counters the notion, true or false, of the artist as a professional eccentric, exclusive, elitist or aloof, interested only in discussion about art and other artists.

Since the late 1960s, Gilbert & George have shared their lives – their spiritual progress – with the viewer through their art. From the earliest days they politely invited the viewer to accompany them – to share the experience of their vision – in walks through nature, in bars and pubs, in the bleak morning light, on dark streets, in vividly coloured visionary vistas, in the strange countries of their own body fluids. And then it seemed, as though through some form of death and reincarnation, thence to more of a ghost world, through several purgatories, of daily tragedy, of paranoia, of anarchy, of masks and barbed wire, the borders closing.

Gilbert & George politely invite their friends, the viewers, into this maelstrom.

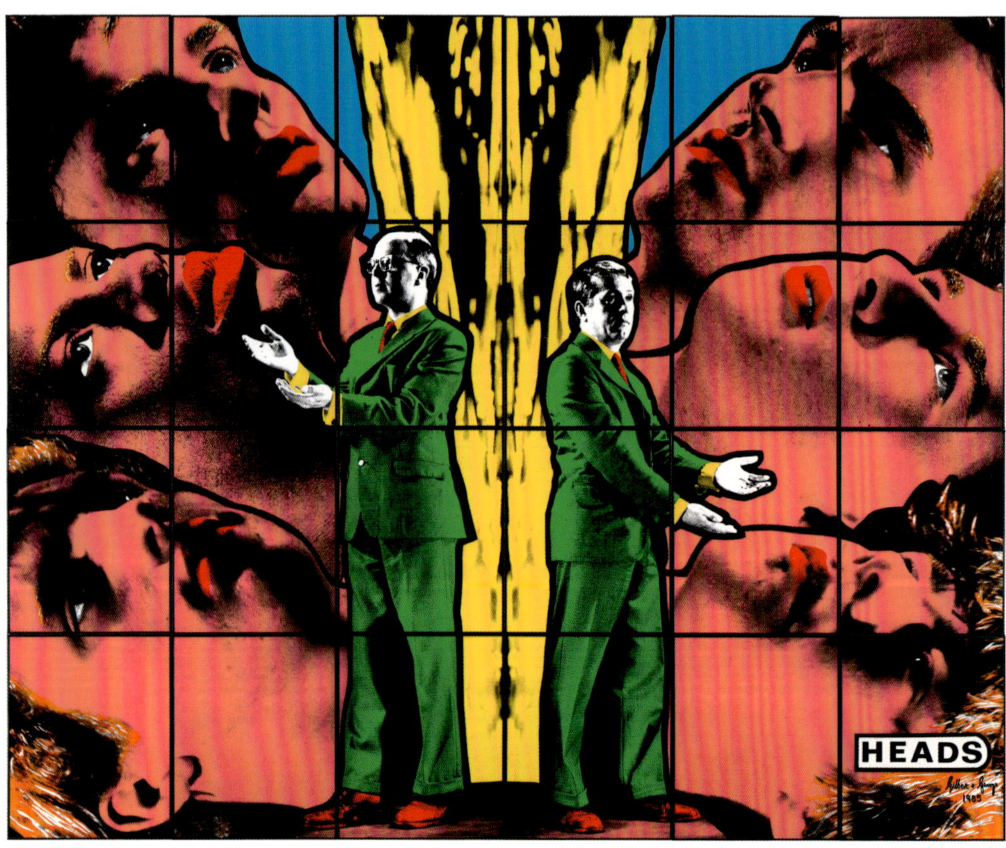

HEADS. 1985. 241 x 301 cm

Twenty-Seven
THE SCREAM OF REASON

THE SCREAM OF REASON is the title of a picture made by Gilbert & George in 1980. Vivid bright yellow, Gilbert & George in semi-silhouette profile, facing one another. A branch with fine, spiky fern-like leaves above their heads.

In their film sculpture, THE WORLD OF GILBERT & GEORGE, the artists are seen as though falling and spinning into a dark vortex that only they can see. They are shouting and moaning and screaming and crying out in fear and distress. George says: 'What a nightmare!'

Another scream of reason.

Everything that you need to know about Gilbert & George can be discovered and experienced by looking at their art. There are no 'right' or 'wrong' ways to look at the art of Gilbert & George; contextual information, while interesting, is not necessary. 'To see the object in itself as it really is' wrote Matthew Arnold, in 1863, on the function of the critic.

And so THE SCREAM OF REASON, for example, is 'about' the mood of such bright, declamatory yellow (the colour of self-harm, in some theories) and the two ordinary-looking modern men facing one another; the foliage above their heads both delicate and 'sharp', as though scalpel-blades or thorns. The epic yellow nothingness behind them.

Why is the picture so compelling and so mysterious?

The picture communicates a moment and a mood, unknowable but memorable. It depicts the consciousness of human relations. Two people facing one another. Its title adds further nuance to its atmosphere. The picture opens up a space, between the figures of Gilbert & George, which feels like a fundamental question.

You could imagine looking at this picture for hours, days. It communicates a vista for contemplation: stark, but not unwelcoming.

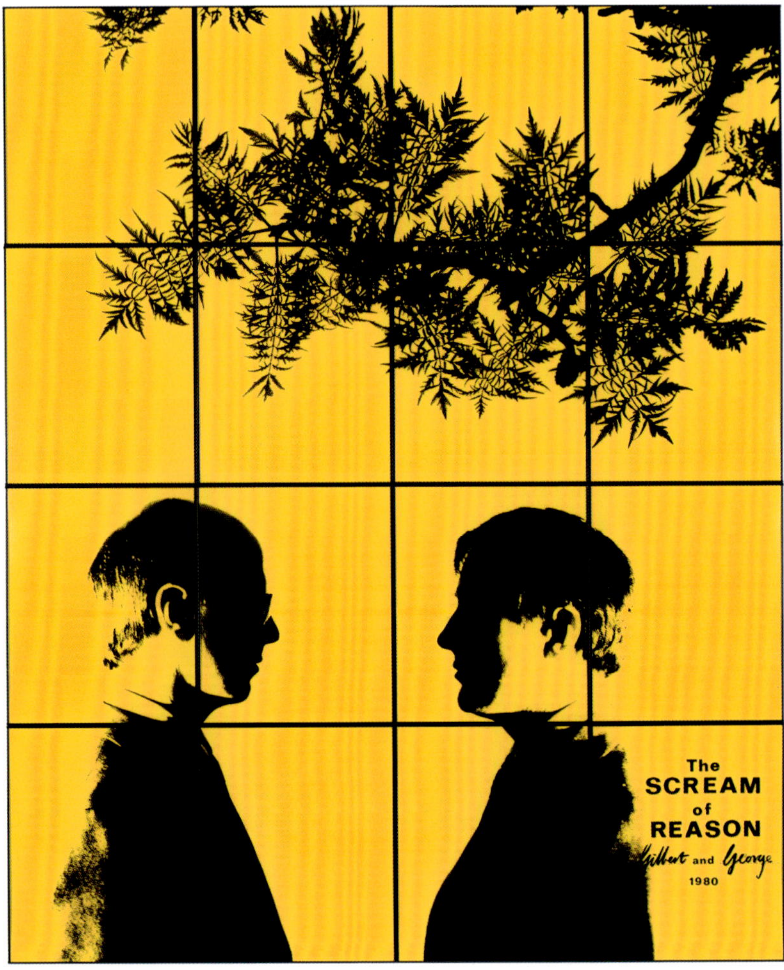

Twenty-Eight
Ancient and Postmodern: Religion in the Art of Gilbert & George

Here are Gilbert & George in prayer; here is Calvary; a youth on a cross; a church reflected and inverted in an autumn puddle on a dull day; a black church face, black cross, black Christ; POWER AND GLORY, SPIRIT OF THE CROSS; AUTUMN FAITH; a urinal in a church; DRUNK WITH GOD; and many crosses and churches, Bible texts and crucifixes; and a statement, 'BAN RELIGION'.

The art of Gilbert & George is filled with religious imagery. The vision of Gilbert & George is fixated on religion. From 1980 onwards, Gilbert & George made many pictures which contained religious imagery or religious subjects.

The temper of the ways in which this religious imagery appears in the art of Gilbert & George is varied in mood yet singular in its critique. Images of Christ or crosses appear stark, mockingly cartoon-like, grotesque or proposed as meaninglessness. In their NEW TESTAMENTAL pictures, Gilbert & George, older, naked, slump, collapse or support one another against backgrounds of magnified body-fluids, and Bible texts that excoriate sodomy or same-sex relationships.

Religious insignia and emblems of superstition are converted in the

← THE SCREAM OF REASON. 1980. 241 x 201 cm

art of Gilbert & George into flamboyant caricature, mutant-gothic, over-ripened ornamentation, becoming leering trinkets or visually choreographed, extravagant patterns. Crosses multiplied into a mockery of their religious symbolism. Imagery of Christ on a crucifix is mirrored and divided and mutated into monstrous form. Gilbert & George naked at the foot of a cross made out of shit.

Here are youths and marching youths and bored teenagers. The secular modern world: the city spread out like an ocean, alive, sleepless. And here are Muslim women wearing burkas, talking into mobile phones, on the wet East London busy workday streets. The medieval and future worlds combine in the present moment. The image of these Muslim women, their exotic-looking, matt-black masking, cultural-religious garb and their personal technology feels like the most contemporary image of modern life on Earth.

Religion threaded through the modern city. Ancient and postmodern, of many moods. Separatism, radicalisation, fundamentalism, ordinary communities, individual believers. Here are frontiers between streets. The imprint of religious law and religious teaching on a world of digital technology, social media, new drugs, brute secular urgency, night buses and cycle couriers.

The art of Gilbert & George opposes religion, determinedly.

The vision of Gilbert & George sees prejudice, torture, conflict, persecution, indoctrination, terrorism, murder, social and sexual control carried out and enforced in the name of religion. In the art of Gilbert & George, religion is depicted as joyless, bleak, decrepit, decadent, dangerous.

THE SCAPEGOATING PICTURES – AIRS, for example, or

WHITECHAPEL – communicate the alien, futuristic, science-fiction, quotidian, ordinary, unstoppable, self-absorbed, multi-technological, multi-faith city. The city is both wired and tensed by technology and religion.

The art of Gilbert & George does not oppose or blaspheme against the concept or reality of God but neither is it accepting of God. The art of Gilbert & George invites the viewer to question their feelings about religion or religious beliefs.

In THE WORLD OF GILBERT & GEORGE, a series of images illustrate the phrases of the Lord's Prayer: Gilbert & George in prayer, 'Christ' scrawled on a lamp post, two soldiers marking time, the rooftops of East London, an unknown youth, a plate of food, and so forth. It is a powerful sequence of images that correlates the modern city to the words of the most important Christian prayer.

The secular modern city and religion are two of the principle subjects of the art of Gilbert & George, and are often combined in the particular view of life communicated in an individual picture or group of pictures. In some of these pictures, it feels as though it is the secular that is enshrined, worshipped, empowered with ceremony and sacred meaning, while religion is shown as terrestrial, debased, empty, bullying and cold.

The art of Gilbert & George therefore rejects religion as historical, man-made and murderous, a means of social control, oppression and bigotry. The excommunication, execution and torture, in the name of religion, of those not obedient to despotic theocracies. The theft of God as a meaningful concept to enforce terrestrial power and political war.

The blasphemous, anti-religious texts and images in the art of Gilbert & George can encourage the viewer to contemplate the nature of modern goodness, modern religion, the secular world, the nature of evil and the nature of God, to make their own decisions, to re-think their idea of faith, to search in their own hearts for instinctual or intellectually reasoned truth.

The endless streets and strangers, the seeming randomness of events, the history of suffering in one city, the responsibility or not of one stranger to another, the dismantling of prejudice and bigotry, the nature of love, the challenge of self-dislike, the challenge of being disliked, the challenge of being alone, the challenge of belief and self-acceptance, the reality of reality are all subjects that can be seen in the art of Gilbert & George.

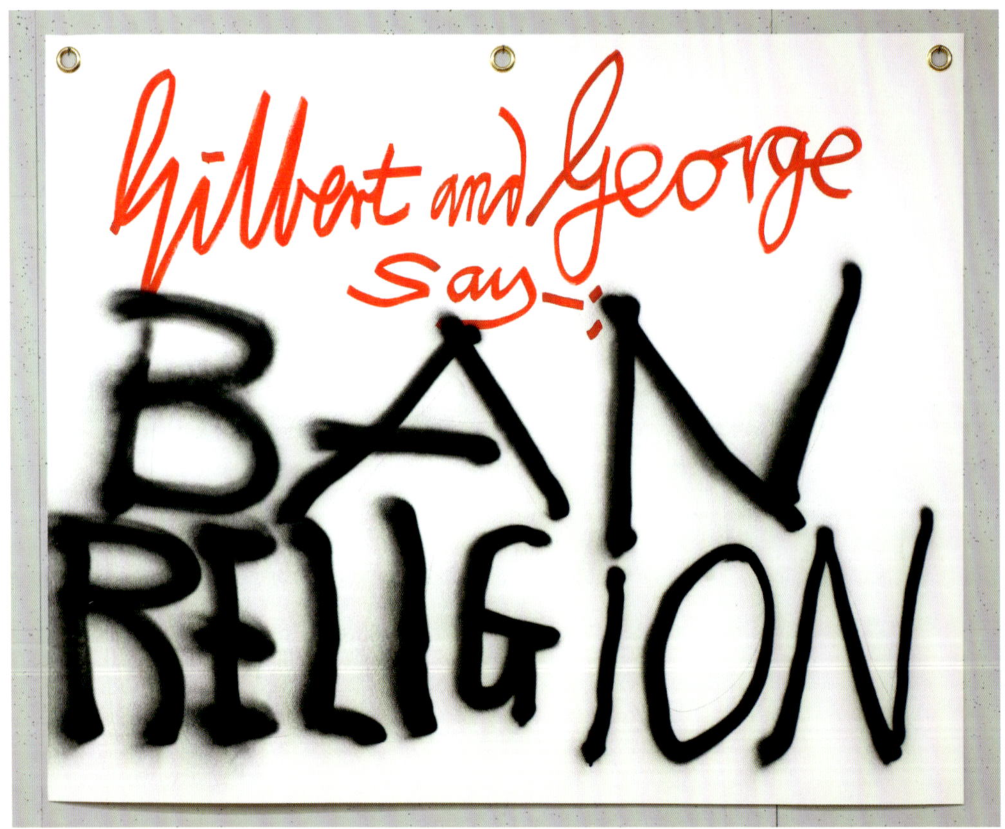

BAN RELIGION. 2015. One of the Banners which also declared 'FUCK THE PLANET, BURN THAT BOOK, DECRIMINALISE SEX, FUCK THE TEACHERS, GOD SAVE THE QUEEN, FELLATIO FOR ALL, fuck HIM, MAKE CUNNILINGUS COMPULSORY and fuck Him'.

Twenty-Nine
MARK OWEN SUCKS LEE'S COCK:
Maleness in the Art of Gilbert & George

Male youths, male sex, male bodies, Gilbert & George. The art and vision of Gilbert & George speculate on a masculine world.

This world is not homosexual, although homosexuality exists within it and is depicted in some of the art of Gilbert & George.

To the viewer who looks, the art of Gilbert & George shows love, anger, sex, mystery, fear, romance, nature, religion, beauty, confusion, struggle and wonder.

Sex is all sex; the nude is all nudes; youth is all youth. These realities stand in the art of Gilbert & George to be their messy awkward selves, rather than exemplars of artistic form.

The art of Gilbert & George communicates the truths of their vision. Because Gilbert & George are communicating their truth, their art and vision are alive before the viewer. The vision of Gilbert & George is a male vision, but the feelings communicated by their art are common and universal and can be experienced by men or women, homosexuals or heterosexuals.

The art of Gilbert & George is not defined by maleness or same-sex relationships. Maleness and sexual choice are secondary to the communication of universal feelings, as experienced as true by Gilbert & George.

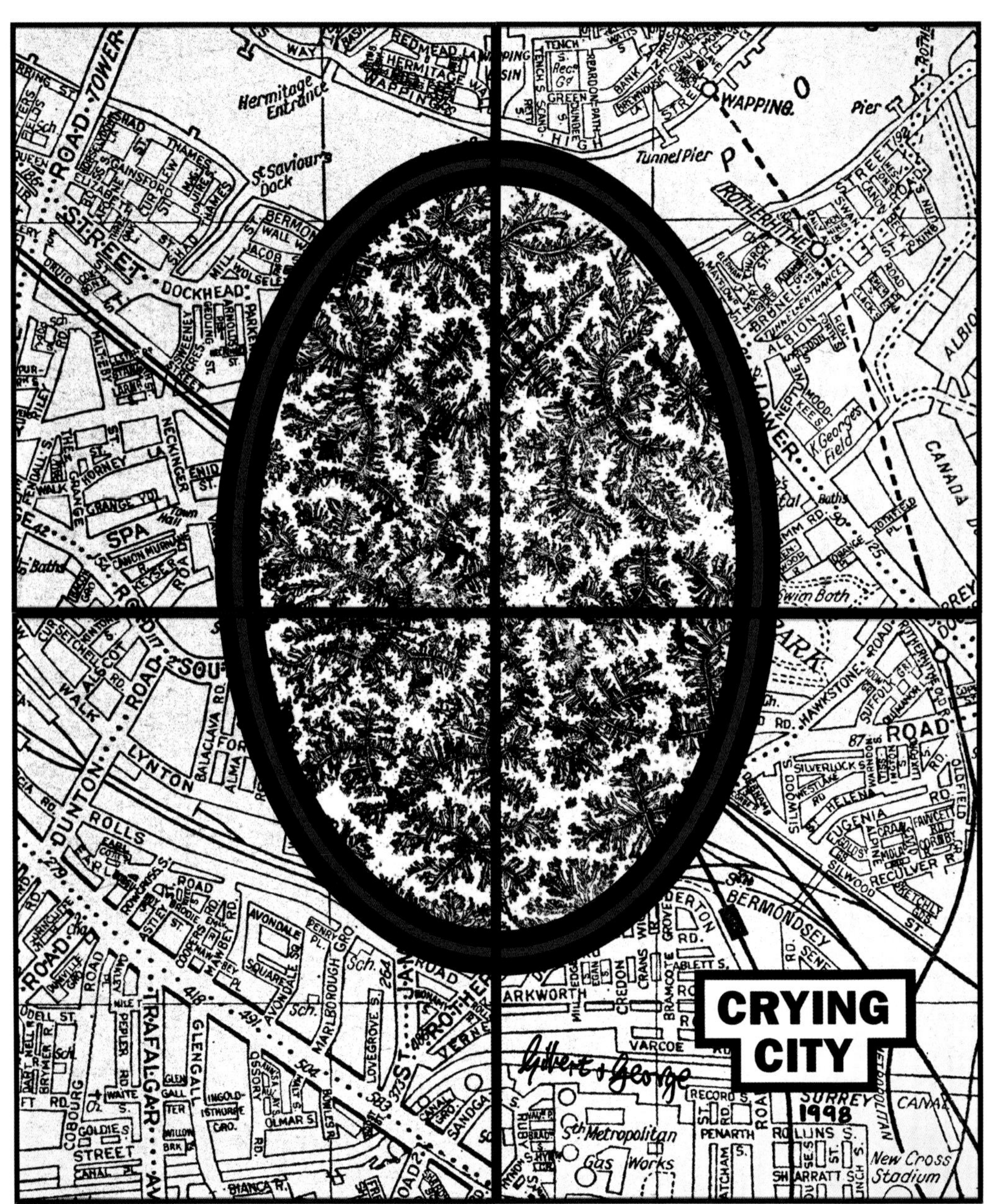

CRYING CITY. 1998. 151 x 127 cm

Thirty

Aesthetic Anaesthetic: Gilbert & George and the Disruption of Complacencies

Designers solve problems; artists create problems.

The art of Gilbert & George disrupts perceptual and ideological complacencies. Does this picture bore you? Why does it bore you? What do you mean by 'poetic'? Or 'empty'? Or 'visionary'?

Gilbert & George conceive it as their task to create difficulties everywhere. Their art is not created to make the viewer's experience easier, but harder.

This is achieved in their art by focus and concision.

Each picture or sculpture by Gilbert & George is made of a very small number of image-subject elements, presented to create the most immediate visual and emotional impact: street maps, magnified body fluids, Gilbert & George; or, Union Jack design, bare trees, brickwork, street maps, Gilbert & George; or, newspaper headlines, net curtains, reflections of Gilbert & George; nitrous oxide canisters, streets, Gilbert & George.

The titles of their pictures and sculptures are directly descriptive, referring to a detail or design element, but always poetic, forceful, sharp, evocative. The RUDIMENTARY PICTURES, for example: BLOOD

ATTACK, CRYING CITY, NAKED CEMETARY, PISS GARDEN. While the titles of THE LONDON PICTURES read like an index of modern tragedy – the stark power of single words that bring a world to life.

Other titles make astute yet associative connections, strange yet precise. A picture of a leafless branch: INTELLECTUAL DEPRESSION. A picture of two jauntily dressed junior mannequins against a background of empty nitrous oxide canisters, with reflections of Gilbert & George to left and right: DALSTON.

It can sometimes feel as though Gilbert & George have to 'prevent' themselves, in order to retain the truth of their vision, from being as poetically, conceptually and aesthetically entrancing and artistically 'correct' as they could so easily be.

Gilbert & George can create seductive beauty, slick minimalism, postmodern Pop, intense romanticism and stark conceptual aphorism. They understand precisely every nuance of different 'artistic' forms. But these seductions of art – that would relax and please the viewer; and slip without effort into the establishment canon of contemporary art – are the bitterest enemy of the disruption, provocation and singularity that is the art and vision of Gilbert & George.

Gilbert & George understand the relation of their art to aesthetic beauty; and Gilbert & George distance their art from the anaesthetic properties of aesthetic beauty.

Whenever Gilbert & George can create art that soothes – with filmic atmosphere, modern cool, semantic and aesthetic poise – they do the opposite: immediately creating new art which will disrupt and unsettle; appear ugly, grotesque or brutal; cheap and of the street, like trashy kitsch; or an East End pimped hooligan car, flashy, annoying, loud and in-your-face.

The art of Gilbert & George is unwaveringly oppositional. It only reveals its aesthetic beauty and incisive poetry in details, or retrospectively. The moods and simultaneous presences of past, present and future in the art of Gilbert & George are always alive and in flux. As time passes, the viewer sees different layers and dimensions, depths and directions in their art, from different periods. This is because the viewer is bringing their age and accumulated emotional experience to the age and accumulated emotional experience of the picture.

The art of Gilbert & George is a mirror.

The profound and fundamental modernity of every piece of art that Gilbert & George have created since they became Gilbert & George has remained and intensified. Look at pictures they made thirty years ago, ten years ago.

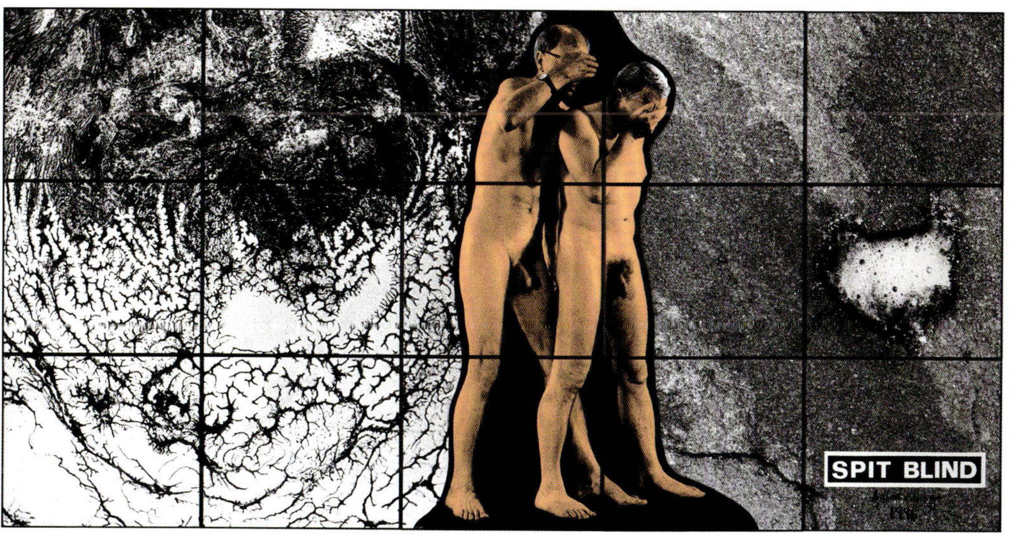

SPIT BLIND. 1996. 190 x 377 cm

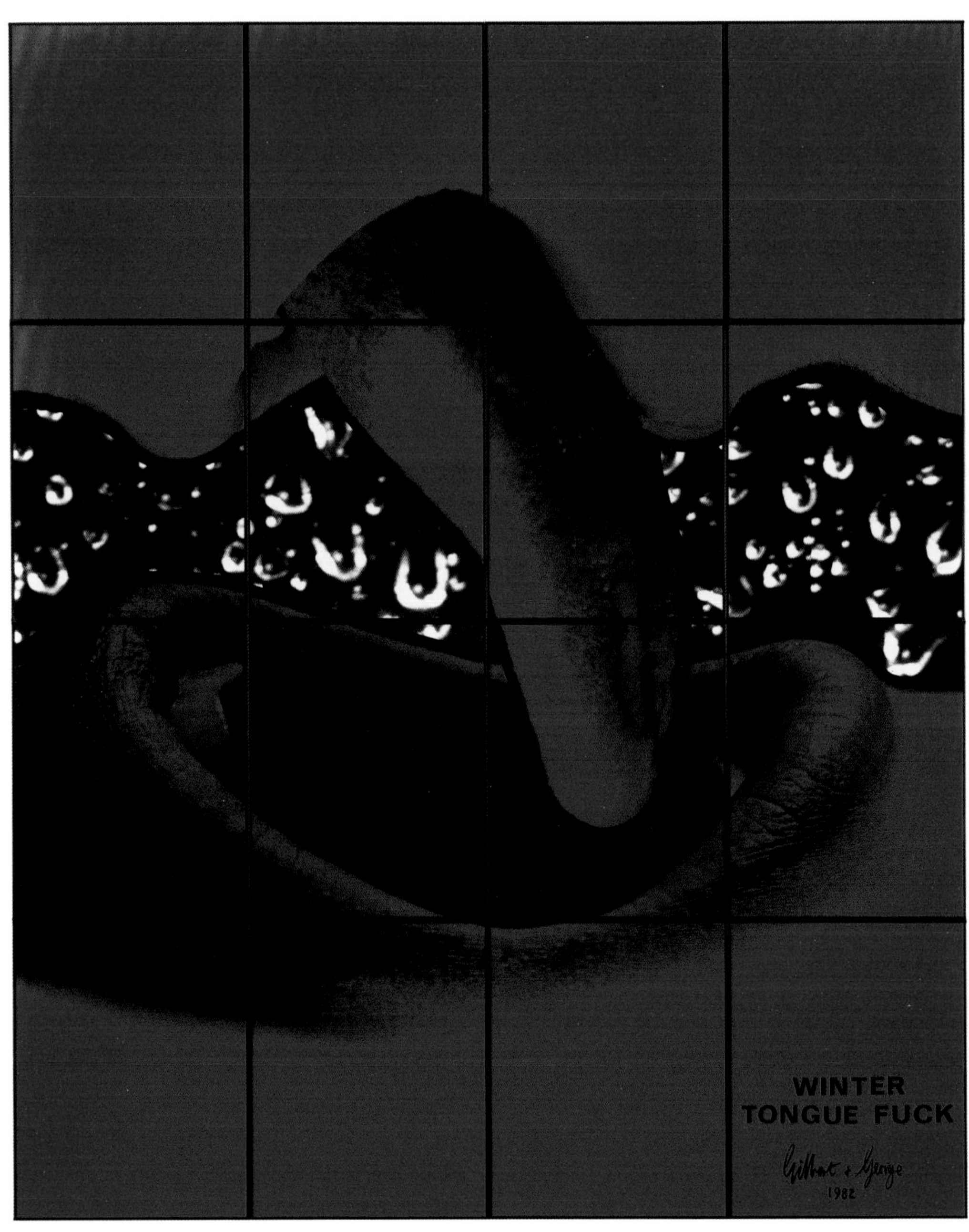

WINTER TONGUE FUCK. 1982. 241 x 201 cm

Thirty-One

Gilbert & George See Art in the Crowd

In their early years together, Gilbert & George, having nothing, wrote announcements and invitations, limericks, BOOK SCULPTURES, of thoughts and feelings, rules, laws and visions.

One such text-drawing-sculpture, made in 1970, is titled TO BE WITH ART IS ALL WE ASK….

Gilbert & George recount how when they were out walking, they thought they caught a glimpse of Art – that (or whom) they were seeking wholeheartedly, obsessively, passionately, like acolytes, their guru – in the form of a sandy-haired man ahead of them on the busy pavement.

They lost him in the crowd.

The writing and imagery of this text share with the recollection of a vivid dream the quality of being both fragmentary, elusive and extraordinarily precise. To lose something cherished in a dream can be a keen experience of pure love.

Gilbert & George write:

We do realise that you are what we really crave for and many times we meet you in our dreams. We have glimpsed you through the abstract world and have tasted of your reality. One day we thought we saw you in a crowded street, you were dressed in a light brown suit, white shirt and a curious blue tie. You looked very smart but there was about your dress a curious wornness and dryness. You were walking alone, light of step and in a very controlled sense. We were fascinated by the lightness of your face, your almost colourless eyes and your dusty-blonde hair. We approached you nervously and then just as we neared you you went out of sight for a second and then we could not find you again. We felt sad and unlucky and at the same time happy and hopeful to have seen your reality.

Art personified as a neatly dressed stranger in the street, always a few steps ahead.

The vision and art of Gilbert & George are literal and visionary; committed to both vernacular realism and living archetypes; to an experience of the visible and invisible natures of modern humanity; and to art as a communication of these things.

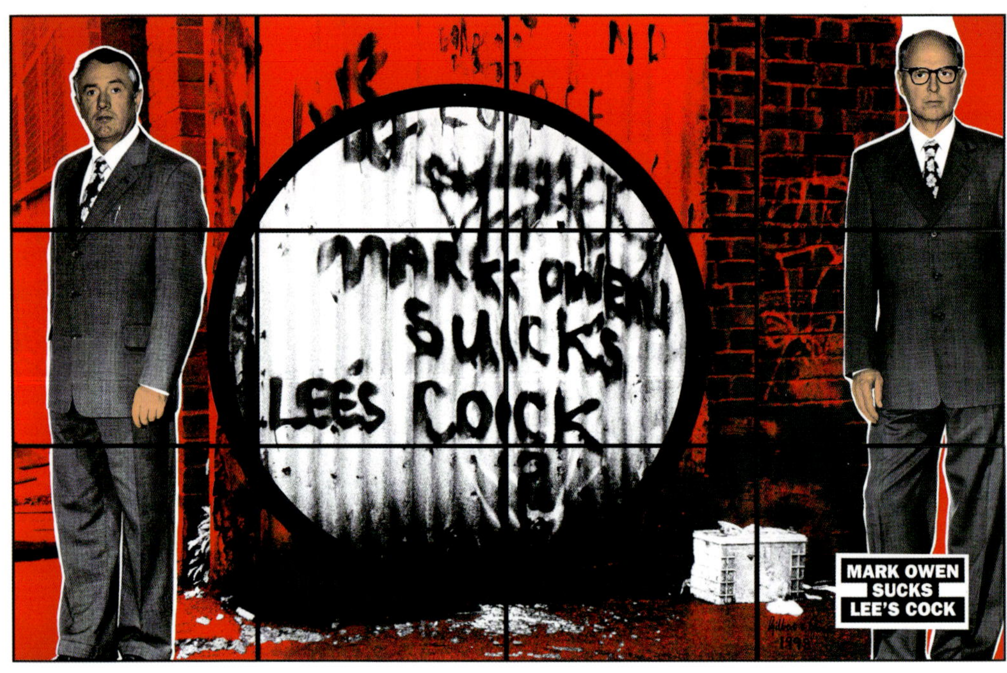

MARK OWEN SUCKS LEE'S COCK. 1998. 190 x 302 cm

To be with Art is all we ask…

Gilbert & George the sculptors Autumn 1970

OH ART, what are you! You are so strong and powerful, so beautiful and moving. You make us walk around and around, pacing the city at all hours, in and out of our Art for All room. We really do love you and we really do hate you. Why do you have so many faces and voices? You make us thirst for you and then to run from you escaping completely into an normal life: getting up, having breakfast, going to the work-shop and being sure of putting our mind and energy into the making of a door or maybe a simple table and chair. The whole life would surely be so easeful, so drunk with the normality of work and the simple pleasures of loving and hanging around for our lifetime. Oh Art where did you come from, who mothered such a strange being? For what kind of people are you: are you for the feeble-of-mind, are you for the poor-at-heart, or are you for those with no soul? Are you a branch of nature's fantastic network or are you an invention of some ambitious man? Do you come from a long line of arts? For every artist is born in the usual way and we have never seen a young artist. Is to be an artist to be reborn, or is it a condition of life? Coming slowly over a person like the daybreak. It brings the art-ability to do this funny thing and shows you new possibilities for feeling and scratching at oneself and surroundings, setting standards, making you go into every scene and every contact, every touching nerve and all your senses. And Art we are driven by you at incredible speed, ignorant of the danger you are pushing and dragging us into. And yet Art, there is no going back, all roads only go on and on. We are happy for the good times that you give us and we work and wait only for these titbits from your table. If you only knew how much it means to us, transporting from the depths of tragedy and black despair to a beautiful life of happiness, taking us where the good time are. When this happens we are able to walk again with our heads held high. We artists need only to see a little light through the trees of the forest, to be happy and working and back into gear again. And yet, we don't forget you. Art, we continue to dedicate our artists' art to you alone, for your pleasure, for Art's sake. We would honestly like to say to you, Art, how happy we are to be your sculptors. We think about you all the time and feel very sentimental about you. We do realise that you are what we really crave for, and many times we meet you in our dreams. We have glimpsed you through the abstract world and have tasted of your reality. One day we thought we saw you in a crowded street, you were dressed in a light brown suit, white shirt and a curious blue tie, you looked very smart but there was about your dress a curious wornness and dryness. You were walking alone, light of step and in a very controlled sense. We were fascinated by the lightness of your face, your almost colourless eyes and your dusty-blonde hair. We approached you nervously and then just as we neared you went out of sight for a second and then we could not find you again. We felt sad and unlucky and at the same time happy and hopeful to have seen your reality. We now feel very familiar with you, Art. We have learned from many of the ways of life. In our work of drawings, sculptures, living-pieces, photo-messages, written and spoken pieces we are always to be seen, frozen into a gazing for you. You will never find us working physically or with our nerves and yet we shall not cease to pose for you, Art. Many times we would like to know what you would like of us, your messages to us are not always easily understood. We realise that it cannot be too simple because of your great complexity and all-meaning. If at times we do not measure up or fulfill your wishes you must believe that it is not because we are unserious but only because we are artists. We ask always for you help, Art, for we need much strength in this modern time, to be artists only of a life-time. We know that you are above the people of our artist-world but we feel that we should tell you of the ordinariness and struggling that abounds and we ask you if this must be. Is it right that artists should only be able to work for you for only the days when they are new, fresh and crisp? Why can't you let them pay homage to you for all their days, growing strong in your company and coming to know you better? Oh Art, please let us all relax with you. Recently Art, we thought to set ourselves the task of painting a large set of narrative views descriptive of our looking for you. We like very much to look forward to doing it and we are sure they are really right for you.

TO BE WITH ART IS ALL WE ASK.

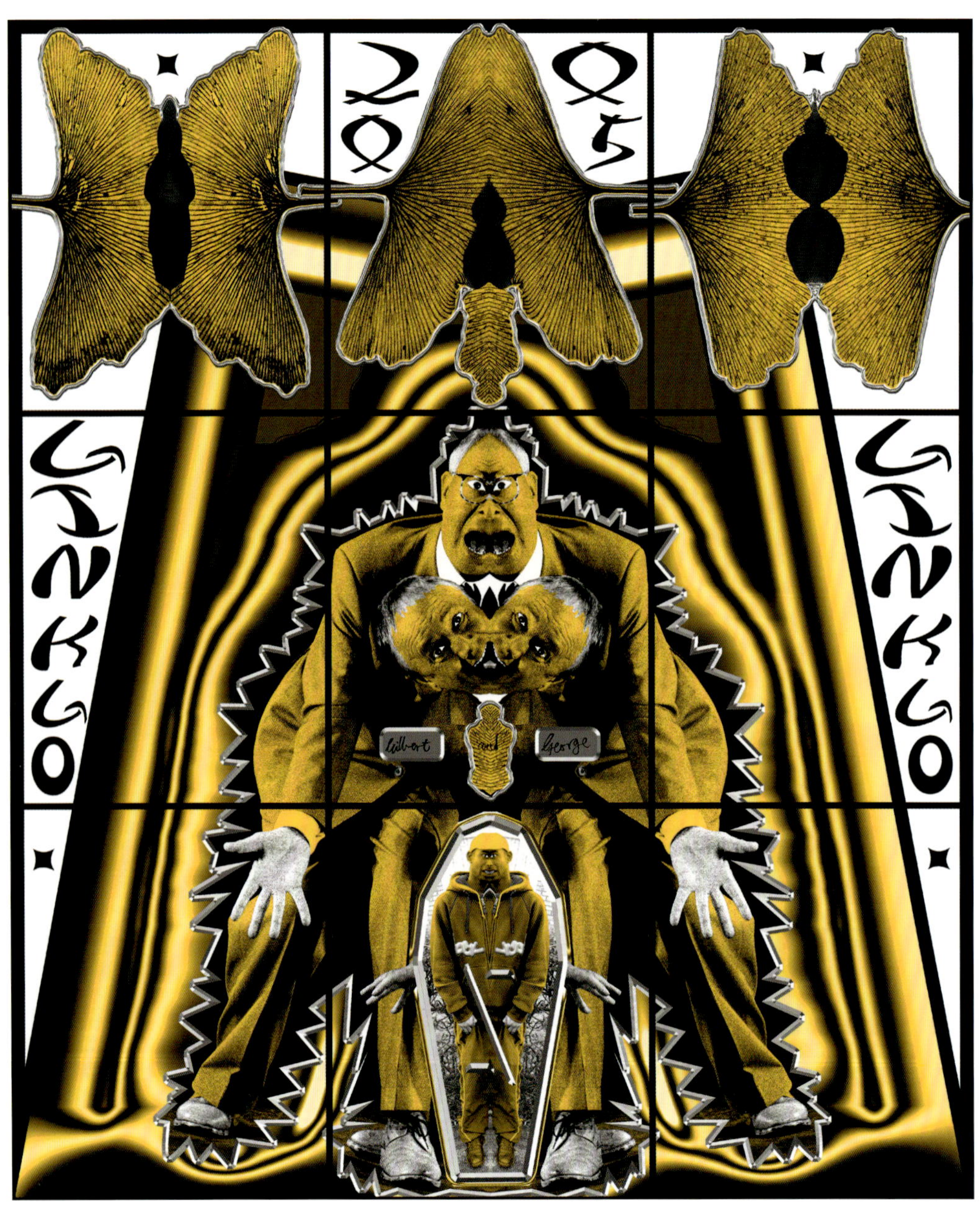

GINKGO GINKGO. 2005. 253 x 213 cm

Thirty-Two
Totally Automatic: The Lexicon and Writings of Gilbert & George

Words, texts and language play a very important role in the art of Gilbert & George.

Factual, descriptive, stream-of-consciousness, dirty words, formal, swearing and, in the final analysis, automatic.

Gilbert & George use angular, outlandish, funny, peculiar, distinctive words as titles for their pictures: GAD, GIMP, GINKGO GINKGO, FINGLE FANGLE, HAUNTERS, APOSTASIA, GASSIE, HABDABS, KYBOSH, SHEBANG, WATTLE.

Words that sound alien, composite, old slang, comic, futuristic.

Gilbert & George use language to further their intimacy with the viewer and also to celebrate the different forms and moods that language communicates – a semantic palette.

Their first use of language was formal – a polite and friendly address to the viewer.

Then, SHIT and CUNT – the prankster-provocateur manifesto summarised.

Limericks and strange, dream-like, stream-of-consciousness prose in book form. Simple yet visionary texts in which Gilbert & George make clear, revealing statements about their state of being as artists. Part journal, part lucid dreaming.

From their BOOK SCULPTURE, SIDE BY SIDE, for instance, these lines on 'Modernity', printed verso to a picture of a country church by the bend in a lane, trees and hedgerows in full leaf and blossom, Gilbert & George admiring the view:

Sweet solace is ours for we are old fashioned enough to see this ancient building. Old-fashioned are our clothes and eyes but our outlook is ultra-modern. And so here we must recognise sadness as the key to our past and future. Where is the balance in which to be two beings with this lovely scene of an old church in such charming trees and front and side and surrounds.

Gilbert & George use language in a manner that is both conversational and of reverie: a commentary on their coming-to-consciousness as artists, as though every pore of their being was unusually opened to the intoxication of potent feelings and insights. A lot like love. SIDE BY SIDE – like Andre Gide's *Fruits of the Earth* – is a hymn to life.

Gilbert & George write:

Art is strong wine for young heads, so be merry and buoyant and in the swim. Be respectful to the moonlight's spell for soon the dawn will come. Collect these golden pieces in their journey downwards like rain. Learn swimming.

The art of Gilbert & George includes the world contained in words; a sound, a place-name, an event. Gilbert & George allow factual data to generate its own strange poetry, that is the poetry of itself, rather than a poetry inspired by and created for it.

When Gilbert & George make a group of pictures, the titles of the pictures comprise their own language-sculpture. For example: MEDALS, MOONS, POINTERS, SLEEPY, STREETERS, SWEAR, WE ARE, WORLDS.

The potency of lists is an aspect of the art of Gilbert & George. Words become incantatory, brewing, enfolding. The simultaneity of presence and anonymity in graffiti, slogans, propaganda, classified advertisements; street language, through which the city speaks in tongues.

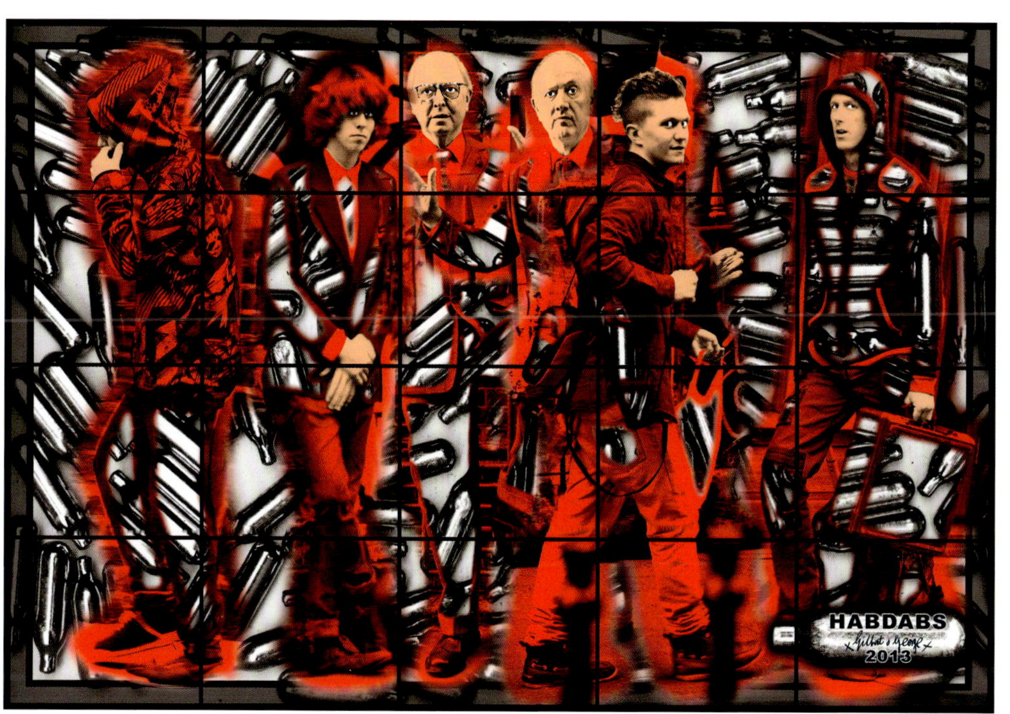

HABDABS. 2013. 254 x 377 cm

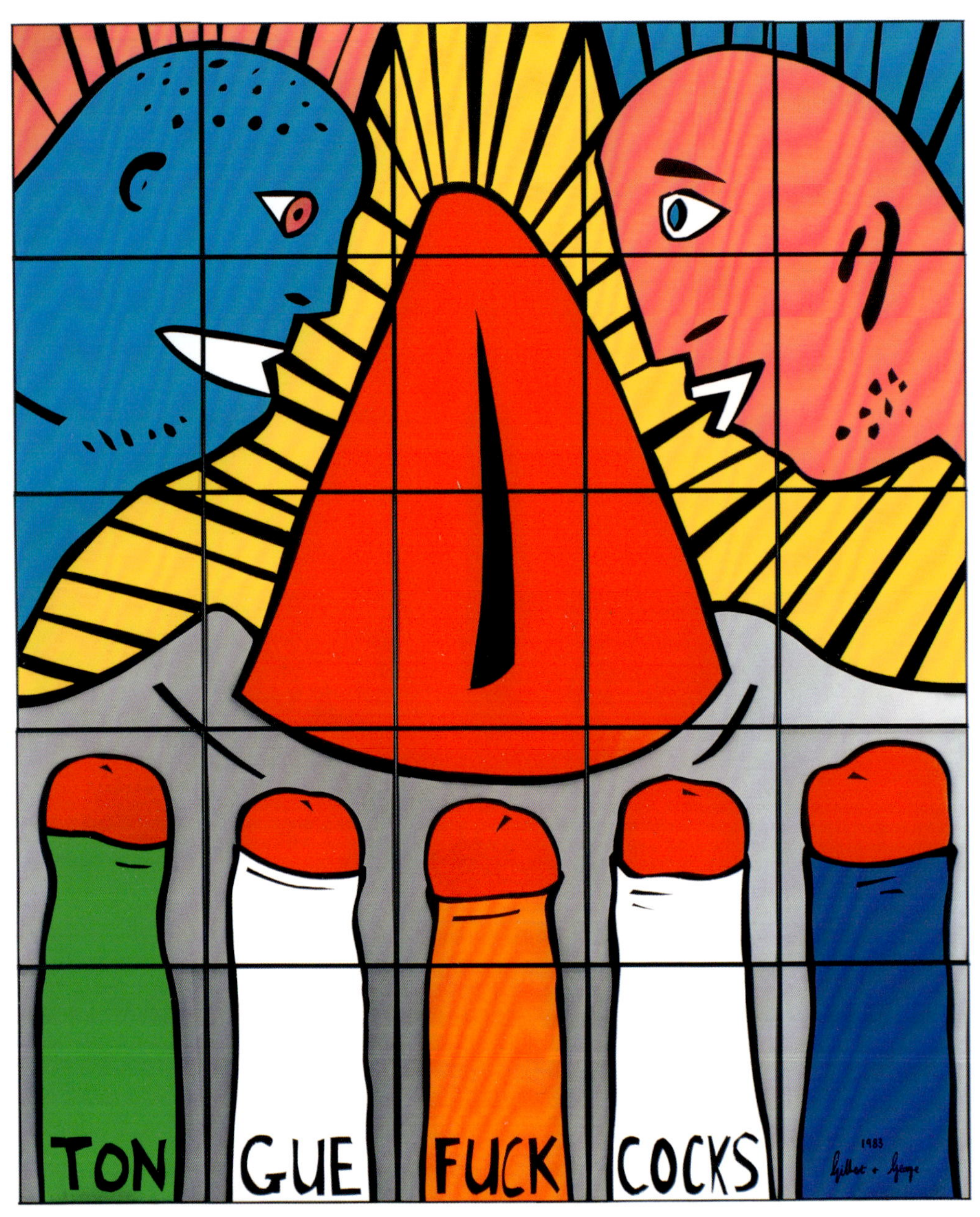

TONGUE FUCK COCKS. 1983. 300 x 250 cm

Thirty-Three
Gilbert & George with Youth on Their Side

Since 1968, successive generations of young people have been fascinated, excited, amused and entranced by the art of Gilbert & George. The reasons for this also provide an astute description of the art of Gilbert & George. The qualities in their art that youth has responded to include:

Drama and spectacle.

Extremism.

Weirdness.

Intensity of image and colour.

Outsider images: other youths, cool modern youths, tramps, alcoholics, Gilbert & George possessed, crazy mutant-transformers.

The reversals, games and contrasts of radical and reactionary, conformism and disaffection, personal conservatism and cultural taboos.

Obscenity. Shit, piss, blood and semen.

The glamour of youth. Youth as heroes.

Aggressive modernity.

The recognisable city.

Shock. Exhibitionism. Crudity.

Comedy, absurdity, the fantastical and the grotesque.

Sex energy.

Profanity, insolence, irreverence and provocation.

Romance.

The conversion of life into art.

Aphorisms and slogans.

Psychodrama. Moodiness. Give-a-fuck attitude.

Anarchy, revolt, atheism and opposition.

From Shakespeare to Elvis to this year's model, the condition of youth is passionate, dichotomous, prone to extremes, desiring, believing, despairing, reckless, enquiring, restless, romantic, daring, death-wishing, loving, strong, extravagant, self-aware, comic, tragic, vulnerable, heroic, trusting, wary, violent, sexual, capricious and moody.

The art of Gilbert & George expresses all of these states, as experienced by Gilbert & George, as witnessed by Gilbert & George, as desired by Gilbert & George, as mourned by Gilbert & George.

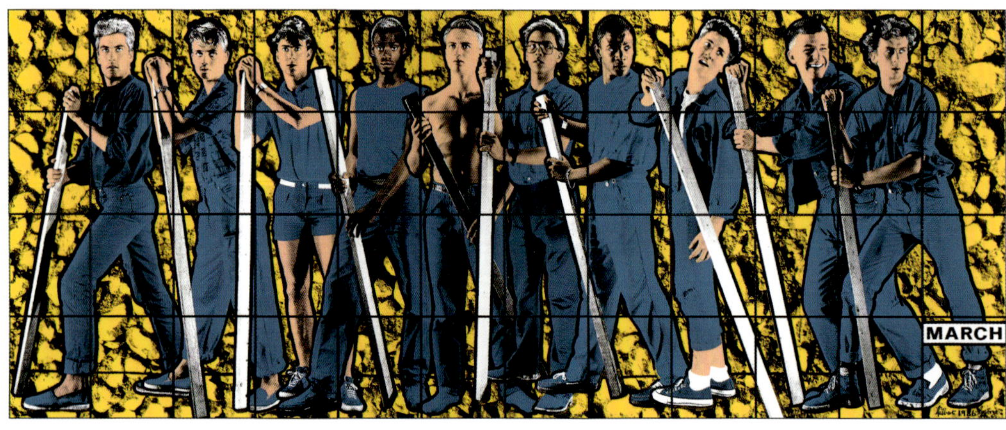

MARCH. 1986. 242 x 608 cm

Thirty-Four
Opposition and Reversal Part Two

In defining their art and their vision, Gilbert & George cite the Victorian architect A.W. Pugin: '… not a style but a principle'. ['style', noun: 'a particular procedure by which something is done.' 'principle', noun: 'a fundamental truth or proposition that serves as the foundation for a system of belief or behaviour or for a chain of reasoning.']

Making art about life, Gilbert & George first made art about being outsiders, alone, with nothing; then they made art about drinking and drunkenness. This was their truth. (Why did artists not make art about their lives, asked Gilbert & George, rather than art about art? The blind-drunk sex-crazed minimalist, for example, who gets up the following morning and thinks very hard about drawing a single short straight line.)

They entered the nauseous, brutal, dark shadow of hangover, to emerge more profoundly immersed in their vision of life and art.

Contemporary art and its cultural infrastructure, as Gilbert & George see it, is obscurantist, thus elitist, exclusive, looking down on those outside its world, insular, self-referential. In addition, pro-non-British, ideologically policed, blinkered, formalist, rejecting of realism, backwards-looking in form, anti-Royalist, self-obsessed, anti-figuration, hence rejecting of a shared reality, deeply and suspiciously conservative, whilst posing as boundlessly liberal, thus also hypocritical, fashion and status conscious in ideology, rejecting of historical tradition and snobbishly intellectual.

The art of Gilbert & George is therefore predicated on the singular, ruthlessly efficient principle of direct and total reversal of all of the values – processes, ideologies, idioms – upheld or enshrined by contemporary art, as they perceive it to exist. Their art in different media is based on this artistically holistic position.

They befriend all materials and subjects they know no 'serious' contemporary artist would pause to consider, from litter to leaves, and in a manner likewise. They oppose the jargon-laden language and 'experimentalism' of contemporary art with a mix of polite formality and insinuations of zombie-music hall comedy.

Fiercely alone, inflexible, indifferent to cultural and artistic fashions, they create an ideological force-field around themselves that is comprised of a ceaselessly updated tension of opposites: home counties appearance, obdurate, inscrutable psycho-drama: barbed ambiguity; impassive dead-headed cosmic tour guides; monster-bellied bogeymen; the tongues stuck out; the 'V' sign flicked; the hand reaching for the other's hand. Thrown through vertiginous vistas of life and death symbolised. The crouching black boy grins; the cold moon rises; sex delirium; body fluid 'landscapes' like a journey to the centre of the Earth.

Gilbert & George make art from an unwavering, intensifying, contrary-declamatory modern anti-art principle.

Gilbert & George used the paradox embodied in their pose as the catalyst and basis for the aggressive modernity of their vision: the pictures show drunks, grey skies, urban brutalism, teenagers, vandalism, somber architectural silhouettes, night streets, religion, street politics. The more the suited artists smile and nod like mild-mannered freshmen seminarians, the more they mutate into ceremonially masked spirit-creatures of a paranoid digital brutal mega-city (see, for instance, their pictures EVIIR, NCP or MILE END), the more interrogatory, jarring, depressed, confrontational, volatile, seedy, threatening, intransigent and savage their art becomes.

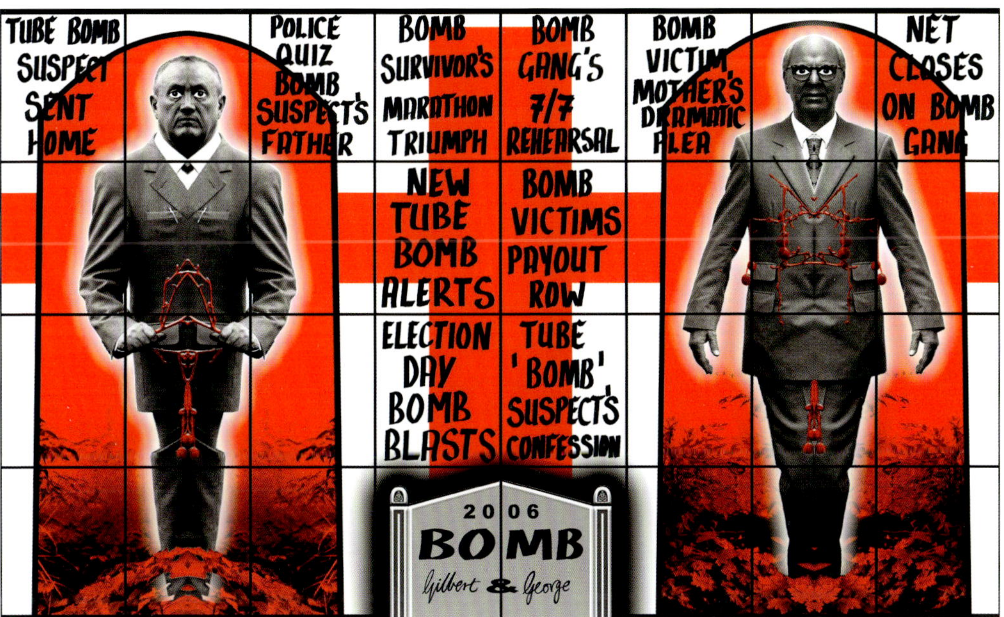

A detail from the middle section of the triptych BOMB. 2006. 336 x 705 cm

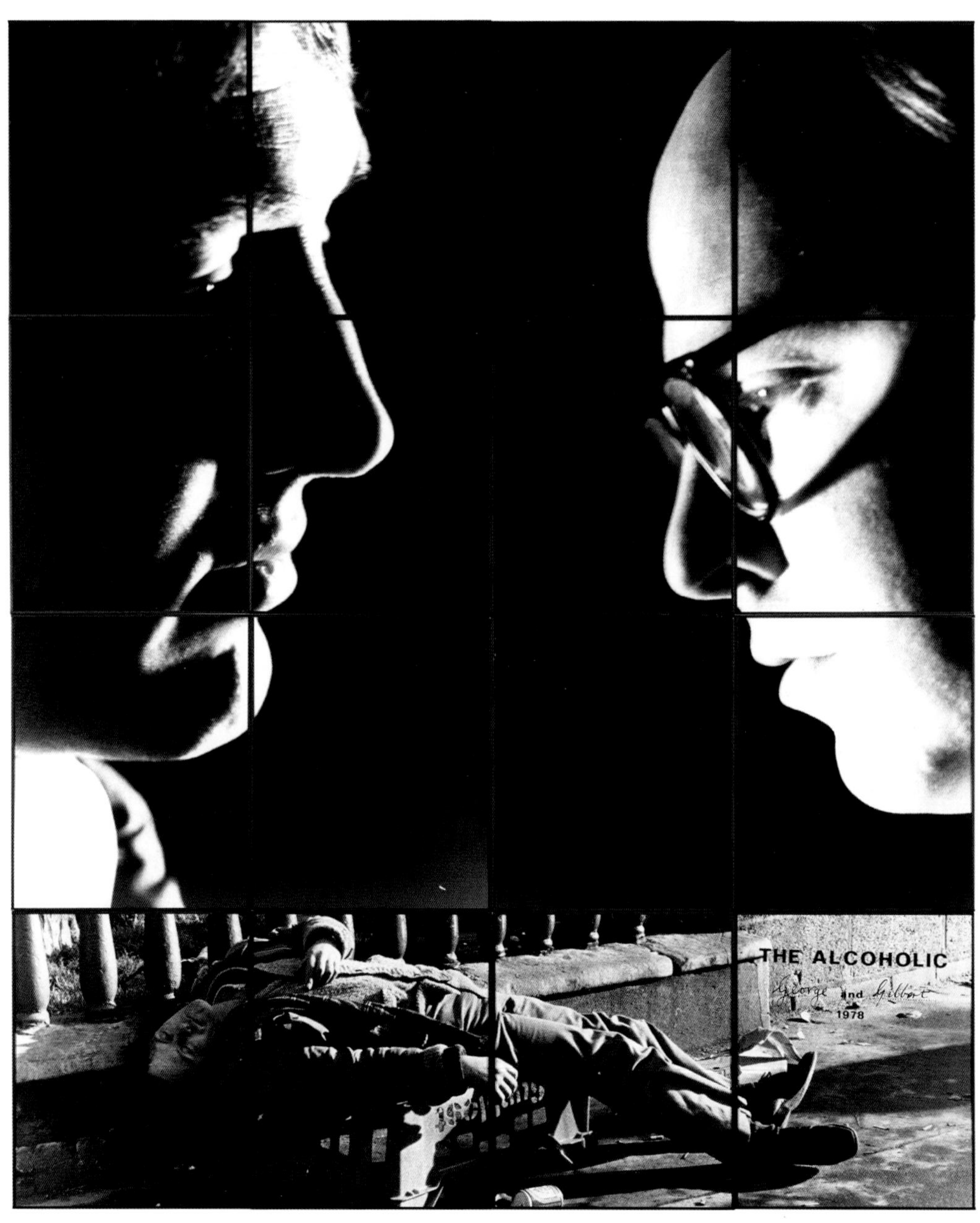

THE ALCOHOLIC. 1978. 241 x 201 cm

Thirty-Five
Gilbert & George and the 'Unreal City…'

The viewer looks at a picture by Gilbert & George – sunburst on a banking tower, back streets, barbed wire, burglar alarm, burka-women, by-laws, traffic, TWENTY-EIGHT STREETS (haunted streets), RED MORNING HATE, WORLDS, THE NINE DARK PICTURES, the seeming infinite directory of loveless sex – and sees the unreal city in the real city.

'Unreal city, under the brown fog of a winter dawn…' – T.S. Eliot sets the scene for his modernist update of Dante's souls in hell in *Waste Land* (1922) as the city clerks stream over London Bridge. Eliot noted, 'For in Dante's Hell souls are not deadened, as they mostly are in life.' Dante writes: 'We met a troop of spirits, who were coming alongside the bank; and each looked at us, as in the evening men are wont to look at one another under a new moon…'.

Baudelaire writes: 'O swarming city, city full of dreams, where ghosts accost the passers-by in broad daylight!'
['Fourmillante Cite, cite plein de reves, Ou le spectre en plein jour raccroche le passant…'.]

As annotated in the *Poems of T.S. Eliot* (2015), Eliot's image of the 'unreal city', City of London, is tailed by a reminiscence of Bertrand Russell – and in imagery reminiscent in temper, as ancestor, to that in the art of Gilbert & George:

After seeing troop trains departing from Waterloo, I used to have strange visions of London as a place of unreality. I used in imagination to see the bridges collapse and sink, and the whole great city vanish like a morning mist. Its inhabitants began to seem like hallucinations, and I would wonder whether the world in which I thought I had lived was a mere product of my own febrile nightmares.

A century on, the viewer looks, for instance, at the JACK FREAK PICTURES of Gilbert & George and sees the collapse of the modern city into a sinister kaleidoscope zombie vision of medals and flags and monster mutants and music hall turns. A lineage of imagery. The city is the unreal city, so resolute in its variform unreality, inherited by Gilbert & George in 1968, who hymn the real city's unreality, making insinuated, but in feeling overt, relations between the living and the dead.

And somewhere along the way – 1977, when Gilbert & George make their DIRTY WORDS PICTURES, seems to mark the place – the modern modernist city seems to reach critical mass: rotted corrugated iron, damp-stained concrete, stagnant cold.

Beyond that point, it seems the city recreates itself, becoming postmodern, fragmented, accelerated, monolithic, the insides on the outside – and remains as unreal as it was for Eliot, recalling Dante or Baudelaire, or Dickens on his insomniac 'night walks', seeing the hidden human city, the nocturnal misery and suffering. His notes, ancestral to the modern and postmodern 'unreal city', a record of a city's soul, transcribed within or beneath the shape-shifting art of Gilbert & George.

For what is the art and vision of Gilbert & George if not a moral record of events and activities within the modern city, as seen by one who lives in the transit of past and future? To re-quote from SIDE BY SIDE: 'Old-fashioned are our clothes and eyes but our outlook is ultra-modern.' (Oscar Wilde wrote: 'The highest criticism is the record of one's own soul.')

The 'unreal city' in the art of Gilbert & George becomes increasingly visionary, inhabited by spirits of varying temper and Gilbert & George themselves possessed. Always a record of modern events, decisions, moods, activities, that create and leave their own moral signature, which cannot be erased.

Paul Elmer More of St Louis, Missouri – humanist critic and writer, conservative Christian apologist, author of *The Great Refusal: Being Letters of A Dreamer in Gotham* (1894) and link in the literary chain between Dante and Eliot – succeeds Dickens in his envisaging of the dead among the city's living, confronting the passage of their lives. He writes:

... so numerous... this vision was given to me, and the hurrying eager multitude of the street were but shadows of humanity, unreal things seeking an unreal good. Who shall say that the unseen dead do not flock through our cities, leading over again in shadow-wise their former lives? Who shall say that to some they are not visible, jostling against the living amid the crowded streets, in the very light of day?

More's vision chimes with that of Gilbert & George (see for

instance their major picture *DEATH HOPE LIFE FEAR*), in turn chiming with that of Dickens, as he describes the spirits on Christmas Eve filling the narrow city street beneath Scrooge's window, anguished at being unable to turn to good all that they had left undone in life. Unable, that is, to rewrite their moral signature. The real city and the unreal city collide and become one: the moral city. That is also the subject of the art of Gilbert & George. Dickens to play:

The air was filled with phantoms, wandering hither and thither in restless haste, and moaning as they went. Every one of them wore chains like Marley's Ghost; some few (they might be guilty governments) were linked together; none were free. Many had been personally known to Scrooge in their lives. He had been quite familiar with one old ghost, in a white waistcoat, with a monstrous iron safe attached to its ankle, who cried piteously at being unable to assist a wretched woman with an infant, whom it saw below, upon a doorstep. The misery with them all was, clearly, that they sought to interfere, for good, in human matters, and had lost the power forever. Whether these creatures faded into mist, or mist enshrouded them, he could not tell. But they and their spirit voices faded together; and the night became as it had been when he walked home.

The viewer can think of the art of Gilbert & George in these terms. As though refracting Dante, Eliot or Dickens, in their visionary mode.

Detail from VALLANCE ROAD. 2013. 302 x 444 cm →

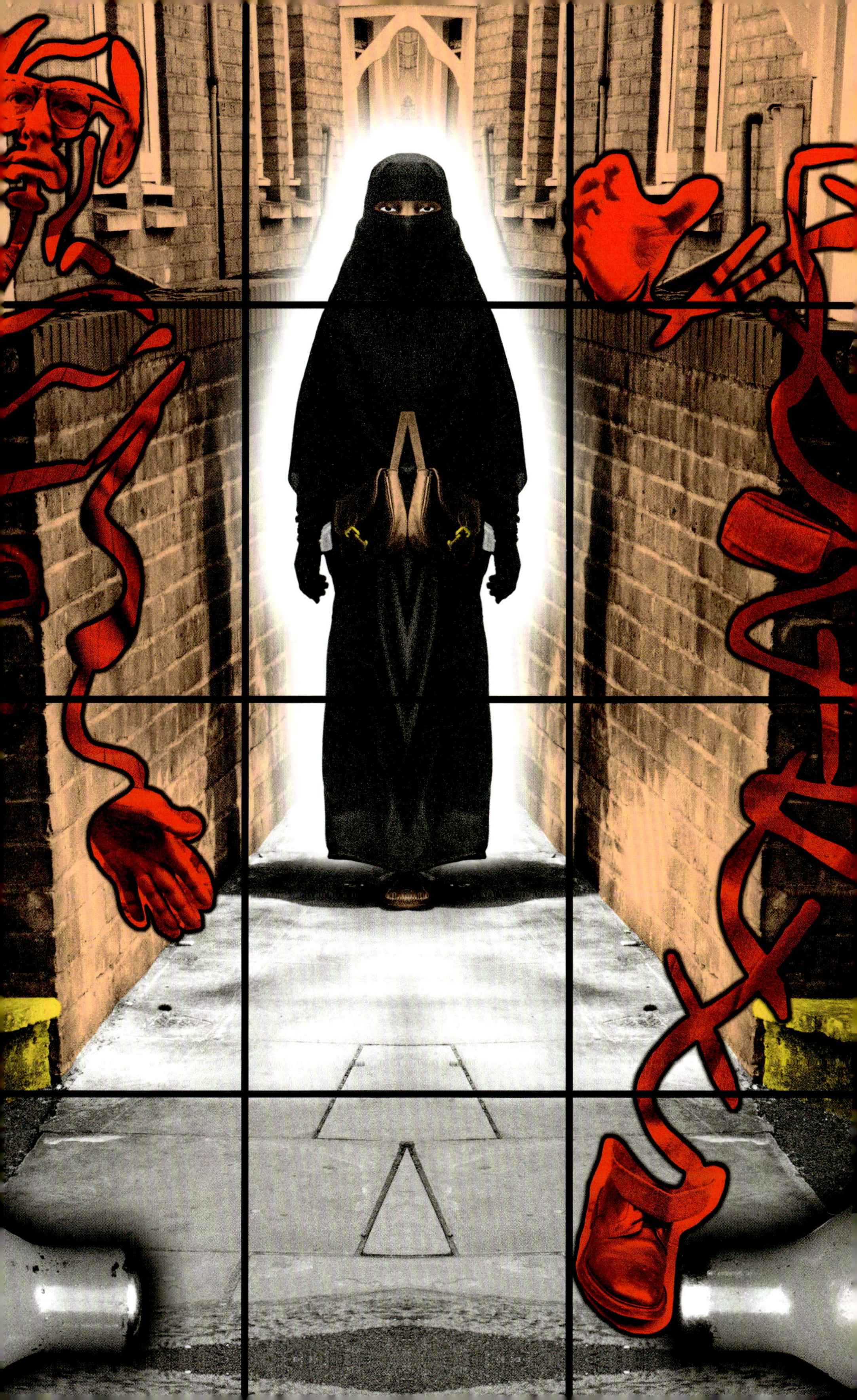

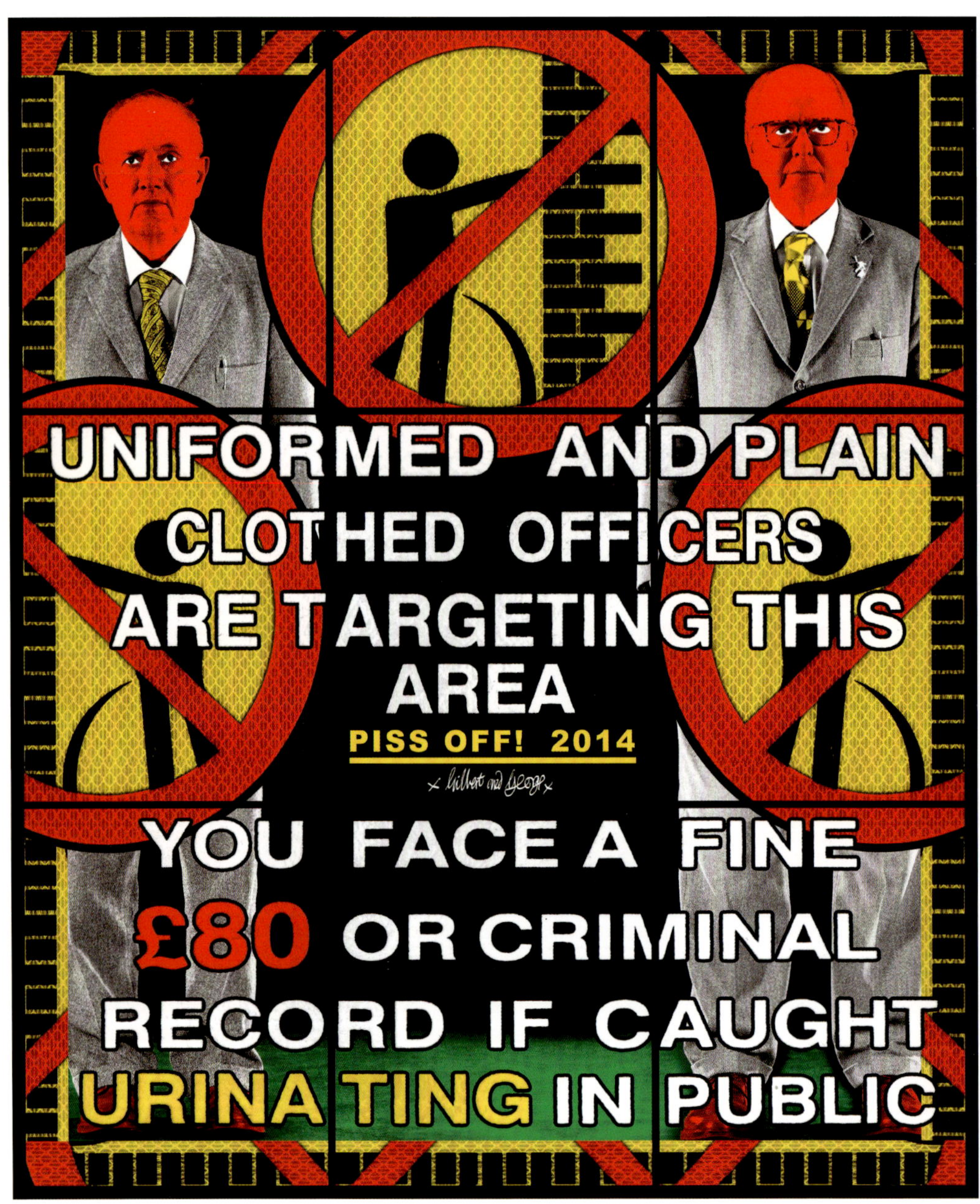

PISS OFF! 2014. 226 x 191 cm
One of THE UTOPIAN PICTURES, which were first shown in Singapore.

Thirty-Six
Gilbert & George: Reveries of the Solitary Walkers

As though bound to walk the endless streets….

The vision and art of Gilbert & George survey the continuum of their times, from East End slums, fags and gold top, to the soaring towers of digital money markets.

In the rigidity of their artistic principle, and the dynamics of their relentless pose, Gilbert & George echo Stravinsky's maxim: 'Whatever diminishes constraint, diminishes strength.'

In order to maintain their vision and create their art, Gilbert & George must maintain and even tighten the principles by which they are Gilbert & George; to allow themselves respite from the *Laws of The Sculptors*, for example (which Gilbert & George laid down for themselves in 1969) would compromise entirely the continuum of their art.

The art of Gilbert & George is an alibi for the dissemination of a principle: their vision of life and art.

Since meeting, Gilbert & George have pursued their reveries as solitary walkers, finding in the city streets those subjects responsive to their mood. Common venue of common human experience and feelings, from boredom to moments of dream-like epiphany: in rain on a windscreen, strangers, mad propaganda, shop fronts….

And a mile from London Bridge station, the old flats and tower blocks stretch away like a grey ocean to a palely misty horizon. Pubs, shops, yards, churches, cinemas, markets, the numberless streets suggesting depths as well as distance. Depths of time, place and lives lived…. At Loughborough Junction, Peckham Rye, Ruskin Park, Denmark Hill, Streatham High Road. Concrete towers, dank urinous subways, black riveted bridge girders dripping, broadways and precincts, above bedsits and cold kitchens, rain, minicabs, funeral parlours, night buses, Star of India, phones unlocked. Thousands upon thousands of streets, to Hackney, Dalston, Haggerston, Finsbury Park, Stoke Newington, Wood Green.

Amidst these streets, Victorian and Georgian chapels and halls; experiments, creeds and visions; plans and tracts for living and dying; intoxication, Ouija and sexual freedom; angels in the branches of a tree; laughing gas, sex workers, anarchists and mediums; dedicated to duty and sacrifice, names on a war memorial; locked subterranean gentlemen's public convenience; tailors; a drinking fountain; human shit, blood, semen, urine and sweat; signs; condensation streaming down the inside of net curtained café windows, forty winters ago; skinheads.

Time begins to seem not linear but foldable. The reveries of solitary walkers *contra mundum* – 'Oh, London, London, our delight!'

In their art, Gilbert & George appear bound to walk, and bound to the city. They traverse the quotidian streets, while also occupying a cosmic, absurd, supernatural, archetypical, allegorical, ritual-ceremonial world, in which they are transformed – as artworks – into magical versions of themselves: flâneur-seer-prankster-libertines, at once imperious and empty-headed, lustful and ascetic, monstrous and impassive, exhausted stooges, vulnerable seekers-after-truth, city sprites, inscrutable nocturnal sentinels, lovers of beauty and witnesses of fate.

Each picture is stark yet vibrant, confrontational and dense with feeling. The pictures are brutal and direct, at times primary coloured, at others poisonously coloured (toxic-seeming young grass green, sickly mauve pink, rust orange). On first encounter, red, blue and yellow or red, white and black, inlaid with monochrome imagery, appear to predominate, muscularly assertive, declamatory, utterly synthetic, at times like a fluorescent dusk. The colours seem psychologically primal, converting space and image into tableaux that merge atmosphere, impression and *mise-en-scene* in a manner that has the simultaneous precision of feeling and narrative illogicality of a dream.

Such bright, venomous colours, yet strangely lit. Such cold monochrome, tensed with panels of warning, mad or angry red. Imagistic scenarios that seem rigid with the formality of ritual and ceremony, as though a ghost world or parallel reality that the figures depicted (youths, traffic, the artists themselves) were haunting in Jungian avatar form.

The artists stand side by side within the copper coloured hemisphere of a blotch blotted upturned leaf. Dressed in blue suits, with blue shirts and blue ties, they appear wholly constructed as a supreme pose: their bodies are outlined in black, the block of blue colour on their clothes is solid and dense; they stand in identical, statesmanlike, somewhat Maoist attitudes, each with one hand raised as though in oration or oath. Preachers or converts. Their eyes are demonically red. From their open mouths extrude stringy, scrawny bouquets of bright green vegetable matter….

A low-rise urban horizon of chimneys, rooftops, nameless industrial-looking premises in London's old East End. This drear landscape is bright yellow, beneath a blank yellow sky speckled with tiny black silhouettes of birds, to the right and left…. Gilbert & George add ceaselessly to the empire of their vision. A place of reversal and confrontation, ever increasingly direct and overt, hammering the opposition, bold enough to aim at storming God in his most secret strongholds.

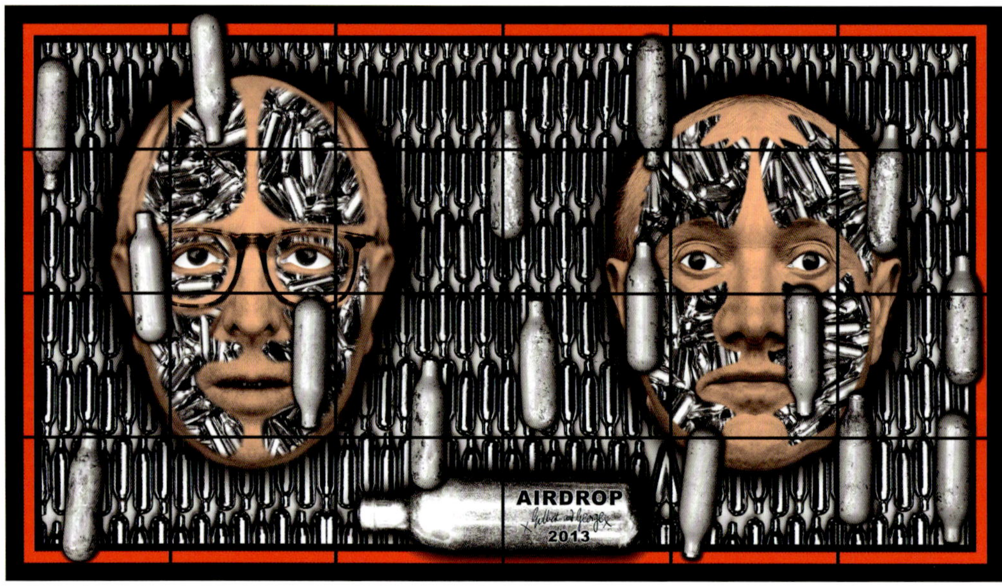

AIRDROP. 2013. 254 x 453 cm
A SCAPEGOATING PICTURE.

Thirty-Seven
The Serious Jest

The smiling bashful polite young men called 'Shit' and 'Cunt'. Extravagant roses in their button-holes. Something of Charlie Cairoli and Paul.

A little marked-out area of wasteland beneath a railway arch. The same young men, facing a building site (a block of flats, scaffolding) sing along to a music hall song. A ragged line of adults and a handful of young children watch them, expressionless.

The young men go to the country, neatly dressed. One has a walking stick. They admire the scenery: a lake in a park. Some light conversation.

Now they're drunk, in the pub. Then collapsing, thrashing about. Then sober, silent, vulnerable to the day.

Here they are chatting on the steps of Somerset House. And again on the Embankment. Big black buildings, blank white skies. One smokes. He might be a progressive junior don.

Darkness and streets enfold them. Their own night walks through the London nobody knows: the alcoholic, the queue, the doleful Pakistani boy. A car on a bridge on a bright bleak day… 'O City City,

I can sometimes hear, Beside a public bar in Lower Thames Street....'

And now it's fifty years later. They've had the romance of the century. Possessed, or in a trance, white-suited, silver-haired, the two men dance in bright green undergrowth, as heavy footed as Breughel's peasants. Each holds a sprig of plane tree twigs, like a symbolic wand or Morris dancer's flag. The dance is unsmiling.

A magical process has occurred; an irreversible transformation.

The serious jest.

Phoenixology – the science of dying and returning to life; if the good Lord is willing, and the creek don't rise.

FIN

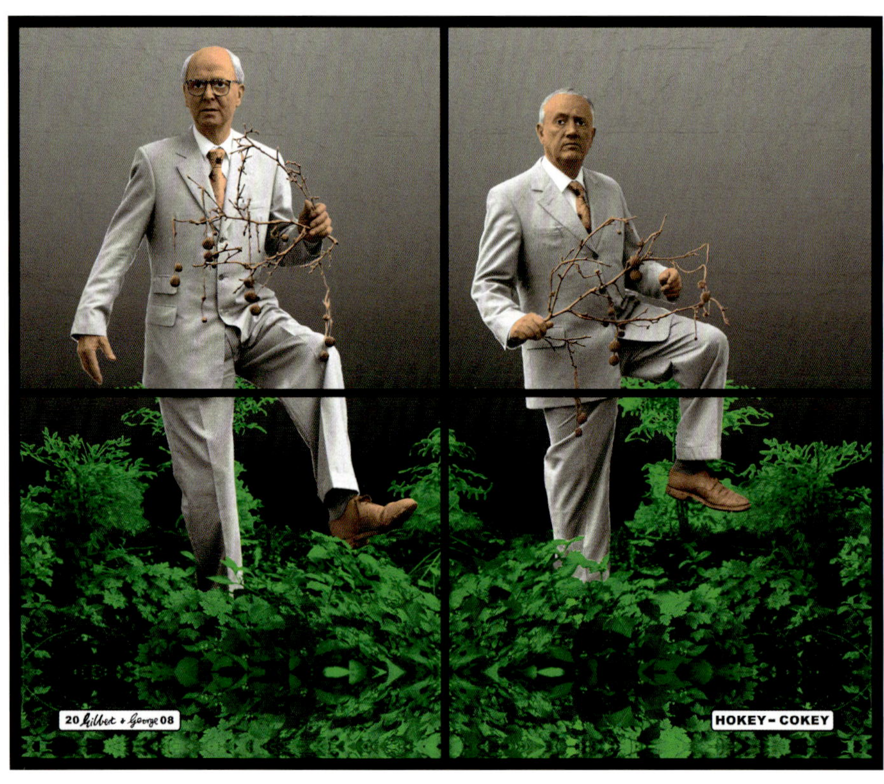

HOKEY–COKEY. 2008. 127 x 151 cm A JACK FREAK PICTURE.

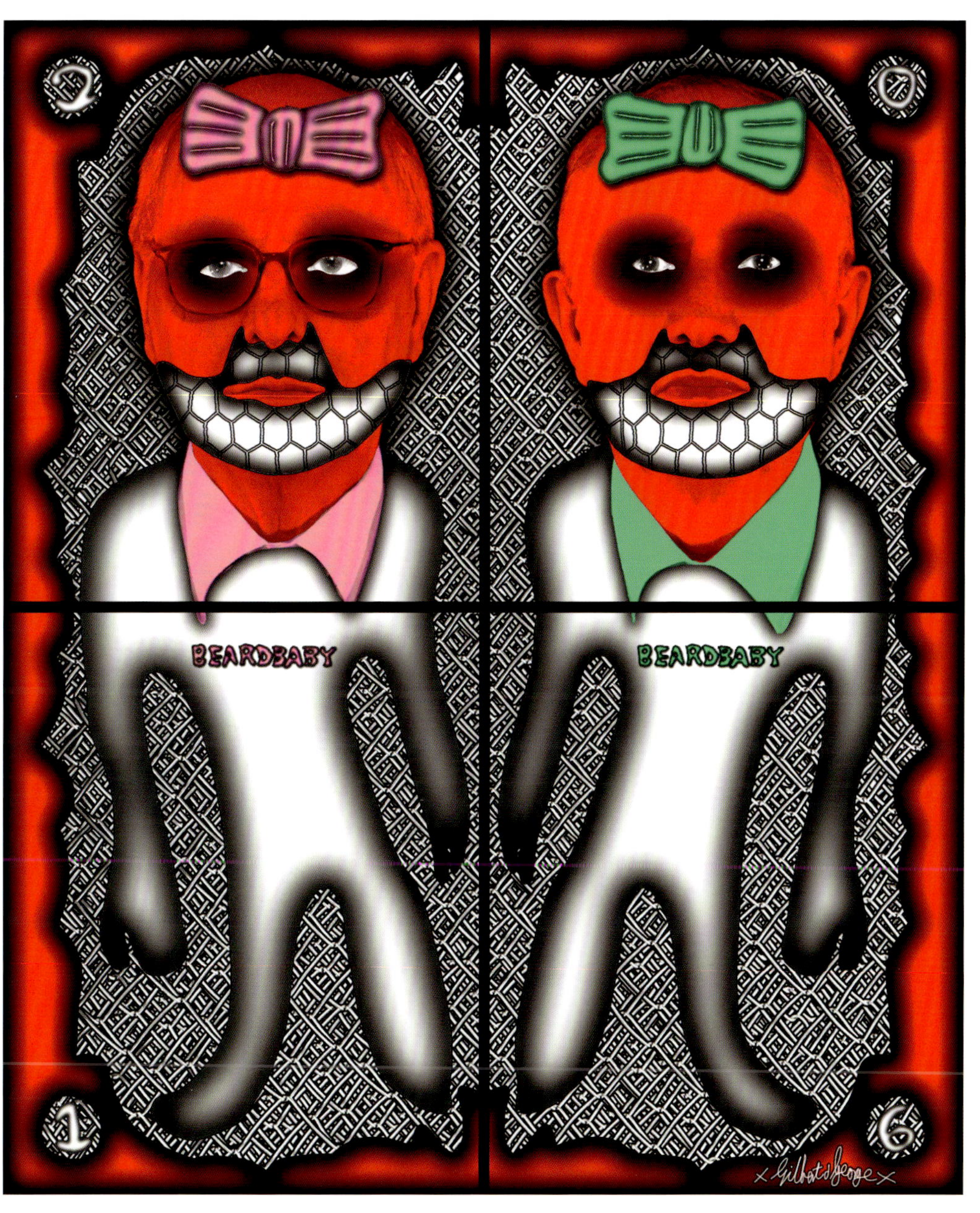

BEARDBABY BEARDBABY. 2016. 151 x 127 cm
One of THE BEARD PICTURES.

Index

Published by HENI Publishing, London

ISBN 9781912122028

A catalogue record for this book is available from The British Library.

Author: Michael Bracewell
Designed by: Gilbert & George
Production: Hurtwood Press
Publishing Manager: Phoebe Adler

Printed in Italy